3. 20

THE
COMMUNION
OF SAINTS

DIETRICH BONHOEFFER

THE
COMMUNION
OF SAINTS

A DOGMATIC INQUIRY INTO
THE SOCIOLOGY OF
THE CHURCH

HARPER & ROW, PUBLISHERS
NEW YORK AND EVANSTON

THE COMMUNION OF SAINTS

LIBRARY OF CONGRESS CATALOG CARD NUMBER:
64-10749

F-U

Foreword

The student of Bonhoeffer who wishes to know the sources of his 'religionless interpretation of biblical concepts in a world come of age', the worldly Christianity of the letters from prison, will have to turn to Bonhoeffer's early writings. There he will find both the basis and the starting-point for the ideas in the letters. The letters, it is hardly necessary to say, read more easily than those early works.

Sanctorum Communio is Bonhoeffer's first work. He was only twenty-one when he presented it, in 1927, as a dissertation to the Theological Faculty in Berlin. Difficult and overloaded though it is, in many respects unclear and youthful in style, nevertheless it moves clearly across the continental map of theology of that time into new country. It begins from two conflicting bases. First there is the sociological school, which had a powerful effect on Berlin theology of the twenties by way of Troeltsch. Bonhoeffer had studied in this atmosphere and learned its language. He worked in Harnack's seminar, but under Seeberg he turned to systematic theology. The second base was dialectical theology. Though it was making stormy advances in Germany, it had not then found a single advocate in Berlin University. Its concern was not with the sociological and statistical understanding of the church, but with its strict and sole source in revelation. In spite of Harnack and Seeberg it was this theology to which the young Bonhoeffer now became attentive. He was attracted by the impossible. What he tried to give in *Sanctorum Communio* was a sociological theology of the church, or a theological sociology. He turned to this task with immense self-conscious power.

Both these bases, the sociology and the theology of the church, have by no means lost their pressing importance for us to-day in, our view of the church, whether we regard them as reconcilable or not. The revelatory character of the church points to its *raison d'être*, its sociological character points to its reality and concreteness. Both elements, the *raison d'être* and the this-worldliness, were to be constant motives in Bonhoeffer's develop-ment. They may be discerned even in his later formulations concerning religionless Christianity.

For his first effort, which was so much more diligently worked over than his last, Bonhoeffer found at that time no readers. It took him three and a half years to get *Sanctorum Communio* pub-lished, in the midst of the German inflation, at an impossible price. The work had to be shortened, and he had to subsidise the publication himself. The publisher reproached him for not helping to make the work known. A friend wrote to him that few would see what he was after. The Barthians would not see, because of the sociology, and the sociologists likewise because of the Barth. It was the bold individuality of the letters from prison, following the individuality of *The Cost of Discipleship*, which forced attention back upon his first work.

In fact Bonhoeffer was never interested in making his writings better known. He never drew the attention of his students to them. The book *Sanctorum Communio* soon disappeared from his view, because he was too heavily engaged with the thing itself, the *sanctorum communio*. He was always ready to describe the thing itself in a new way. For this very reason it is both exciting and rewarding for us to read how Bonhoeffer regarded the church when he began his work, and to see what his answers were then. Both continuity and discontinuity can be seen.

If we are attracted by Bonhoeffer's later views, and want to find the answers to his questions, then we are on more solid and controlled ground if we add to our considerations this pre-cocious and astonishing essay.

Eberhard Bethge

Contents

CONTENTS

CONTENTS

Preface

This study places social philosophy and sociology in the service of dogmatics. Only by this means did the structure of the Christian church as a community seem to yield itself to systematic understanding. The subject under discussion belongs to dogmatics, not to the sociology of religion. The inquiry into Christian social philosophy and sociology is a genuinely dogmatic one, since it can be answered only if our starting-point is the concept of the church. The more theologians have considered the significance of the sociological category for theology, the more clearly the social intention of all the basic Christian concepts has emerged. Ideas such as 'person', 'primal state', 'sin' and 'revelation' are fully understandable only in relation to sociality. The fact that every genuinely theological concept can be correctly comprehended only when set within and supplemented by its special social sphere is proof of the specifically theological nature of any inquiry into the sociology of the church.

This book was written more than three years ago. I was unable completely to revise it before it went to press, but had to be content with rewriting it in parts. In view of the course the subsequent debate has taken, this is a defect. My justification for publishing the book in its present form is the basic approach adopted in dealing with the problem, which now as then seems to me the right and profitable one.

I should like particularly to thank Herr Geheimrat Reinhold Seeberg, who from the outset has shown a most friendly interest in this work. My thanks are due also to the Minister for Science, Art and Education for the help accorded me in getting the book printed. It was the *Notgemeinschaft für deutsche Wissenschaft*, together with a grant from the Reinhold Seeberg foundation, which made publication possible. For this too I should like to express my thanks.

July 1930

A note on the translation

This translation is based on the third German edition of 1960. That edition had substantial additions, printed in an Appendix, which had not appeared in the earlier editions. They had been removed partly at the wish of the publisher, partly to please Reinhold Seeberg, Bonhoeffer's teacher in Berlin. In this translation these additions have been incorporated in the main text. This version therefore corresponds more closely to the original text of the author than even the latest German edition.

The task of translation has passed through various hands. However, the undersigned undertook to revise the entire text, and must take responsibility for the final version.

R. Gregor Smith

THE
COMMUNION
OF SAINTS

CHAPTER I

Towards a definition of social philosophy and sociology [1]

If this introductory chapter were to present and criticise the many different attempts at solving the problem of these definitions, it would swell to a monograph. As our concern is with the material and not the method of sociology, we shall not develop the whole problem of method. Moreover, a discussion of method may be found in most of the larger sociological works.[2] It will suffice if we discuss the problem briefly and give our own attitude to it.

It is characteristic of the situation that when chairs of sociology were asked for by the universities, and the ministry of education requested statements about the aim and the object of the science of sociology, the statements were so varied that no uniform picture emerged. It is further characteristic that almost every new work on the subject suggested a new goal, or a modification of a previous goal; and the number of works increased enormously. And if we examine the principles of the great 'classic' works, we are appalled at the confusion even in the most fundamental matters. The historical and psychological reason for this seems to me to lie in the fact that the chief material interest of most sociologists is to be found in the political and economic or historical field. Sociology has therefore a particular relation to these disciplines. But this means that a clear view of the real object of sociology is lost; yet this real object does not seem to me to be too difficult to define. Economic politics, comparative religion and the philosophy of history were all presented as though they were sociology. The word 'sociology' was used, but the concept was quite unclear. A dozen different things from all sorts of fields of knowledge were named as the real object of sociology, instead of one which might be held to constitute its essence.[3] In this confusion it might seem impossible to find any uniform lines. Nevertheless I think that certain clearly emerging types may be distinguished at least among the chief sociological works.

In a well-known essay Troeltsch[4] has made such a distinction, into two groups, the first 'historical-philosophical-encyclopædic', and the second 'analytic and formal'. It is the latter, the more recent, which has established itself in the universities as scientific sociology.[5] It deals with the 'relations and connections within the group and its products'.[6] Its object is 'society', not as constituted of elements, that is, individual persons, but 'so far as it is the bearer of inwardly established interactions between its individual members'.[7] The basic category of sociological thought must therefore be relation.[8] And questions must be asked concerning social forces as well as kinds of relation.[9] Since the time of Simmel 'social forces' are taken to mean such constitutive concepts as love, subordination, mystery, conflict, etc. By 'kinds of relation' is intended, for example, the classic distinction made by Tönnies between community and society.[10] On this basis there arises the question of the products of society, such as culture, economic life, and 'materialising of the objective spirit' (see below).

So far we have looked at the problem of the object of sociology. But the significance of sociology is equally that it is also a fundamentally new method (similar to induction in its time), for the investigation of historical, psychological and political problems, which it believes it can solve only by knowing inter-human relations. The method is applied to the problems of language, of religion, of the state, and takes the ground from under the theory that all these goods were invented by individuals. It is true that as a method sociology always presupposes the concept of the object, on the basis of which the linguistic problem must be considered. Basically, this means that in order to grasp a great number of historical problems a consideration of the social form is important. That is, sociology adds something to the other disciplines. For this concept Simmel coined the term 'sociological method'.[11]

The chief representatives of this analytic and formal study are Tönnies, Simmel, Vierkandt and von Wiese[12] in Germany, in France Durkheim[13] with his great work, *Totemism as a Social Phenomenon*, Tarde with his discovery and account of the imitative instinct in its significance for sociology,[14] and in England McDougall.[15]

The historical-philosophical group acknowledges Comte[16] and Spencer[17] as their originators. Among them may be named Schäffle,[18] Spann,[19] Oppenheimer[20] and Müller-Lyer.[21] This group aims at describing the historical course of social life, and its historical and philosophical basis. Sociology here becomes a collective name for all the humane sciences, and thus without being aware of it renders itself superfluous. In seeking too many objects it fails to find one. Thus in Oppenheimer[22] sociology simply becomes a universal science. For a discussion of this matter Troeltsch's essay is the most convenient *locus*.

In opposition to this weakening of the concept formal sociology takes as its object the 'forms' of society.[23] Though we are in formal agreement with this limitation of the problem, we feel bound to define the content differently. We cannot regard the problem as solved by the method of formal sociology. We agree, so far as it concentrates on the problem of society; we disagree, so far as it regards the content as consisting simply of relations and interactions, we disagree also in respect of its normal method. Our first disagreement concerns the social and philosophical basis on which formal sociology builds, namely, the theory of atomism. This is most clearly expressed by von Wiese and Vierkandt, in their teaching about relation.

As might be expected it is their concept of persons which we must oppose. There are here two apparently different courses of thought. Starting from the fact of change brought about by the environment (an officer on duty, and in his family, a scholar in his profession, and, say, in politics, or a child with a weaker and stronger child), first the conclusion is drawn that the person is not a unity, and the decisive emphasis is laid upon the power of relationships. Man is regarded as a product of social relationships, to which, it is true, he contributes his little share.[24] Alongside this idea[25] there is a second, that distinguishes man, as an isolated structure, at rest, from the 'forces which play between persons in relative independence from them'.[26] At first glance this seems to involve sheer contradiction; but there is unity of view here. Basically, persons are here regarded as firm objects, whose social 'capacities' permit and establish relations with other persons. Man as a person is therefore not of interest. What is of sociological interest is the forces which play between persons. These forces can transform the person's social sphere, but the personal kernel is untouched. If such an isolated personal kernel is once granted, the whole investigation remains in the sphere of an atomist and individualist theory of society, however carefully the idea is worked out of a mutual penetration within the social sphere. In this Vierkandt is more cautious than, for example, von Wiese.[27] But basically they are agreed: we are presented with a multitude of isolated I-centres, which can enter into an outward connection with one another through some stimulus.

Now it would be quite wrong to identify the philosophical individualism of this social theory with the atomist theories of the individual, say of the Enlightenment. Formal sociology does recognise and evaluate positively the basic significance of man's living in society for his whole spiritual life. It is only the social and metaphysical ordering of the social phenomenon which fails to carry conviction. It is not sociology itself, but the social philosophy which underlies it, which is atomist. Nor is this state of affairs equally clearly expressed by all formal sociologists. But when these matters of principle are discussed, the conclusions are plainly as I have described them.[28]

When the social and philosophical insights are deepened, the object of sociology takes another form. But the concept of the object in this teaching involves a method which we must likewise reject, namely, the empirical and scientific method. The procedure is to enumerate and to arrange the many possible interactions. Most typical is von Wiese. But in fact this is not a sociological achievement at all, but at most the gathering of material for sociological study. In saying that a proper grasp of the concept of the object in sociology depends on the most profound social and philosophical insights into the nature of the person and of society, we realise that the view we shall give of this concept, and of sociological method, can only be confirmed as our concrete study of the problems proceeds.

All the same, we give here the concept of social philosophy and sociology with which we shall work. Social philosophy and sociology, being two disciplines with different subject matter, should be strictly distinguished.[29] If this is not done, there arises a hopeless confusion of terms, though of course individual results may be largely correct. The two disciplines are related through sociology building on the results of social philosophy. The sociologist may be unaware of these results. Moreover, the permanent norm of sociology is found in social philosophy. Neither discipline is a natural science; they are both humane sciences. As independent disciplines they have their own subject-matter.[30]

Social philosophy investigates the ultimate social relations which are prior to all knowledge of and will for empirical community, and the 'origins' of sociality in man's spiritual life and its essential connection with it. It is the science of the original and essential nature of sociality. It is a normative science in so far as its results supply the necessary corrective for the interpretation of actual social conditions. Sociology is the science of the structures of empirical communities. Hence its true subject is not the laws governing the origin of empirical social groupings, but the laws concerning their structure. Thus sociology is not a historical but a systematic science. In principle it is possible to do sociology without a basis of social philosophy, so long as this limitation is kept in mind. What is meant by the structure of a community will be fully clarified as we proceed with our investigation. It is sufficient at this point to say that it is not exhaustively expressed by relations or interactions, although these do sustain social activity. Sociology is concerned with tracing the manifold interactions to specific spiritual and intellectual acts of our being which are the peculiar characteristic of the structure. Personal units, however, as centres of action, belong just as much to the structure of a community as the unit of the group as a 'formation'. The general structure of an empirical social grouping is determined by all three.

This state of affairs has its consequences for the method: the sociologist's approach is not morphological and descriptive (as in Durkheim), but is that of the humane studies, concerned, that is, with the essential structure of the spiritual phenomenon of the group. The phenomenological method is derived from the systematic nature of sociology. It seeks to grasp in empirical acts the essential constitutive acts.[31] This method is the only one which can overcome the genetic approach which turns sociology into a mere branch of history.

The sociology of religion is therefore a phenomenological study of the structural characteristics of religious communities.[32] But to avoid misunderstanding it should be noted that the present work on the *sanctorum communio* is theological rather than sociological. Its place is within Christian dogmatics, and the insights of social philosophy and sociology are drawn into the service of dogmatics. We wish to understand the structure, from the standpoint of social philosophy and sociology, of the reality of the church of Christ which is given in the revelation in Christ. But the nature of the church can be understood only from within, *cum ira et studio*, and never from a disinterested standpoint. Only by taking the claim of the church seriously, without relativising it alongside other claims or alongside one's own reason, but understanding it on the basis of the gospel, can we hope to see it in its essential nature. So our problem has to be attacked from two, or even from three, sides: that of dogmatics, of social philosophy, and sociology.

In the next chapter we shall show that the Christian concept of the person is real only in sociality. Then we shall show, in a social-philosophical section, how man's spiritual being is likewise possible and real only in sociality. Then in a purely sociological section we shall consider the structures of empirical communities, being by that time in a position to refute the atomist view of society. Only then, through the insight we have acquired into the nature of community, shall we be able to come near to a conceptional understanding of Christian community, of the *sanctorum communio.*

CHAPTER II

The Christian concept of the person and the concepts of basic social relation

A. THE FOUR SCHEMES FOR THE CONCEPTS OF BASIC SOCIAL
RELATION IN THE LIGHT OF THE CHRISTIAN CONCEPT OF THE
PERSON AND OF BASIC RELATION

Every concept of community is related to a concept of the person. The question about what constitutes community can only be answered by asking what constitutes a person. Since the aim of our inquiry is to understand a particular community, namely, the *sanctorum communio*, we must investigate its particular concept of the person. Concretely this means that we must study the Christian concept of the person. In understanding the meaning of person and community, we shall also have said something decisive about the concept of God. For the concepts of person, community and God have an essential and indissoluble relation to one another. It is in relation to persons and personal community that the concept of God is formed. In principle, the nature of the Christian concept of community can be reached as well from the concept of God as from the concept of the person. In choosing the latter as our starting-point, we cannot reach a soundly based view of it, or of community, without constant reference to the concept of God.

We shall now discuss the Christian concept of the person and its concept of basic social relations in the light of the four schemes for the concepts of basic social relations in philosophy. The question is not about some social area in man which might have a religious or other origin, nor about empirical communities of will or merely social acts; but about basic ontic relations of social being as a whole. It is these which establish the norm and the limit for all empirical sociality, and this proposition is of the utmost significance for the concept of the church. Since it is basic ontic relations which are to be discussed, it is not the types of social theory but their philosophical precursors which we shall adduce.

1. In Aristotle man becomes a person only in so far as he partakes of reason. The collective form, as more nearly approaching the genus, is therefore ranked higher than the individual person. Man is a ζῶον πολιτικόν, the state is the highest collective form, preceding by its nature all individuals. The individual only partially achieves identity between the νοῦς παθητικός and ποιητικός, just as in Plato's *Timaeus* only the reasoning, that is, the universal, part of the soul is immortal.[1] Essential being lies beyond individual and personal being. The antithesis between man and his destiny is the antithesis between the individual and the universal—or, in the language of social philosophy, between the individual and the race. Aristotle's concept of God is thus impersonal.[2]

2. It was Stoicism with its concept of ἡγεμονικόν which for the first time in the history of philosophy formed the concept of the ethical person. A man becomes a person by submitting to a higher obligation. This obligation is universally valid, and by obedience to it persons form a realm of reason, in which each soul, submissive to the obligation, is at one with eternal reason and thus also with the soul of other persons.

But here too, in spite of the emphasis upon the ethical and 'personal', that which really makes a person goes beyond the individual. It is the ethical and reasoning life of the person which is his essence, and it is so in abolishing him as an individual person.[3]

The first difference in principle between the Aristotelian and the Stoic teaching is that for the Stoic the I is self-sufficient, and reaches the full height of reason without any other; whereas with Aristotle it is the genus, presented in the idea of the state, which possesses the height of reason, so that the individual can be thought of only as a part of the genus. One man enters into connection with another only as he approximates to the genus and transcends individual life. The genus is opposed to the individual as something absolutely superior and conceptually primary. For the Stoic the concept of the genus offers nothing new in principle. The existence of a realm of reason merely indicates the existence of a realm of like beings. Thus for the Stoic the person is something finished in itself, complete, and final. The realm of reason is still thought of as a realm of persons. What is important for us in this is that the basic scheme is not a metaphysical and intellectual one of the individual and the universal, but that the individual and the universal are closely interwoven, and the person is regarded as somehow ultimate. Hence the relation of moral person to moral person is always thought of as a relation of like to like, and this is the basic relation of social philosophy.

3. Epicureanism, with its starting-point in Democritus's atomic theory, which it applies to the social and ethical spheres, maintains that life in society serves only to heighten the pleasure of each individual. Social life is thus purely utilitarian, based on a συνθήκη, and is inconceivable as a natural community. Each individual is completed by the individual pleasure which separates him from every other individual. Each person confronts the other as alien and unlike, since each is aiming at the highest pleasure. Here nothing remains either of the ethics of Stoicism or of Aristotle's intellectual philosophy of mind. Epicurean teaching reappears during the Enlightenment. It is characterised by a defective concept of spirit, a negative description which can be interpreted as a theory of basic relations, in which no original, significant or essential relation of spirit exists between men; the connecting threads are sheerly utilitarian. Basically, every man is alien to every other. *Status hominum naturalis est bellum omnium contra omnes* (Hobbes).[4] On this basis all social structures arise, and are thus purely contractual. In this and the following two chapters this theory is implicitly criticised.

4. Descartes's transformation of the metaphysical question into an epistemological one also changed the view of the person. In Kant the development of the epistemological concept of the person has made the perceiving I the starting-point for all

philosophy. His synthesis of transcendental apperception resolved both the I-Thou relation and the opposition of subject and object in the higher unity of mind, of intellectual intuition. This meant a fresh attempt in philosophy to master the problem of basic social relations.

In this historical survey our only purpose is to show how various philosophical approaches deal with the problem of social relations, and how the relation of one man to another, or to the genus, have been conceived. We emphasise that we have so far not committed ourselves about a possible social province in man, or said anything about empirical social relations. But we have looked at the possible relations of person to person from the standpoint of the various philosophical concepts of the person. We have met with four basic approaches: 1. the Aristotelian scheme of the universal and the individual, the genus and the individual, 2. the Stoic and Christian, of person and person, 3. the Democritean, Epicurean and Enlightenment view of an atomist society and 4. the view of German idealism, expressed in the subject-object relation of epistemology.

It is now possible to show that between the first and the fourth type, despite their different starting point, there is a basic kinship. Both types see the meaning of the subject to consist in its entering into the general forms of reason. What is additional in the epistemological view of the individual (in idealism) is its regarding all that is opposed to the object as an object of knowledge; this is basic both to Fichte's ethical idealism and to Hegel's logical idealism. But subject and object are not final opposites, but in being recognised as such they are resolved in the unity of intellectual intuition.

This brings us to our first systematic question, concerning the philosophical basis of a Christian doctrine of person and community, in which we must criticise the basic schemes we have described. The need to have some concept of the person arises, as we have already said, from the very nature of our task, which is to understand the specifically Christian community of persons, the *sanctorum communio*.

It is a precondition of this investigation of the Christian

concept of the person and the basic social relations that neither should be somehow abstracted from empirical social structures. But both must be conceived of quite generally, in order to be applied to the special case of empirical relations with basic social relations. Empirical relations extend across a social realm, a group of social acts, which are not our immediate concern. We are asking, rather, whether a person must necessarily be thought of in relation to another person, or whether a person is conceivable in an atomist fashion; and this leads to the question of what are the basic relations between persons. That is why in our historical introduction we discussed the philosophical background of each social theory, and not the history of the social theories themselves. In brief, we are dealing not with the empirical fact of communities of will, and the specific sociological problem of the interaction of wills, but with basic ontic relations of social existence. Our problem, therefore, is the metaphysic of sociality.

This part of our investigation is therefore not sociological, but theological and philosophical. In this way we hope to find a norm in these basic matters for empirical sociology. It is the basic ontic relations which provide the norm for all empirical social life. This is of the greatest significance for a concept of the church.

In thus presenting basic social relations from the standpoint of Christian dogmatics we do not mean that they are religious; they are purely ontic, but seen as such from the Christian perspective. This provides us with the conditions for a positive presentation of the philosophical basis of the Christian doctrine of persons and basic relations. We must look for the scheme by which basic Christian relations are to be understood.

We first ask whether the philosophical schemes are satisfactory. The metaphysical scheme involves a basic overcoming of the person by absorbing it into the universal. The epistemological subject-object relation does not advance beyond this, since the opposition is overcome in the unity of mind, in intellectual intuition, but there is no distinction between the subject-object and the I-Thou relation; but the latter is absorbed in the former. Fichte makes no advance on Kant when he speaks of the self-conscious I as arising from the Not-I. For his Not-I is not I, but an object. Both are in the end resolved in the unity of the I. Hegel, too, sees the I as arising at the point where it is drawn into objective spirit, and reduced to absolute spirit. Thus here too the limit set by the individual person is in principle overcome. Basically it is the concept of spirit which unites all these systems, and indeed the concept of spirit as immanent. Such a concept is bound to lead to the consequences which idealism in fact drew.[5] The I is a person so far as it is spirit. Spirit, however, as Kant says, is the highest principle of form, comprising and overcoming all material, so that spirit and the universal are identical and the individual loses its value.

Immanent spirit as the highest principle of form is formal law. This holds true of ethics as well. Any exposition of Kant's ethical formalism which claims to find in it the basis for the freedom of a material ethic is in error.[6] For the reasoning person the supreme principle of action is universal validity. This definition of the person was taken over by Fichte. But though he has much to say about individuality, he makes no advance on Kant. The goal of reason is satisfied by the individual accomplishment of his task, his duty. One I is like another. Only on the basis of this likeness is a relation between persons conceivable at all. Admittedly, this is true only in regard to basic relations; for empirical social relations Kant recognised the decisive importance of antagonism.[7] It is the destiny of the human race that it should disappear in the realm of reason, in which persons, completely like and unanimous, are separated only by their different activities, and determined by universal reason or by one spirit. But this union of like beings—and this is the chief point—never leads to the concept of community, but only to that of sameness, of unity. But this is not a sociological concept. Thus it may be seen that the subject-object scheme never leads to a sociological category.[8]

With this conclusion we have formed the presuppositions for a positive presentation of the specifically Christian view. But we do not wish just to present this view; we wish to suggest a Christian

27

philosophy in place of the idealist philosophy of immanence. And we hope we may offer results which might determine the direction of a Christian social philosophy.

The Christian concept of the person may now be defined as constitutive of, and presupposed in, the concept of Christian community; that is, in theological terms, the concept of the person as found in primal man, but in man after the Fall, and that means, not in man living in unbroken communion with God and his fellow-men, but in man who knows good and evil. This concept necessarily builds upon the fact of man's spiritual nature, upon its structural and individual personal nature; but of this we shall speak later. In this general concept, too, the Idealist concept must be overcome by a concept which preserves the concrete individual concept of the person as ultimate and willed by God (cf. next chapter). We must first discuss the specifically Christian concept of the person, in order to make clear the difference from Idealism.

We must reject the derivation of the social from the epistemological category as a μετάβασις εἰς ἄλλο γένος. From the purely transcendental category of the universal we can never reach the real existence of alien subjects. How then do we reach the alien subjects?[9] By knowledge there is no way at all, just as there is no way by pure knowledge to God. All idealist ways of knowledge are contained within the sphere of the personal mind, and the way to the Transcendent is the way to the object of knowledge, to grasp which I bear within me the forms of mind: thus the object remains an object, and never becomes a subject, an 'alien I'. Certainly a subject can also become an object of knowledge, but in this case it is transferred from the social to the epistemological sphere. These spheres can be in principle so separate that in epistemological realism no social sphere may be recognised, and in radical epistemological idealism, that is, solipsism, the social sphere may be fully recognised. This means that neither sphere can be reduced to the other. We have now to show what we mean by the social sphere.

So long as my mind is dominant, and claims universal validity, so long as all contradictions that may arise with the perception of a subject as an object of knowledge are thought of as immanent in my mind, I am not in the social sphere. This means that I enter this sphere only when some barrier of principle appears at some point to my mind. This can happen in the intellectual sphere, but not in the epistemological-transcendental sphere: the idealist's object is not a barrier. What matters is not the nature of this barrier, but that it should really be experienced and acknowledged as a barrier. But what does this mean? It is the concept of reality which must be discussed, the concept which idealism has failed to think through exhaustively but has identified with self-knowing and self-active mind, involving truth and reality. The person has command of his own ethical value, possesses the dignity of being able to be ethical, and—so far as he is a person—having to be ethical. The boundary between obligation and being does not lie on the boundary of man as a whole, but in idealism the dividing line runs through man. Of course, in so far as every obligation, taken seriously, postulates ethical transcendence, idealism could at this point have paused for reflection. But with Kant's 'You can, for you ought' it moved from ethical transcendence to the immanence of a philosophy of mind.[10] From this it followed, as the necessary consequence of a one-sided epistemological philosophy, that the reasoning person had command of his own ethical value, entered by his own strength into the ethical sphere, and bore his ethical motives within himself, as a person equipped with mind. The real barrier was not acknowledged. This is possible only in the ethical sphere; this does not mean, however, that the barrier must have only an ethical content. As we have already said, it can be purely intellectual, that is, it can be experienced, for instance, in the conflict of perceptions. But the experience of the barrier as real is of a specifically ethical character. But we have still to say, in criticism of idealism and its implications, what we mean by reality. This brings us to the problem of time.

Kant taught that the uninterrupted flow of time should be understood as a purely intuitive form of our mind. As a result his thinking, and that of the whole of idealism, is in principle timeless. In Kant's epistemology this is obvious; but in ethics, too, he did not consciously get beyond this view. The same starting-points which could have led to the perception of the real barrier might also have overcome timeless thinking in ethics, without prejudicing the absolute ethical claim. Fichte, with his conception of individual duty, came nearer to it, but he too was a long way from the radical change which was required. Despite their constant emphasis upon the primacy of ethics, both are under the persistent influence of their epistemology. We do not dispute the epistemological view of time as a pure intuitive form. But we start from other considerations. Like Fichte and Kant we emphasise the absolute nature of the moral demand, and relate it to the person faced by it. At the moment when he is addressed the person is responsible, or, in other words, faced with a decision. This person is not the idealist's reasoning person or personified mind, but a particular living person. He is not divided in himself, but it is the entire person who is addressed. He is not present in timeless fullness of value and spirituality, but he is responsible within time, not in time's uninterrupted flow, but in the value-related—not value-filled—moment. In the concept of the moment the concept of time and its relations of value are included. The moment is not the briefest part of time, as it were a mechanically conceived atom, but the time of responsibility, of relations of value—let us say, of relations with God—and essentially it is concrete time, where alone the real moral claim is realised. And only in responsibility am I fully aware of being bound to time. It is not by my having a reasoning mind that I make universally valid decisions, but I enter into the reality of time by relating my concrete person in time in all its particularities to this obligation, by making myself morally responsible. Just as sound for the musician and sound for the physicist lie in different spheres of knowledge, so with time for idealist epistemology and the Christian concept of the person, without the one sphere abolishing the other.

Thus from our concept of time there follows an idea which is quite meaningless for the idealist: the person is continually arising and passing in time. It is not something timelessly existing, it has a dynamic and not a static character; it exists only

when a man is morally responsible; it is continually recreated in
the perpetual change inherent in all life. Every other concept of
person cuts through the abundance of life of the actual person.
The ultimate reason for the inadequacy of idealist philosophy to
grasp the concept of the person lies in its having no voluntarist
concept of God, and in its lack of a profound concept of sin (as
we shall show); and joined to these defects is its attitude to the
problem of history. The idealist conception of the person does
not indicate an accidental logical defect, but is inherent in the
system. Idealism has no conception of movement. The movement of the dialectic of mind is abstract and metaphysical,
whereas the movement of ethics is concrete. Further, idealism
has no understanding of the moment in which the person is
threatened by the absolute demand. The idealist moralist knows
what he ought to do, and, what is more, he is always in principle
able to do it, just because he ought. Where is there room for
distress of conscience, for infinite *Angst* in face of a decision?

This brings us close to the problem of reality, of the real
barrier, and thus of basic social relations. It is a Christian
recognition that the person, as a conscious person, is created in
the moment when a man is moved, when he is faced with responsibility, when he is passionately involved in a moral struggle,
and confronted by a claim which overwhelms him. Concrete
personal being arises from the concrete situation. Here too, as in
idealism, the encounter lies wholly in the mind. But mind means
something different in each case. For Christian philosophy the
human person comes into being only in relation to the divine
person which transcends it, opposing and subjugating it. The
autonomy of the mind, in the idealist individualist sense, is unchristian, since it involves the human mind being filled with
absolute value, which can only be ascribed to the divine mind.
The Christian person arises solely from the absolute distinction
between God and man; only from the experience of the barrier
does the self-knowledge of the moral person arise. The more
clearly the barrier is recognised, the more deeply the person
enters into responsibility. The Christian person is not the bearer
of the highest values, but the concept of value is to be related to

his being as a person, that is, to his creatureliness. Every philosophy of value, even one which makes the value of the person the supreme value (Scheler), is in danger of depriving the person as such, as God's creature, of his value, and of regarding him as a person only so far as objective, impersonal value is apparent 'in' him. But this prevents any understanding of basic personal and social relations.

When the concrete ethical barrier is acknowledged, or when the person is compelled to acknowledge it, we are within reach of grasping the basic social relations, both ontic and ethical, between persons.

The concept of the barrier is decisive here. We must now examine its form and structure, as experienced by the person. It is not given in the relation between the individual and the universal. The person is not simply the individual, and the individual is not as such involved in the fall and sin (Schelling). But the metaphysical concept of the individual denotes immediacy, unlike the ethical concept of the person, which denotes ethical and social reflection. From the ethical standpoint man is not 'immediately' mind by and in himself, but only in responsibility to 'another'. It is in this sense that we think of the ethical concept of the individual as the basic concept of social relations; for the individual cannot be spoken of without the 'other' also being thought who has set the individual in the ethical sphere. It might be objected that the 'other' has hitherto meant God, but now we have suddenly introduced a concept of social relation, and speak of the 'other' as another man.

We must, however, recall what was said at the beginning about the connection between God, the community and the individual. Moreover, the individual exists only through the 'other'. The individual is not solitary. For the individual to exist, 'others' must also exist. But what is this 'other'? If I call the individual the concrete I, then the other is the concrete Thou. But what is the philosophical status of 'Thou'? First, every Thou seems to presuppose an I, which is immanent in the Thou, and without which a Thou could not be distinguished from objects. Thus Thou would seem to be equal to the 'other I'. But this is only correct within limits. Beyond the limit set to epistemology there is a further limit, set to ethical and social knowledge, or discernment. The other may be experienced by the I simply as Thou, but not himself as I, that is, in the sense of the I that has become I by the claim of a Thou. In the sphere of moral reality the Thou-form is fundamentally different from the I-form. But since the Thou, too, confronts me as a person, as a thinking and effective mind, it must be understood as an I in the general sense, that is, of self-consciousness and so on (cf. next chapter). But the two I-forms must be strictly distinguished. The Thou, as a form which has reality, is independent in principle, over against the I in this sphere. Its essential difference from the idealist object-form is that it is not immanent in the mind of the subject. It is a barrier to the subject, it activates a will with which the other will comes into conflict, as an I for a Thou. If it is objected that the other is the content of my consciousness, and immanent in my mind, then the point has been missed about the different spheres, of which we have spoken above. The transcendence of the Thou has nothing to do with epistemological transcendence. This is a purely moral transcendence, which is experienced only by the man who makes a decision, which can never be demonstrated to someone standing outside. Thus all that is to be said about the Christian concept of the person can only be grasped by one who is himself involved in responsibility.

I and Thou are not just interchangeable concepts, but they comprise specifically different contents of experience. I myself can become the object of experience for myself, but I can never experience my own self as a Thou. It is perfectly possible for another man to become for me an object for the contemplation of his life as an I; but I can confront him only as a Thou. I can never become a real barrier for myself, but it is equally impossible for me to leap over the barrier to the other. My I as a form of Thou can only be experienced by the other I; my I as a form of I can only be experienced by myself. Thus in the experience of a Thou the I-form of the other is never immediately given. This means that I can be shown limits by a Thou which is not an I in the sense of the I-Thou relation. So the Thou-form is to be defined as the other who places me before a moral decision. With this I-Thou relationship as the basic Christian relation we have left the epistemological subject-object relationship behind. Similarly with the concept of the Thou as the other I. Whether the other is also an I in the sense of the I-Thou relation is something I can never discover.

The important question arises, how the I-Thou relationship may be thought of along with the concept of God. Is the idea of God to be included in the category of the Thou? I know of no philosophical system which has completely taken over the Christian I-Thou relationship between God and man. In the age of classical philosophy even the concept of God as personal was rejected. *Omnis determinatio est negatio,* said Spinoza, and his words were determinative for a long time. And if in dogmatics, in more recent times, it was found possible to make a philosophical application of the concept of person to the concept of God, this may have reacted on philosophy, when you find the attempt, as for example in Max Scheler, to do the same thing. But it is interesting to note that where a personal concept of God is advanced, there is always an effort made to keep it from being too concrete and specific. In theology, too, this may be seen happening not infrequently. Scheler is equally emphatic about the personal nature of God (on the basis of a 'sociological proof') and about the impossibility of God's relation to man being an I-Thou relation. Can we nevertheless maintain the I-Thou relation? We know God as the absolute, that is, however, also as self-conscious and spontaneously active will. This expresses formally and metaphysically the personal nature of God as pure mind, whose image is present in every man, as the remnant of God's likeness. Now it does not conflict with such a concept of God that he may be experienced by us as a Thou, that is, as an ethical barrier; further, this experience of God as Thou has *a priori* no effect on his I, either as being individually limited or as itself ethically addressed. If God is for us—that is, is active will over against us—this does not mean that we are a barrier for God. This has its application for the concept of God. God is impenetrable Thou, and his metaphysical personality, conceived of as absolute self-consciousness and self-activity, does not affect what we have said about his being as I.[11]

We might be accused of great one-sidedness. What of all that might be said about the philosophical concept of the person? In fact we have not left the ethical situation. But our intention has simply been to confront the Christian concept of the person with the concept of idealist metaphysics. The positive gains of the idealist concept will be made clear in another context. Meantime we must maintain that the centre of the Christian concept of the person lies elsewhere than in idealism. The attempt of the former to reach the concrete reality of the other was bound to fail, for we have to do with two spheres which are qualitatively different. On the idealist path, from the idea of the universal we come at best to the possibility of the other. The other is a postulate, just as the entire conception of the historical element in Christianity is a postulate for idealism (Christology). On the epistemological and metaphysical path one never reaches the reality of the other. Reality cannot be derived, it is simply given, to be acknowledged, to be rejected, but never to be established by proofs, and it is given only to the moral person as a whole. The Christian concept of the person rightly sees itself as a view of the whole person. Every idealist construction uses the concept of mind in order to cut through the living entirety of the person. The Christian concept affirms the whole concrete person, body and soul, in its difference from all other beings in its moral relevance.

What form do these basic relations of persons now assume? Does the proposition that the Thou is not necessarily an I, not conflict with the concept of community based on persons? Is not the person in the last resort completely isolated? For it is only with the Thou that a person arises, and yet the person is completely isolated. It is unique, separate, and different from other persons. In other words, the person cannot know but can only acknowledge the other person, 'believe' in him. There is the limit for psychology and epistemology, for the personal being of the other is a moral reality which cannot be grasped by psychology as a fact or by epistemology as a necessity.

B. THE CONCEPT OF GOD AND BASIC SOCIAL RELATIONS AND THE CONCEPT OF THE I-THOU RELATIONSHIP

The problem is the relation between the person, God, and social being. The I arises only with the Thou; responsibility follows on the claim. 'Thou' says nothing about its own being, but only about its demand. This demand is absolute. What does this mean? It claims the whole man in his claimlessness. But this seems to make a man the creator of the other's moral person, which is an intolerable thought. Can it be avoided? The person-forming activity of the Thou is independent of its personal being. Now we add that it is also independent of the will of the human Thou. No man can of himself make the other into an I, into a moral person conscious of responsibility. God, or the Holy Spirit, comes to the concrete Thou, only by his action does the other become a Thou for me, from which my I arises. In other words, every human Thou is an image of the divine Thou. The character of a Thou is in fact the form in which the divine is experienced; every human Thou has its character from the divine Thou. This is not to say that it is not a Thou, but a quality derived from God. But the divine Thou creates the human Thou, and because God wills and makes it this human Thou is real, absolute and holy, like the divine Thou. Here we might speak of man as God's image in virtue of his effect upon the other man (cf. below, the discussion of community of spirit, where one man becomes Christ for the other). But since one man's becoming Thou for another does not in principle alter anything about the Thou as a person, it is not his person as an I that is holy, but the Thou of God, the absolute will, here visible in the concrete Thou of social life. The other man is Thou only in so far as God makes him this. It is only in God that the claim of the other resides; but for this very reason it is the claim of the other.

To sum up: the person in his concrete life, wholeness and uniqueness, is willed by God as the ultimate unity. Social relations must therefore be understood as built up interpersonally upon the uniqueness and separateness of persons. The person cannot be surpassed by an a-personal mind, or by any 'unity' which might abolish the multiplicity of persons. The basic social category is the I-Thou relation. The Thou of the other man is the divine Thou. So the way to the other man is also the way to the divine Thou, a way of recognition or rejection. In the 'moment' the individual again and again becomes a person through the 'other'. The other man presents us with the same problem of cognition as does God himself. My real relation to the other man is oriented on my relation to God. But since I first know God's 'I' in the revelation of his love, so too with the other man: here the concept of the church finds its place. Then it will become clear that the Christian person achieves his true nature when God does not confront him as Thou, but 'enters into' him as I.

Hence the individual belongs essentially and absolutely with the other, according to the will of God, even though, or even because, each is completely separate from the other.[12]

It could be objected that we have not come to grips with the real problem of idealism, in that (1) we have not inquired about the essence of the person, but have dealt with its origin, and (2) so far as we have discussed the content of the personal we have been biased in the direction of the ethical, and have ignored man's 'spirituality', as though it were not an attribute of the person. To (1) we reply that it was no mere accident that we were driven from the question of the essence to the origin of the person. The Christian person—though not only the Christian person—consists in this continual coming into being. To (2) we reply that man's 'spirituality', with its moral and religious capacities, is certainly indispensable as a presupposition for moral growth as a person. This has already been affirmed, and it will be further developed in our discussion of the primal state.

Thus what follows in the next chapter must be regarded as also containing the presupposition for what has been said so far.

CHAPTER III

The primal state and the problem of community

Three main groups of ideas provide us with the doctrine of the primal state. First, in contrast to the ethical and ontic relations which have just been discussed, we shall show the real community of God and man *in statu integritatis*. Second, we shall discuss the relation of human spirituality and sociality in general. Third, we shall investigate the essential social forms. Our task therefore falls into three parts, a theological, a socio-philosophical, and a sociological. If the first part gives the original image of the church, the second and third parts provide the criteria for the sociological problem of the church. And before we reach the church's concept of community the primal community must be broken by sin, and quite new ontic relations established as basic. These have been to some extent described in the previous chapter, so far as they are not directly connected with evil will and are still real in the community of the church. We shall then have to show the remarkable intentions towards community which are found in the concept of sin, and how these were overcome in the revelation in Christ and yet are still active in the church. The concept of Christian community appears as determined by its inner history. It cannot be grasped 'by itself', but only in a dialectic of history. In itself it is broken. Its inner history becomes clear in the concepts of the primal state, of sin, and revelation, all of which are fully understood only when seen as aiming at community. It is therefore impossible to present the concept of the church without placing it in this inner dialectical history. It is of its essence that it still bears within itself the community of sin and is real only by the constant overcoming of this community of sin.

The theological doctrine of the primal state can serve only one purpose, to construct dogmas about man's original spirituality in a state of integrity. Moreover, what is of interest is the original state of man's religious and moral life. If we regard man as a free spiritual being created by God, then we must combine this idea with the idea that God created man in a direct relation with himself, in the direction of himself. There can be no objection to describing this freely affirmed direction as morality and religion. The person, then, as a freely created spiritual being, can be defined as the unity of a self-conscious and spontaneously active spirit.[1] This concept of the person, in contrast to the ethical, may be termed the universal-spiritual-metaphysical. Clearly the person is considered as a structural unity, so that there is no possibility of absorbing the structures in sociality. We have already seen that the person is willed by God as the ultimate unity, purely as a concrete person in absolute uniqueness and separation from other persons, as the creation of God. To this we now add the structural closed entity of this metaphysical concept, so that we reach a pure concept of the person, in which sociality is based purely on persons. The relation of sociality and persons will be discussed in the socio-philosophical section. The reason why we cannot define the person solely in the universal-spiritual sense is that while this definition is necessary, it is insufficient. All that we have said did presuppose the person in the sense of this definition, but it is insufficient because it is formally so universal that it includes man in his original state, in his natural state, as well as in his sinful and redeemed state. In other words, from the Christian standpoint it is irrelevant, and does not penetrate to the sphere of reality. It lifts man out of the animal world, makes it clear that he is not to be regarded as a

truncus; but the definition is possible only when the limits are
seen which are set to it by the Christian concept of the person.
Our aim is to present the concept of the person which holds true
within history, that is, after the Fall. This aim is justified because
(1) in a real sense history only begins with sin, in that the factor
that makes history possible, namely death, is bound up with
sin, and (2) if our chief question concerns real Christian community then the metaphysical concept of the person yields nothing; we need a definition of the person which has a Christian
content. The whole of idealism is unaware of any cleft between
the primal state and the Fall, or of the significance of this cleft
for the person and the view of community. It is this recognition
of the inner history of the concept from the primal state to sin,
that is, in the depths where we ascribe to sin a qualitative reality
in connection with history, that we make a fundamental separation from idealism. Origin and *telos* are an unbroken continuum
for idealism, and are synthesised in the concept of 'essence'.
All that interferes with this, on the one hand sin, on the other
hand Christ, cannot disturb this essential and necessary continuum. This straight-line conception of the history of the spirit
abolishes anything specifically Christian. Neither sin nor
salvation can alter the essence of this history.

To return: if the metaphysical concept of person is taken in
a positive Christian sense, that is, in the direction of God, then
we have the concept of person which belongs to the primal state.
Is there any connection with a concept of community? Undoubtedly man in the primal state must be thought of as being in
immediate community of service with God, as we find in Genesis
1 and 2. It is the concept of the church which first makes it clear
that this immediate community means something more than the
ontic I-Thou relation. This community is a real connection
of love between an I and an I. In the Christian concept of God,
known to us from the revelation in Christ, but also from the
church of Christ, the community of God and social community
belong together. We shall have to give our reasons for this
assertion later. So we maintain that the immediate community
of God demands also the immediate community of man, that the

latter is a necessary correlate of the former, and that it is no accident that we read in Genesis 2.18: 'It is not good that the man should be alone.' The immediate community of God is documented in the immediate community of man. But what does immediate community mean? In the community of God it clearly means, first, the absolute identity of purpose of the divine and the human will, within the relation of the creative to the created, that is, the obedient will. In other words, within the relation of ruling and serving. The idea of a community of love and of this connection of ruling and serving appear together here, in this image of the primal state, anticipating their connection and distinction in the ideas of the kingdom of God and the rule of God. In religious language, certainly, this community is built upon immediate and mutual love; but because love rules when it serves we have the problem here of a pure association of authority (*Herrschaftsverband*): by limitless serving God rules limitlessly over men. In that God establishes this law for community, man serves him limitlessly in fulfilling it, and God rules over men. Among men, therefore, immediate love must take other forms, since the absolute ruling character of a creative will over a created will falls away, and mutual service is a common service under the rule of God. But since all persons are created unique, even in the community of love the tension between wills is not abolished. This means that conflict as such is not the consequence of the fall, but arises on the basis of common love for God, in that every individual will strives to reach the one goal of serving the divine will, that is, serving the community, in its own way. Let this suffice for the present. When we consider the concept of the church we shall be able to disclose the wealth of relations in this. In the last resort we can speak of these things only because we know the church of Jesus Christ. In the logic of a complete dogmatics the source of these ideas is to be found in the concept of the church, whereas in the logic of the doctrine of the primal state they are a necessary consequence of man's religious and moral disposition in relation to God.

As a supplement to these findings we attempt a biblical exegesis. This must not be regarded as the source for what we have said, which in the last analysis comes from the revelation in Christ, and is valid even if the biblical exegesis is faulty.

It is certain that the chief motif in the story of Genesis 1-3 is the individual perfection of Adam in his primal state. But we think we find traits which indicate the basic social relations of this state: Adam is created as the crown of creation. He is lord of the beasts and of all created things. But he does not come to a full development of his spiritual nature. So the woman is created as his companion: 'it is not good that the man should be alone' (Genesis 2.18). We learn only indirectly, from the Fall, something of the nature of this community. The woman is seduced to disobedience by the serpent, and the man by the woman. Scarcely has the step been taken to the conscious act of disobedience when the man and the woman realise their sexual difference, and are ashamed in one another's presence. A cleavage has entered their hitherto unbroken and childlike community of obedience and innocence. With the loss of immediate communion with God the immediate social community is also lost. Between man and God, as between man and man, a divisive power has come, the power of sin. The medieval symbolism for the Fall puts a tree in the centre, with the serpent coiled round it, and on either side the man and the woman, separated by the tree from which they disobediently ate.

That the narrator sees sexuality as the power which now stepped between human beings, had a devastating effect upon the doctrine of original sin. But this result is not our immediate concern. What is important is that the narrator sees some kind of separation arising through the Fall, that is, through the moral act of rebellion against God, by which the original community of God and man is lost to man. Nor is this separation removed by the following sentence: 'And they became one flesh.' Rather, we perceive here the extremely complicated dialectic of human community, of which more later. The narrator thinks of divine and human community as in some way belonging together; since this community is destroyed by moral failure it clearly has moral character originally, and is part of the divine image in man in the narrator's view. It is sufficient to note that divine and human community are in some way part of the original moral and spiritual life of man, and that means, part also of his future life, in accordance with the parallel between Adam and Christ, the primal state and the last things. And this points us to the church.

It has always been recognised that man in his primal state must be thought of in communion with God. But it has very seldom been noted that this belongs with social community. In speaking of the church in Adam's time there was no thought of any communal relation, but only of the preaching of the divine word at mankind's beginning, in the sense of Augustine's words, *ecclesia, quae civitas Dei est, cui ab initio generis humani non defuit praedicatio (De Civ. Dei.* xvi.2). So far as I know, Schleiermacher was the first to speak of the communal relation in the primal state (*The Christian Faith*, para. 60.2). But even he says only that 'the inner union of the race-consciousness and personal self-consciousness' forms part of man's original perfection. This is intended to ensure the possibility of mutual communication and of the communal relation in religion; for it is only in the race-consciousness that men meet one another, and without it they could not have a communal relation. This must be an original relationship, since outside community we are not given any 'living and vigorous piety'. But the idea disappears after Schleiermacher. So far I can see, it was not till Reinhold Seeberg, in his *Christliche Dogmatik* (i, para. 22.1), in his teaching about man's innate spirituality, that the idea of sociality was suggested as belonging to man's original nature, thus restoring to dogmatics an important doctrine, without which the ideas of original sin and of the church cannot be fully understood.

This brings us to the second problem of the doctrine of the primal state, to the question of the connection between original, innate human spirituality and sociality. Our attention must be directed not to the Christian and moral fulfilment of empirical community, but to the meaning of the proposition that it is not good for man to be alone, to the meaning of the creation of woman, that is, of life in sociality. It will appear that all Christian and moral content, as well as the entire spirituality of man, is possible and real only in sociality. Not only do the concepts of sin and of the church become more profound, but a way opens up to a Christian evaluation of community life.

C. THE SOCIO-PHILOSOPHICAL PROBLEM: HUMAN SPIRITUALITY AND SOCIALITY

The problem of this section is the relations between man's spirituality and sociality. We shall show that man, as spirit, is necessarily created in a community, and that his general spirituality is woven into the net of sociality. This is extremely important in providing a clarification of the relation between the individual and the community, and the right background for the typology of community; on this basis we can clarify the problem of the religious community and the church.

1. *Personal being as structurally open*

First a general matter. In speaking in what follows of I and Thou and their relations we shall be using the words in a basically different sense from that of the preceding chapter. 'I' is not the person summoned up or awakened by the Thou. 'Thou' is not the unknowable, impenetrable, alien other. But we are now moving in a different sphere. Here we have to show that man's entire so-called spirituality, which is presupposed by the Christian concept of person and has its unifying point in self-consciousness (which must also be discussed in this context), is so constituted that it can only be seen as possible in sociality. If we have also to show that self-consciousness arises only with the other, we must not confuse this with the Christian I-Thou relation. Not every self-conscious I knows of the moral barrier of the Thou. It knows of an alien Thou—this may even be the necessary prerequisite for the moral experience of the Thou—but it does not know this Thou as absolutely alien, making a claim, setting a barrier; that is, it does not experience it as real, but in the last resort it is irrelevant to its own I. It is in this sense that I have now to speak of this general spiritual presupposition.

There is no empirical social relation of a specifically human kind which does not have a community appropriate to its nature. Thus the typology of social structures, too, is based upon a phenomenology of sociality which is established in spirit. Our first question, therefore, is not about the person with a social will, but about the spiritual person as such, and the way he is bound up in sociality.

Material spirituality in each person is bound up with self-consciousness and self-determination as the authentication of structural unity, and these can be formally defined as the principles of receptivity and activity. Material spirituality is effective in the acts of thinking, self-conscious willing and feeling.[2] These acts are only conceivable as resting on man's sociality, arising from it, and also with it and in it. So this first section deals with the structural openness of the personal unit to sociality, while the following section will analyse the structural closedness of personal being, showing the basic relationship of person and community.[3]

Man is embedded in an infinite abundance of possibilities of expression and understanding. By a million arteries a stream of spirituality has entered him, before he was aware of it, and he can only notice it when he is in the midst of it.

He knows that he understands, expresses, and is understood. The three experiences go together. They are present, potentially at least, in every spiritual act, and all spiritual acts are thus potentially bound up with sociality. In the life of feeling, too, where man thinks he is most isolated, he is certain of being able to express—if not fully, at least to some degree, which provides the limit to any expression—what he feels. This means that he is also certain that he can be understood and can understand the feelings of others. Thus sociality is involved here too.

At this point the concept of basic relations, and the supplementary concept of interaction, are in danger of being confused with empirical theories. It is only in interaction with other spirits that self-conscious thinking and willing are possible and meaning-ful. This we shall have to verify. First, the social phenomenon of speech, which is so closely connected with thought that it may well be said that it largely makes thinking possible, and has been given precedence over thought, the word over mind.[4]

Speech unites within itself the intention of objective meaning and subjective disposition, as well as empirical objectifying (acoustically and graphically), in which latter the mind simul-taneously acknowledges and overcomes nature in speech. This affirmation of nature (that is, of the sense-world), by means of which communication between persons is made possible (cf. 'the new body', 200f.), does not imply that nature is the con-stitutive element in the social character of our impulses to speak and write. But it is the material which the formative spirit, which is given in social intention, makes fruitful objectively and subjectively. And there is such a close connection between the two that spirit is inconceivable without nature, and human nature inconceivable without the social spirit. The phenomenon of language would be meaningless if the understanding of the hearer or reader were not potentially co-ordinated with every word.[5] With language a system of social spirituality is set within man; in other words 'objective spirit' has become effective in history.

Will must not here be regarded as will to communion, but purely phenomenologically, if serious misunderstanding is not to arise.

In contrast to impulse, will is the united activity of self-determination and self-consciousness. Will is always self-conscious; that is, in carrying out an act I myself am the centre and the unity of the act. This act of the individual person is possible and real only in sociality. There is no self-consciousness without community, or rather, self-consciousness arises together with the consciousness of being in community. And the will is by its very nature dependent on other wills. The first proposition has been maintained frequently in recent philosophy, and I should say has been essentially solved by Paul Natorp.[6] It is an unsolved riddle just how and when self-consciousness arises, genetically, since a study of one's own person is in this case excluded by the nature of the problem. All we can do is try to interpret aright the fact of self-conscious spirit, and this seems possible only within spiritual sociality. In knowing myself as 'I', I lift myself out as a unity from the vegetative spiritual state of the community; and simultaneously the being of the 'Thou' as the other self-conscious spirit rises up for me. We could turn this round and say that in recognising a Thou, an alien conscious spirit, separate and distinct from myself, I recognise myself as an 'I': I become aware of my self-consciousness.[7]

The consciousness of the I and the consciousness of the Thou arise together, and in mutual dependence. 'Self-consciousness, and with it self-conscious willing, develops solely in and with the communion of one consciousness and another.'[8] Thus the will, too, as an activity arising from self-consciousness, is possible only in sociality. Further, it is of the nature of the will as an activity that it is effective in community. Will arises where there are 'oppositions'. And strictly only another will can be an opposition of this kind. When it is a matter of removing a natural obstacle, it is not really the will which experiences opposition, but one's natural strength (or the will's means of organisation). The will itself experiences opposition only in the will of a person who wills something different. It is only in the struggle with other wills, in overcoming them and making them part of one's own will, or in being oneself overcome, that the strength and wealth of the will are deployed. Such a struggle takes place in miniature wherever man lives in the community of the I-Thou relation. For where person meets person, will clashes with will, and each struggles to subdue the other. Only in such encounters does the will reach its essential determination. As an isolated phenomenon the will is without meaning. Here again we come upon the basic significance of sociality for human spirituality.

A brief glance at man's emotional life shows that here too, where he is most isolated, there is a certain consciousness that expression is both possible and required, that is, that understanding by others plays a part. In addition, there are certain acts of feeling, experiencing, and rejoicing along with others, which direct the individual's life to that of others. Acts of pleasure, of sympathy, and of erotic love have also this social direction.

To sum up, man's entire spirituality is interwoven with sociality, and rests upon the basic relation of I and Thou. 'Man's whole spirituality becomes evident only along with others: the essence of spirit is that the self is through being in the other.'[9] The I and the Thou are fitted into one another in infinite nearness, in mutual penetration, for ever inseparable, resting on one another, in inmost mutual participation, feeling and experiencing together, and sustaining the general stream of spiritual interaction. Here the openness of personal being is evident. But the question arises: is there any point in still speaking of I and Thou, if everything is now apparently one? Is not every apparently individual phenomenon just a participation in the one supra-individual work of the spirit?

2. *Personal being as structurally closed*

The idea of personal openness threatens to turn into that of an a-personal spirit. With the beginnings of spirituality the I plunges into a sea of spirituality. It awakens and finds itself existing in the midst of this sea. It can only live in this context, and it knows that every Thou it meets is borne along by the same stream. But the characteristic form in which all this takes place is the form of the Thou. That is, man knows that his I *is* real only in the relation with the Thou. Clearly, then, he is not just the reservoir for a certain amount of objective spirit, a receptive organ, but an active bearer and member in this whole context of relations. Otherwise there would be no I-Thou relation, and no spirituality. The more the individual spirit grows the more it plunges into the stream of objective spirit,[10] sustaining it; and out of this movement the power for individual spiritual life is increased.

Thus the person's openness requires closedness as its correlate, if we are to be able to speak of openness at all. So the question whether there is an individual being which is untouched by social links must in a certain sense be answered affirmatively, if the idea of the I-Thou relation is not to be abandoned. On the other hand there is a danger that in trying to save the idea of an a-social core of personal being we might be thinking atomistically. A basic change of this kind would matter a great deal for our view of the church.

The tragedy of all idealist philosophy was that it failed to break through to personal spirit. But its tremendous merit (and that of Hegel in particular) was its recognition that the principle of spirit was something objective, reaching beyond everything individual, and that there was an objective spirit, the spirit of sociality, which was something in itself as opposed to all individual spirit. It is our task to affirm the one without denying the other, to keep the insight without joining in the error.

That the personal unity is closed is attested by self-conscious- ness and self-determination: in both there is complete separation from everything social, and both consist of introversive acts. The structural unity of the I is established as an experience in the experience of the Thou; it cannot be constituted by acts; acts rather presuppose it, and are directed towards it. We recall the distinction of principle we have made between structure and intention.[11] Here the basic synthesis between social and individual being comes to light. The individual personal spirit lives solely by virtue of sociality, and the 'social spirit' becomes real only in individual embodiment. Thus genuine sociality leads to personal unity. One cannot speak of the priority either of personal or of social being. We must hold firmly to the fact that alongside those acts which are real only in sociality there are also purely introversive acts. It is clear that the latter are also possible only in a person living in full sociality—than which there is indeed no other kind of person. So far as experience is concerned these acts isolate the I from the Thou completely;[12] but on the other hand it is not the intimate act which constitutes the person as structurally closed. Rather, no social intention is conceivable without this structural closedness, just as no intimate act is conceivable without the corresponding openness. On the other hand, the social intention is directed towards openness of the person, and the intimate act towards his closedness. But it is wrong to distinguish in the person an inaccessible, completely isolated core and a completely open layer surrounding it. The unity and the closedness of the whole person are presupposed together with sociality. No Thou can be experienced except by an I, which means that the Thou can never be experienced in a purely epistemological context. Thus the only question asked in idealist philosophy concerning the I and the Thou—the question of Fichte concerning the synthesis of the world of spirits—is wrongly put. For it proceeds from the assumption that I and Thou can be thought of as entirely unrelated, and then questioned about the point of unity, which somehow must exist. The question about the other soul, about being with the other, is not sufficiently filled with the knowledge of the unity of all spiritual happenings. The question starts with the individual, thought of as isolated and somehow seeking connection with others.[13] So we hold to our conclusion about the equilibrium between personal and social being.

Does the social unity, then, extend beyond the personal interactions? In what way is this conceivable? Or is it completely contained in them? In theological language, does God mean by community something that absorbs individual man, or is God solely concerned with the individual? Or are the community and the individual both willed by God as having their own significance? Is objective spirit nearer to God than subjective spirit, or is it the other way round? Or do both stand side by side beneath God's will?

If the equilibrium between social and personal being is to be maintained, what meaning does the community acquire as a metaphysical unity in relation to the individual? We maintain that the community can be understood as a collective person, with the same structure as the individual person. To think of the community as man on a larger scale, rather in the style of modern organology,[14] that is, with the aim of subordinating the individual to the whole, is an idea known since the time of Plato. This subordination must be rejected, as contrary to the equilibrium we have spoken of; but the question remains whether, besides the individual, there is not an individual collective person in which the individual participates, which goes beyond the individual but is incomprehensible without the correlate of individual personal being.[15] The question is the metaphysical possibility of such an assumption, the idea of equilibrium or of the monadic image in sociality. With the concrete application we shall deal later. In my empirical consciousness I myself represent the community, and I do not hypostatise the community in this way: my consciousness does not wish to ascribe to the community any being outside myself. But this empirical view must be overcome. Social unity is experienced as a centre of acts from which the social unity operates. It is self-conscious, and has a will of its own, though only in the form of its members. To conclude from this that the collective person is impossible is a typically empirical objection. A community is a concrete unity. Its members must not be thought of as individual: the centre of action does not lie in each member, but in all together. This unity is the starting-point for our thought, for one does not reach the one from the many, and an individualist starting-point precludes understanding of the situation. It is not that many persons, coming together, add up to a collective person, but the person arises only through being embedded in sociality. And when this happens, simultaneously the collective person arises, not before, yet not as a consequence of the arising of the individual. That is, the collective person exists only where individual persons exist. But since the collective person as a centre of acts is possible only as a concrete purposive community, it can only be possible where the individual person is a real part of the concrete community. The question of the 'body' of this collective person, and whether the ascription of a body to it has any meaning, will be discussed later. Litt's objection that in inter-personal relations one cannot jump from individual to collective persons, and that all social being is exhausted in I-Thou relations, is not in my opinion conclusive. I-Thou relations are also possible between a collective person and an individual person. For the collective person is in fact also an individual person. It is only when collective persons are included in social intercourse that the richness of this can be properly grasped. To grant the collective person, then, does not limit the basic sociological category of I-Thou relations; rather, in the eyes of God, the all-embracing Person, collective and individual persons have the same structure, both closed and open, with mutual completion, and social and introversive intentions within a structural unity. Yet we still shrink from asserting the reality of the collective person. As the problem of reality can be solved only from the ethical standpoint, the question must first be discussed how far ethical, personalist categories are applicable to a collective person. Clearly this will be important for the idea of the church.

We now have the basis for a theory of the formation of empirical communities. They must all be built on those basic relations which are given with the personal life of every man. This net of sociality in which man lives is prior to all will for community: the real relations in this sociality are still to be found even if empirical community is consciously and entirely rejected. Clearly, Leibniz's doctrine of the monad will be of help in understanding these basic social relations: individual beings, completely closed—'monads have no windows'—and yet representing, reflecting and individually shaping the whole of reality, and so finding their own being.

What is the theological significance of these observations? Man is not conceived of by God, the all-embracing Person, as an isolated, individual being, but as in natural communication with other men, and in his relation with them not satisfying just one side of his otherwise closed spiritual existence, but rather discovering in this relation his reality, that is, his life as an I. God created man and woman, each dependent on the other. God does not desire a history of individual men, but the history of the community of men. Nor does he desire a community which absorbs the individual into itself, but a community of men. In his sight the community and the individual are present at the same moment, and rest in one another. The structures of the individual and the collective unit are the same. Upon these basic relations rests the concept of the religious community and the church.

THE PRIMAL STATE AND COMMUNITY

D. THE SOCIOLOGICAL PROBLEM

I. *Social community as community of will*

Where men are brought together by sheer impulses it is not possible to speak of human society. The impulses of imitation, subordination, sociability, and in particular of hunger and sexuality, man has in common with the animals. Specifically human community is present only when conscious human spirit is at work, that is, when community is based on purposive acts of will. Human community does not necessarily arise from such acts of will, but it has its being in them.[16] Human community is by nature a community of will, and as such it gives meaning to its own natural form. Sociology may therefore be defined as the study of the structures of communities and the acts of will that constitute them; it is a phenomenological and systematic science. The subject-matter is not the origins of the state, of marriage, the family, or religious community, but the acts of will at work within them. Human community is a community of self-conscious beings who have wills.[17]

We must first describe the nature of social grouping in general, and then the concrete types of social acts of will and 'structures'.

It is characteristic of communal acts of will that they are not necessarily directed towards an object outside the person, but that they all point in the same way, that is, towards one another. The one man must in some way intend and will the other, and be intended and willed by him, whether purely for their association with one another, or for some purpose beyond them both. 'Agreement' which lacks this reciprocal relation is simply parallelism, and this is not overcome by the knowledge that the other will is running the same course.[18] The agreement must have this two-way traffic, and only then can we speak of 'unity' of will: it rests upon the separateness of persons. Community is not having something in common—though formally this is found in every community—but it is constituted by reciprocal will. Communities which are founded on merely formal agreement (an audience in a lecture-room, etc.) are not communities of will, but come into the category of the mass or the public (see below). 'Unity' of will means that the content which is intended and willed is identical for all. Here a further distinction arises. 'Unity' must exist absolutely in the will of the community, that is, as formal unity in the sense of 'agreement'; at first it will exist as absolute unity in regard to content as well, that is, in regard to the aim which is beyond the pure will to community. But in the historical development of every community differences of opinion arise concerning the realisation of the aim. These differences often lead to differences regarding the content of the aim, so that the unity of content can only be described as relative. So, too, the formally absolute unity of the empirical community of the church shows in regard to content only a relative unity.

One must never conclude, however, from the unity of will, whatever its nature, that there is some kind of unity of persons, that is, some fusion of persons. Community of will and unity of will are built upon the inner separateness of I and Thou. We have already rejected the idealist argument that the identity of what is willed demands the homogeneity and unity of persons. The man who is united with me in what we intend is structurally just as separate from me as the man who is not so united with me. Between us there is the boundary of those who have been created as individual persons. Only with this conception of community is the Christian idea of a divine community possible. Otherwise such a communion with God becomes unification in the sense of overstepping the boundary of the I-Thou relation, a mystical fusion.

To see the individual person as an ultimate unit, created by God's will, but as real only in sociality, is to see the relations of one with another, built upon difference, as also willed by God. This means that strife is the basic sociological law. Concretely this means that in every social relation there must be an element of partisanship. Only in the conflict of wills does genuine life arise, only in strife does power unfold. This insight is by no means new.[19]

54

Since the Fall there has been no concrete strife in the genuine sense. Hence the very idea of it has been condemned as evil. But even in the strife that has become unholy through evil, will the inmost social links of the human spirit be visible. For it does not mean that the other will is ignored or denied, but it is forced into one's own will and so overcome. Only in the co-operation of wills is their opposition dissolved. This is the 'social synthesis which triumphs over all antitheses of the will and of nature', in which 'the sociality of the human spirit is revealed as a primal force . . . a tremendous reality, which teaches us to understand the mystery of mankind and its history, and to have hope for its future'.[20] This truth is valid not only for the relation between man and man, but also for that between God and Man. Man's sinful will is forced in this struggle into the will of God, and thus community is established.

Community is community of will, built upon the separateness and the difference between persons, constituted by reciprocal acts of will, with its unity in what is willed, and counting among its basic laws the inner conflict of individual wills. This definition is incomplete until we have discussed the theory of objective spirit. But first we must consider the content of what connects one will with another. Only then can the nature of concrete community and the concrete form of objective spirit be clarified.

2. *Typology of social communities*

Bonds between wills can be regarded from the standpoint of the relation between the goal that is willed and the will to community, that is, the direction of the wills. This analysis provides us with an understanding both of the closeness and the looseness of the bond. The other way of looking at the matter is to study the relative strength of the wills. From these two approaches it seems to me that we can get at the nature of every bond between wills, even though in any particular case the analysis may be made more difficult by the presence of a combination of several types.

We begin with the first approach. Every will strives to reach a goal. There are two possibilities for the relation between this goal and the will to community, and in each the will has a different form.[21]

Wills may be 'with', 'beside' and 'against' one another. Only the first leads to empirical social formations. The second is sociologically irrelevant (but see below on the sociological concept of the mass). The third, when developed in a completely pure form, does create real social vitality, but cannot form a social structure. We are left, then, with the first form. When wills are willing with one another, what is willed can be two things. To be with one another can be willed as an end in itself (and this would include willing for one another); or it can be willed as a means to an end. The first we call the 'will for a meaning', the second the 'rational purposive will'. The first we describe in this way because its form of community has no material rational purpose, but it is meaning that is willed and affirmed. Corresponding to these two concepts of will are a 'structure of meaning' and a 'structure of purpose'. Community can therefore be constituted either as a means by a rational will with a pure purpose, or by a will for meaning which acknowledges the value of community as such. In the structure of purpose the unity of what is willed establishes the reciprocal movement of the wills; in the structure of meaning the unity of what is willed is itself represented in this movement. The latter, too, can throw out certain purposes, but they are not constitutive of the structure. When Aristotle says, in the *Politics*, πᾶσα κοινωνία ἀγαθοῦ τινὸς ἕνεκα συνέστηκεν, he is expressing the teleological character of all social structures, for clearly ἀγαθόν here means the good, and a good which is outside the community itself. We dispute the proposition in this form, since it corresponds to a eudaemonist ethic and mistakes the nature of the meaning of community as such. A structure of meaning is not constructed with a purpose, nor can it be explained by means of a purpose. We shall speak of this later.[22]

According to modern terminology—in Tönnies's creative definitions—the first would be called 'community', and the second 'society'. We shall keep his terminology. It would be easy to identify this distinction with the genetic one of associations which have 'grown' and those which have been 'made', between those already existing and those which are willed.[23] The family, the nation and the church would be among the first, limited liability companies, clubs, and perhaps sects (as in Weber and Troeltsch) among the second. But this identification is basically false. A nation is a community in the special sense, but it has not grown, but has been willed, moreover as an end in itself, having its own value, for every community is a community of will. The task of a sociological inquiry is not to disclose the thousands of motives which give rise to a social structure—one may recall von Wiese's chart of relations—but to study the acts of will of which this structure consists. Of course associations which have grown do often coincide with the type of a community, but both methodologically and logically it would be incorrect to identify them. In discussing the psychological differences between the life of a community and the life of a society, we shall discuss the closeness and the looseness of the bond between wills. That is to say, we do not think that the psychological differences actually constitute the types, but that the different acts of will have different psychological consequences.

Scheler is to some extent right to call all communities life-communities, not because the whole of life necessarily runs its course in them, but because man can live in them in the form proper to his vital personal being. The first act of affirmation that he belongs to a community is usually set within a concrete, living, non-formal act, say, conscious participation in the work of the community. Thus children, in love, or trust, or obedience, can belong in this way. For a community, unlike a society, can carry children too. This is not the genetic concept of a community, but the children are in the community as a piece of their parents' will, until they have their own will—an idea which would be meaningless in a society. This is important for the sociological concept of the church. Common feeling, willing and responsibility are the forces of inmost cohesion. The basic attitude is mutual inner interest.

If community is essentially life-community, a society is an association in rational action. It appeals to man to make the greatest possible use of his intelligence, as we see in the search for the most suitable means for the end desired, and the use of the society itself for the man's own ends. This procedure is not un-ethical only because it is agreed, and mutually applied. More-over the other man has to be treated with the great consideration, precisely in order that he may be exploited. This is the basis of the inner self-preservation of a society. The act of will by which a man enters a society must be explicit, and contractually agreed. There is no intimate personal element in this. Along with the communication between purposive wills in a system of means, there is complete spiritual isolation. Each man makes himself responsible for the society only in his own interest. A society has in principle no tradition. The basic spiritual attitude is mutual inner indifference, strictest caution towards the other, leading to reserve and self-assurance, and finally to a conventional amia-bility, so far as this consorts with your purpose. The organised structure of purposes is based on contract as the origin and criterion of the association, and develops into a comprehensive system of means, which are fixed in records and agreements.

From this it is clear that the directness of the bond between persons is expressed in a community by closeness, and in a society by looseness, both in the form of their life and in their psycho-logical attitude. It must, however, be emphasised that no pure type actually exists. There is no community without acts of will which are those of a society, and no society without acts of will which are those of a community, because society is by nature based on community.[24]

So far we have spoken of the way in which the direction of the will is determined, about its purposive intention and its intention of meaning. The question now arises of the relative strength of wills. This can appear as a relation of power and as a relation of authority. In the former the dominated will is activated mechani-cally by the will in power, whereas in the latter there is pre-supposed an understanding of the command by the one who obeys. This is sociologically significant in so far as in an association of power there can be no community, whereas in one of genuine authority community is not only present, but for the most part realised. This is most important for the concept of the church.

Corresponding to the disbalance of strength in an association of authority there is the balance in the 'co-operative association'. This brings us to Otto von Gierke's famous distinction.[25] The concept of a 'co-operative' is applicable only to relations of strength, and is not identical with the concept of community. A co-operative is in this sense a legal and not a sociological concept, since what it expresses is the legal equality of its members. It cannot be applied to living social relations. Concretely, as has been often shown in sociological studies, there is no pure balance of strength between the members of a social structure. In every community which seems to rest upon the dynamic co-ordination of wills there is in fact subordination. We should agree, but with the qualification that where there is an absolute authoritative will there is real co-ordination with those who are ruled. This co-ordination is included in the idea of equality before the law, as in the idea of the rule of God, as we shall show later. But this transforms the concept of the co-operative. It has no sociological significance as a necessary correlate of the concept of authority. The only sociologically new structure is therefore the association of authority. This means that the scheme of community and society is joined to the concept of this association, which may be either a community or a society.[26] The relevance of this for the concept of the church will be discussed later. A discussion of the closer relations between these three sociological types belongs to a detailed sociological study. Empirical social structures such as the army, the school, etc., are to be understood as combinations of these three types.

There is still another social structure which does not fit into the general concept of community, and which can be described as human only because it is formed of conscious beings: namely, the concept of the mass. 'The mass is not real' (Rosenstock). In the mass there is no real social bond between wills, but the wills are regarded as mechanical forces, as it were reacting to stimuli.

That is, they are not bound together by their direction or strength, but in an objectively operative relation, in which their reaction to stimuli is necessary, while their bond with one another is accidental.

Thus the 'mass'[27] in the sociological sense is not just any aggregate of men, but the structure, called into being by external stimuli, which rests upon the parallelism of will of several persons. In the mass the boundary of the personal disappears, the individual ceases to be a person, and is only a part of the mass, drawn along with it and led by it. The mass is a unity which is not supported by the differences between persons and which therefore cannot have any duration. It is the simplest social structure and it gives rise to the most powerful experiences of unity.[28]

What Vierkandt means by the invisible church expresses something that the church to-day has often become—a religious theatre and auditorium. The congregation are the audience, the 'public', they are pleasantly elevated by music and sermon, everyone is pleased to see many others who feel themselves exalted by the same spiritual enjoyment. And of course this feeling of shared joy is invisible, an idea which would be superfluous if it did not intend to say more than this. Vierkandt goes on to quote Goethe in the *Urmeister*: 'Where is there a more pleasant bond in society, where else must men confess that they are brothers, than when they hang on the lips and the features of a single man, and they are borne aloft in a common feeling?' But a common feeling, and knowledge of it, do not make a 'community'. This can be present, but sociologically it is *sui generis*, and the public is no more than a subordinate concept which refers to the mass with its parallelism of wills. The other sociological structures, with their basis in meaning and purpose, are in the midst of temporality.

This gives rise to a new problem. Is the reference to time or duration for these basic sociological concepts something new?[29] Is there a new principle of order here? Basically, the question here is the relation of eternity to the temporal community. This is most important for the idea of the church, though it also goes to the heart of the social structure we are now considering. We have distinguished between a will for meaning and purposive will, a structure of meaning and a structure of purpose, between community and society. The meaning of society is clear. But why should we speak, in connection with community, of 'a will for meaning' and 'a structure of meaning'? Because in this kind of bond the will is not self-establishing, but recognises something established, it is not related to a purpose but to value, because what demands acknowledgment is a structure of values which cannot be grasped rationally or teleologically.[30] Or, to put it from another angle, because community by its nature does not point purposively beyond itself. Unlike many sociologists, we do not consider that it is possible to elaborate the *telos* of a community, a family or a nation, however delicate our insights. A community may have a rational *telos*, but it is not contained within it, the community itself is not this *telos*. It is its very nature that this should be so. Rather, community is permeated with value, as history is, and as value itself lies beyond intramundane limitations. As history by its nature finds its *telos* at the boundary of history (regarded as the end of time, and beyond time), that is, in God, so community is founded in God, and willed by him. History has no rationally perceptible purpose, it comes from God and goes to God, it has meaning and value as such, however broken its origin and its destiny may be. So, too, genuine community, in marriage, the family, the nation, is from God to God, and its *telos* lies on the boundaries of history. This means that the concept of duration, whose boundary lies on the boundary of time, is given with the concept of community. The 'duration' of a community is identical with the duration of history. We are thinking of community as an idea, not as an empirical fact. Concretely, one may think of the communities of blood, such as family and race, or of historical communities, such as the people and the nation, or of communities of destiny, such as marriage and friendship—in their nature as communities they are all from God to God. Nor is there any essential difference between the communities which are found and those which are made, so far as they are communities in the sense defined above.

In contrast, a society as a structure of purpose is purely within history. For the realisation of its purpose it is constituted in history. Its purpose can be the purely personal desire of each individual (earning money, or connections), and with the satisfaction of the individuals the duration of the society is, ideally, at an end. If a society's purpose goes beyond the individual, say over a whole generation, then the duration corresponds to this purpose. If the purpose of the society is the dream of many people to establish the kingdom of God on earth, then its purpose lies at the end of history, which is thought of as the end of time. The category of 'development' appears, which is not found in a community. But the idea of society never goes beyond the idea of the purpose which constitutes it. A purposive association which tries to reach beyond what is temporally possible for it, ceases to be an association. Here the end of history is the end and not a boundary. Thus the idea of a concrete society as purely teleological is necessarily intra-historical, and temporally conditioned.

This description cannot be refuted by an appeal to the empirical difference in duration. For we are speaking of the idea of society, not of its empirical duration. If wills have joined together for the sake of their joining, if a community has been affirmed, irrespective of rational purposive tendencies, then the intentionality in these acts reaches to the limits of time, i.e. to the limits of history, to God: it is 'from God to God'. Here is the entire 'holiness' of human life in community, the relation with God which is found in friendship as in marriage and the life of a people, and thus also the indissolubility of all these structures of life.

Finally, in the sociological concept of the mass we saw that the dynamic and mechanical stimulus on a great number of men was constitutive. 'Stimulus' can only be conceived of in the category of what is temporally conditioned, the temporal 'moment'. If a community is at the boundary of time and a society is bounded by time, then the mass is to be described as being within time.

An association of authority cannot be described here. For it is to be categorised according to whether it is seen as a structure of society or a structure of community.

So far we have analysed the structures of acts of will and the possible types of social life. We can now consider the concept which is of the utmost significance for social philosophy and sociology, one whose use is very confused and yet can be service-able for an analysis of the concept of the church, the concept, namely, of objective spirit.

But before we do this we must give a brief historical excursus on the patristic view, and the view of St. Thomas Aquinas, on the natural forms of human socialisation.

The problem of social formations arose early in the history of theology, as both a philosophical and ethical problem. It was natural that it should arise in the communal life of the state rather than of the church. Is the state a consequence of the Fall, that is, is it sin; or is it willed by God?[31] The answer can be seen as flowing from the two concepts of the world[32] which run through early Christian literature, the one seeing the world as good, as created, the other seeing it as evil, made bad by the evil will. We therefore find the concepts of primary and secondary,[33] of absolute and relative,[34] or of ideal and concrete[35] natural right. The state in itself is willed by God, and good, and it is the con-sequence of sin that the power of punishment and of compulsion is necessary. In their primal state men would also have founded a state. It is noteworthy, however, that the state in patristic literature has essentially social character. Its task is to care for order and welfare. Ideals of state in Hegel's sense are quite absent.[36] The existing state is therefore good and sinful at the same time. This twofold character is found in all social structures, which would also have arisen in the primal state, but now bear flaws. Man is by nature a social being. *Sociale quiddam est humana natura.*[37] This is the general patristic view. The necessary pre-supposition, for all empirical social structures, of the difference and inequality between persons is acknowledged by the Fathers, and moreover as belonging to man's primal state, and not as a consequence of sin. Basic to this view is the acceptance of the organic conception of society. If this was possible as a solution of the problem of the church, as following St. Paul it was thought necessary to believe, then it was also applicable to man's original existence. Marriage and family are the most primitive social structures, undoubtedly willed by God, which were depraved in the state of sin by concupiscence and the punishment of patriarchalism, and then hallowed once more by Christ. Originally, neither the continuation of the race nor the idea of subordination, as the constitutive powers for the family, was connected with sin. Both are good and necessary. In particular, 'equality' is not abolished by subordination. The heavenly hierarchies provide an example of this. Troeltsch's idea of primal equality in the sense of absolute likeness of being does not hold for patristic literature.[38] From the idea of organic equality there came into force the philosophical and ethical justification of private property, derived from Lactantius, Cicero, and Aristotle.[39] There were few who maintained that poverty and wealth are the consequence of sin (Ambrose). Since gainful activity was regarded as natural, and therefore good, buying and selling, and profits and risk, were approved, there arose an explicit acknowledgment of social action in the sense of purposive rationality. The danger of self-seeking was again and again mentioned by the Fathers.[40] But the necessity of commercial activity was not disputed. Thus there was made explicit a basic estimation of all honourable work as having a proper place in the organic social structure.[41]

These basic ideas were taken over and systematised by St. Thomas.[42] Here too his theological system of reason and revelation may be plainly seen. With the help of Aristotle and the idea of organism the life of the state and of society in its Christian form was established and recognised as having natural right. The purpose of the state is essentially the same as in patristic thought. The spiritual superstructure is given with the concept of the church, to which everything is referred.[43] The balance between individualism and socialism is provided by the conception of organism. How far this can be systematically maintained cannot be examined here. It is enough for our purpose to see that both social and communal activity were recognised as belonging to primary ideal natural right, and that social life as a whole was regarded as willed by God. If, as Thomas maintains, mankind is presented as a unity (*unus homo*), then social life is necessary.[44] It is the evil will which depraves everything and introduces self-seeking into the organic common life.

3. *Objective spirit*

Without being aware of it, people speak of objective spirit in a double sense:[45] (1) in the sense in which the spiritual is objectivised in contrast to unformed spirit, and (2) in the sense in which the spiritual is social in contrast to subjective. The basis for both is the recognition that where wills unite, a 'structure', that is, a third thing, previously unknown, arises, independent of its being willed or not willed by the persons joining with one another. This general recognition of the nature of objective spirit was a discovery of qualitative thinking, which arose in Romanticism and Idealism. It is only here that concrete totality arises; it is not a question of numbers, but depends on the way people think of it, and experience it as a phenomenon. Two wills encountering one another form a 'structure'. A third man joining them does not see just the two men joined together, but rather a third thing, the structure itself, opposes his will with a resistance which is not identical with the will of the two individuals, but can be greater than the resistance of the individuals, or—if such an idea were possible—of the sum of all individuals. It is this 'structure' which is objective spirit. Not only does it confront the third man, who is seeking admittance to a society of friendship, as something independent and autonomous, but it also intrudes as a third thing between the two who are bound together in however primitive a structure. The persons thus experience their community as something real outside themselves, disengaging itself from them, and rising above them.

In community the individual is faced by his own objectivised self. His own life has flowed into the community, and stands before him daily as experienced content and form, as a regulative principle for his conduct.

Thus the law of human community is an intermingling of being that is continually moved and of objectivised being. Time fixes every past moment in objectivity, so that the present moment and the past are in conflict. In this conflict the victory is with onward-marching time, which makes objective spirit into the historical and social turning-point between past and future. In objective spirit there is the element of historical movement forward and the expansive element. The first is the reality of its historicity, the second the reality of its sociality. Objective spirit is thus the bond between the sense of history and the sense of community, between the intention of a community in time and its intention in space. Objective spirit is the will effectively operating upon the members of the community. It has individual form. It leads an individual life over and above the individuals of the community, yet it is real only through them. The more the individuals are alive, the more powerful is the objective spirit. It interacts with each individual, and with them all together. To withdraw from it is to withdraw from the community. It has a will for historical advance as well as for the social realisation of its will.

What is objectivised, however, is completely irremovable, whether by one individual or by all together. If the individual cuts himself off completely from the community, then he no longer experiences the objective spirit; but he cannot do more. It must be generally admitted that this is not all that can be set aside, if what is objectivised has been materialised. But what cannot be shown is that there is a difference in principle between the objectivisation in a work of art, so far as it is not experienced as mere matter, and unmaterialised objectivisation.

Objective spirit is found in social as well as communal formations. The more members a community has, the less specialised their awareness of standards will be, the less the inner power, and the greater the outward power. It is easier to immerse oneself in the spirit of a class of school children than in that of a friendship. The difficulty of entering into the spirit of a social formation is independent of the number of its members. Its objective spirit bears none of the marks of personal aliveness. That which in a society is a means to an end (advertisement) is in a community a symbol, corresponding to the difference between them: the society has an end or goal, whereas the community is self-representational. Objective spirit in a society is not affirmed as a value in itself, but only as means to an end: it is an objective structure of purpose. The productivity of objective spirit is here directed to a system of means. If the society is dissolved, this system of means is left behind as materialised spirit, but has lost its inner meaning, since the aim is no longer there. An 'instrument' whose purpose is no longer understood, or no longer of interest, is dead, because the objective spirit which sustained it, and which was simply the means to an end, disappears when the end is lost sight of. A work of art, on the other hand, which bears fulfilment and understanding within itself, in its intention, rests in itself, because the objective spirit which sustained it was an end in itself, and has a life over and above the will of its members.

From all this it follows that society and community have a different view of time. In a community the intention reaches to the bounds of time, in a society it is bounded by time. This eschatological character, which a community shares with history, contains its deepest meaning, as being given 'from God to God'. This is the basis of the 'holiness' of human life in community, whether it is a physical community of blood and race, or a historical community like the nation, or a community of destiny like marriage or friendship. It is in virtue of this holiness that all such human structures are in principle indissoluble. The idea of society, on the other hand, does not go beyond the idea of the goal which constitutes it; it is temporal, and intra-historical. For a society the end of history is really an end, and not just a boundary. (The temporal intention of the mass, as we have already seen, is directed towards the moment.) That is why only a community, and not a society, can become a 'church'. Of this more later.

The most profound difference between the two social forms lies in the fact that we can attribute personal character to the objective spirit of the community, but not to that of the society.[46] It is regarded as an achievement in sociology to have discarded such a metaphysical hypostatisation.[47] It is the fear of Hegel which prompts this view. His idea of the 'spirit of a people' makes the individualist feel uneasy. But we cannot accept the criticism of his idea. This is based upon the empirical idea that there would be no objective spirit without persons, that its existence depends upon persons coming together and parting, the spirit being constituted by the first movement, and destroyed by the second. The interdependence of the individual spirit lives in the objective spirit, but 'it is the triumph of the subjective spirit that the objective structures which it can produce out of itself, with their own value and duration, never win completely free of it, but must always tend back to it in order to be quite real.'[48] It should not be necessary to repeat that the genetic dependence of objective spirit tells us nothing about its ideal autonomy. For subjective spirit, too, as we have shown, is dependent for becoming personal on other spirits, but is nevertheless in principle autonomous. Objective spirit lives its own life, but not in such a way that the life of the individual is absorbed into it, as Hegel suggests, when he says, 'It is mind that has reality, and individuals are its accidents.'[49]

Rather we must say 'in principle everyone can say good-bye, and go his own way.'[50] Nevertheless there is a centre of action which is proper to the experience of community (love, sympathy, rejoicing, etc.) and a particular way of acting in community, alongside other individuals, in the sense of social equilibrium and the image of the monad.

Thus we do not have here the conception of a being of the spirit, called the spirit of a people, rising up with power from metaphysical depths. But in the dialectical movement, in which persons arise, there also arise individual collective persons, and only when this is seen does the richness of the monadic image of social life become clear. Collective persons are self-conscious and self-active.

But it is also clear why no personal character can be ascribed to a society. Objective spirit is regarded only as a means to an end, whereas a person can never be only a means to an end.

Can we speak of the collective person having a body? We

must not confuse this with a theory of organism. This would once again bring us close to the theory of the spirit of a people. Body is not the equivalent of the spirit's executive function, a definition which is certainly false. 'Body' is not an objectively establishable entity, but one which is experienced subjectively. It must not be confused with physical body, the 'flesh' of the Apostles' Creed.[51] Objectively, a dead and a living physical body have the same aspect, but only the latter is 'body'. 'Body' is given in relation to the I; it is the physical body experienced by the I as its possession, with which it has an inner connection, and which it has to some extent at its disposal. In this sense the centre of action of the community experiences all its members, which have affirmed it. The community takes this affirmation seriously, and in this sense has its 'body' at its disposal. In distinction from the idea of an organism there is here the idea of a community of will. The concept of body is important for the concept of the church, as we shall see later.

Those who have followed the course of the argument will certainly now raise the objection that idealism has after all carried the day. For the community of will which has been so emphasised, which is built upon the structural separateness and diversity of individuals, has now become the unity, with its own centre of action. What are we to reply? In fact, with the collective person a new unity does arise, which is something else than the absolute and relative unity found in the identity of what is intended. But this new unity does not annul the specific reciprocal movement of community. The individual persons remain entirely separate from one another. Metaphysically the collective person is autonomous in face of the individual persons, even though genetically dependent on them. In the structure of persons its position is no different from that of any individual person. In the strict sense unity and community are not mutually exclusive, nor are they identical; but they require one another.

In relation to the doctrine of the primal state, we may now say that theologically all the relationships in community which we have discussed can be represented in the integral state, that is, within the community of love, both social and religious, which was originally given, and that therefore the spiritual form (this community of love) and the natural form (the empirical community) are so created that they rest in one another. From this it is easy to draw conclusions about the character of the empirical community.

We have now to show how, with the coming of sin, the spiritual form takes a new shape, and how these altered ethical relationships are related to the unchanged natural forms. The idea of the collective person can then be fully elaborated.

CHAPTER IV

Sin and the broken community

The world of sin is the world of 'Adam', the old mankind; but the world of Adam is the world for which Christ atoned and which he turned into a new mankind, into his church. This did not happen, however, in such a way that Adam was completely overcome, but in such a way that the mankind of Adam still lives on in the mankind of Christ. Thus a discussion of the problem of sin is indispensable to an understanding of the *sanctorum communio.*

Our essential task in this chapter is to reveal the new basic social relationships, between the I and the Thou and equally between the I and mankind, which are postulated by the concept of sin. The argument will bear extensive reference to the concept of the Christian person presented in Chapter Two. The question of the connection of these relationships with natural forms can be treated very much more briefly.

Whereas the previous spiritual form had grown up upon the basis of love, the Fall changed this to selfishness. This gave rise to the break in immediate communion with God, as it did to that in immediate communion with man. This alteration in direction brought about a change in man's whole spiritual attitude. Morality and religion in their true sense are lost to his nature; they are still visible only as forms in legal order and natural religion.

Whereas the primal relationship of man to man is a giving one, in the state of sin it is purely demanding. Every man exists in a state of complete voluntary isolation; each man lives his own life, instead of all living the same God-life. Each man now has his own conscience. Conscience did not exist in the primal state; it was only after the Fall that Adam knew what good and evil were. Conscience can just as well be the ultimate prop for self-justification as the point at which Christ strikes home at man through the law. Hearing the divine law in solitude and recognising his own sinfulness man comes to life again as an ethical person, though in ethical isolation. With sin ethical atomism enters into history. This is essentially applicable to the spiritual form. All the natural forms of community remain, but are corrupt in their innermost core.

But man's perception of utter solitude in his responsibility before God, of the utter particularity of his guilt, encounters another perception, which, even though it seems to run directly counter to the first, does not cancel it out, but rather deepens it still further. The second perception is based upon an insight into the qualitative nature of sin, that the misery caused by sin is infinitely great; this means that it must have not only an individual but also a supra-individual significance. Sin must be imagined as a supra-individual deed, though of course as an individual deed too; it must be at the same time the deed of the race and of the individual. Thus the perception that *in sin* one is to the highest degree alone leads to the other perception that one's sin is to the widest extent shared, so that of inner necessity we are once again directed from the one to the others, without whom the existence and nature of the one could not be understood.

Two problems force themselves upon us here. How should the universality of sin be understood from the point of view of logic and theology? It is not enough simply to suppose it as a fact. Secondly, how should we conceive of the empirical spreading of sin throughout mankind? The idea of the social significance of sin has been developed dogmatically in the doctrine of original sin.

A. ORIGINAL SIN

The doctrine of original sin assumes that sin is spread throughout mankind, and inquires concerning the manner of its spreading. It then gives an account of the way mankind belongs together, is bound together, in the *status corruptionis*. But joined with the account of the spread of sin there are ideas which aim at proving its universality, and it is for this reason that the doctrine of original sin presents some of the most difficult logical problems of all dogmatics.

Theology has suggested various answers to the problem. We give a brief outline of the biblical material.

Throughout the Bible there is reference to the universality of sin (Gen. 8.2, Ps. 58.5, Ps. 14, Job 14.14, Rom. 3.24), but none to original sin (not even Ps. 51.7 or Ex. 20.5, cf. Ezek. 18.2, 20 and Jer. 31.29). Nor does Paul make use of a doctrine of physical original sin. The translation of Rom. 5.12 ἐφ' ᾧ =*in quo* is wrong: this should be rendered 'by which'. The line of thought here is therefore 'through *one* man sin comes into the world,' i.e. into the human race. When Adam sinned, he sinned as an individual and as the race. From eternity God lays upon his sin, as an individual sin and as a sin of the race—i.e. upon mankind from Adam to Christ—the condemnation of death. For with the one sin there is given the 'objectively effective principle' (Seeberg) for all men's further sins. No man will act differently from Adam. That is, as a result of this 'objectively effective principle' the universality of sin is established in principle. Paul does not discuss the empirical form of this, which is the very question of the doctrine of original sin. From Paul we receive no more than the general thought that God imputes to all men the one sin of Adam, and that this is derived from the universality of the condemnation of death. The first question, then, concerns the connection in principle between the one man, Adam, and the whole race; and the second question concerns the empirical nature of the spread of sin—to which latter question Paul gives no answer, a fact which has its reasons.

A brief historical survey will show how these two basic sociological and ethical problems have been dealt with in the history of theology. This will give us a starting-point for a systematic presentation.[1]

We begin with Augustine. The essence of original sin is the

guilt of all mankind, introduced by Adam and continued by physical propagation; it is shown in the corruption of the natural state of all men, in concupiscence, which is deserving of punishment. Concupiscence is regarded as the punishment consequent upon the primal sin. Sin must somehow be man's own act, for a moral view presupposes that there is an identity, however brought about, between the guilty and the punished. Thus, in line with Rom. 5.12, it is maintained that all men were 'in Adam'. Being 'in Adam' is a necessary but an inadequate basis for punishment. The guilt which occurs 'in Adam' must be 'reckoned': this is the meaning of the 'imputation'; and the punishment which is the consequence, namely, concupiscence, is simultaneously given. But original sin and original evil go together so closely that Augustine can describe original evil as the reason for the reckoning of guilt: that is, he calls concupiscence itself a sin, and not just the punishment and the place where further sins can arise. Original sin and original evil continue by physical propagation. A question arises here concerning Augustine's view of mankind's basic social relations. The social and philosophical concepts which give significant help here seems to me to be (1) original evil, (2) man's 'being in Adam', and (3) *imputatio*.

When Augustine considers the whole of mankind, his first feeling is that he belongs to a race which has been struck by a terrible and overwhelming fate, and is distorted and corrupted in every element of its life, in its very nature. A fearful punishment has been imposed upon it. As conceivers and as conceived the members of the race are indissolubly connected to one another, and at the very nearest point of this connection the most terrible fate is also to be found. For it is sexual concupiscence which Augustine regards in this way. Its very naturalness assures the universality of the fate. With terrific intensity of feeling Augustine recognises the power of the *natura vitiata*, of original evil. In that unbridled age he shudders before the immense power which *concupiscentia* has in the world. This power, which not even the will can command, which again and again brings even the saints low, and leaves not a single man untouched, must have some special religious and metaphysical significance. Mankind lives in its endless thrall. Thoughts of this kind are the devastating utterance of a man who ascribes to the powers of nature a significance which is at once metaphysical and borne by destiny. These thoughts lead logically to the conception of the *massa perditionis*, the mass which endures a tragic destiny, seen as a natural happening.[2]

But in this pessimistic, almost Manichaean view there are also to be found the means for overcoming it. In the bodily consciousness of every man, which is given with sexuality, he is aware both that he possesses something quite personal, and that he is a natural being beyond his life as a person. Augustine, thinking the first along with the second, is able not only to relate natural corruption to personal guilt, regarding the corruption as the punishment for the guilt, but he actually makes concupiscence the reason for the ascription of guilt: for concupiscence itself is guilt.[3] Concupiscence is still a power, but not like an earthquake or a thunderstorm. It is connected with man's bodily nature and thus with the person; and yet again, it is quite independent of the person. This twofold nature of Augustine's thought is clearly expressed in the image borrowed from Rom. 5.12, that we were all 'in Adam', that is, in a purely biological and natural sense, but at the same time this expresses the guiltiness of each man. The contradiction here is to our way of thinking extreme. Augustine's strongest words for the purely personal and spiritual reference are 'we were all that Adam' (*pecc. mer. et rem.* I, 10, 11). That is, our will is like Adam's, and thus we ourselves have done what Adam did. The thought of personal guilt is strongly emphasised, but at the same time the idea of original sin seems to have disappeared. Although Augustine constantly strove to understand personal guilt as truly personal, he was always led astray, by the thought of infant baptism, to false biological views of the human race. Yet we must acknowledge that besides the concept of the mass we have another, which we can describe as the concept of the kingdom of ethical persons. The cleft between the two ideas is most clear in his doctrine of the imputation of Adam's sin. Here Augustine suggests a middle position between the two views already described. It is joined to the first view, so far as mankind is regarded as a biological unity, and to the second view, so far as it tries to express the idea of personal guilt. Its problem is how to derive personal guilt from the biological unity of mankind in Adam. It cannot solve this problem, for it is a view which contains inner contradictions. Adam is regarded in a twofold way, as primal father and as representative of mankind: first as the conceiver, and second as the one in whom the will of all mankind reposed: as *caput seminale* and *morale*, to use terminology from a later age. Adam's willed deed is imputed to man as his own. So biological and ethical views of mankind struggle vainly with one another. But for Augustine the dominant interest is in the universality of sin rather than individual guilt: the biological view prevails over the ethical.[4]

It was Luther who put all the weight on man's ethical guilt, and overcame the biological view of the race which had been derived from the notion of physical reproduction. In the 'willing of the I' he found the essence of original sin, that is, in a personal ethical act. He thus maintains simultaneously that sin is both inexcusable and universal. In orthodox teaching this view has not been preserved.

It was Schleiermacher who saw once more the significance of original sin as a social and philosophical problem. He brought to the problem a new biological view. He thought it was easy to regard sin as inherited, but in that case the concept of sin was misleading (*The Christian Faith* II, para. 69). Original sin is on the one hand the sinfulness which is present in man, but beyond his actual life (para. 70), and on the other hand it is the guilt of each man towards the other, and thus to be described as the total deed and the total guilt of the human race (para. 71). Sinfulness, in the form of sensuality, is innate in every man, and he actualises it by free self-confirmation 'in real sins'. The first man possessed this innate sinfulness as something original (para. 72.5). Real sin increases the 'disposition', that is, of sinfulness, and so becomes the 'effective original sin', which impels others, as well as itself, to real sin (paras. 71.1, 72.6). The individual should see himself

76

as the subject of original sin only in actual sin. But since actual sin necessarily happens, it is clear that every man would have acted as Adam did, so that Adam's sin can rightly be called the sin of every man. No one can regard sin as something individual, but rather it arises as something communal from the self-consciousness which is extended to the consciousness of the race. Everyone knows his sinfulness as dependent on the guilt of others, but he also knows that his own real sin is the basis for the sinfulness of others. Therefore not only has every man made himself guilty, but everyone also lives in a total life of guilt, which both relieves him and weighs upon him. So on the one hand everyone is 'the representative of the whole race' (para. 71.2), and on the other hand the concept of original sin is correctly applied only when it is related to 'the entirety of the race', in which it 'cannot likewise be the guilt of the individual' (para. 71.2). This means that the individual is relatively relieved of the burden by the totality. It is the race which is the subject of original sin, as at first it was the individual in his actual sin who was regarded as the subject. Schleiermacher undoubtedly saw correctly that the concept of sin is fulfilled in a social and collective understanding. But in place of an ethical and social category he has introduced a biological category, with a partial metaphysical foundation. Sin is sensuality, a hindrance to the consciousness of God, that is, something negative, and not an ethical category. The emphasis lies on a theory of heredity interpreted as a physical fact. Thus Schleiermacher concentrates on establishing the inheritance of sin—the part of the problem which is unbiblical; he loses touch with the biblical content.

Partly in opposition to Schleiermacher, partly in dependence on him, Ritschl developed his doctrine of the kingdom of sin. On his view the subject of original sin is mankind as the sum of all individuals.[5] The biological view, but also sin as original, disappear from this teaching. Moreover, we may, as I think, find a substitute not in Ritschl's idea of a sum of individuals, but only in the idea of a collective person (see below).

In the twentieth century the tendency is to set aside the problem of how sin is inherited. The most recent justification of a doctrine of original sin is to be found in the Roman Catholic philosopher Scheler, with whom we shall have to deal briefly.

We take up the threads of our systematic presentation, and must attempt to understand in ethical terms some basic sociological concepts, such as the race, ascribing or imputing, and collective person, before we attempt to understand the meaning of the church.

The guilt of the individual and the universality of sin should be conceived of together. The individual's guilty act and the guilt of the race must be joined in our thinking. So far as we mean by 'race' the concept of the biological species, we weaken the ethical seriousness of the concept of guilt. We must therefore find a concept of the species which is suitable to Christian ethics. We have to understand the human species in terms of the concept of sin. Hitherto it has only seemed possible to understand what the human species is, in terms of nature. Children, idiots, and normally developed people had all, it seemed, to be included equally. But this necessarily led to a view of sin, of sacraments, and of the church, that was ethically indifferent. From this it follows that the Christian concept of guilt is incompatible with a biological concept of the species. So the concept of guilt must not be understood in terms of the concept of the species, but viceversa. In this way we reach an ethical collective concept of the race, which is able to meet the requirements of the idea of the race's sin. The individual is then established as the self-conscious and self-active person, which is the presupposition for ethical relevance. And the race is understood as consisting of such persons.

The idea of the sin of the race and the individual must be discussed from the standpoint of the Christian concept of the race, of mankind. How is it possible to conceive of the individual's act of guilt and of the guilt of the race together, without making the one the basis for the other, that is, excusing the one by the other? Augustine evidently thought that it was the sinful general act which formed the basis for every individual act, and basically Anselm and St. Thomas Aquinas do not advance beyond this position. Ritschl's thought takes the directly opposite course, proceeding from the sum of individual sins to the concept of the kingdom of sin, and thus not finding a sufficient basis for the universality of sin. Everything clearly depends upon finding the general act in the individual's sinful act, without making the one the basis for the other. An ethical category must be related to the individual as an individual person. This, however, is not to exclude the social element, but to postulate it together with the individual person. Man is the race precisely in being an individual. This is the definition which is adequate to man's spirit in relation to the basic social category. If the individual spirit rebels against God in the sinful act and thereby rises to the utmost height of spiritual singularity—since this is its very own deed against God, occasioned by nothing outside it—the deed the man concerned is doing is at once the deed of the human race (no longer in the biological sense) in his person. In acting thus he lapses not only from his personal destiny but also from his destiny as a member of the race, so that with every sin it is the whole of mankind which falls, and in principle none of us is distinct from Adam—which also means, however, that each of us is the 'first' sinner. This relation between the individual and the race also corresponds to the monadic image presented in the section on social philosophy, the image in which every single monad 'represents' the whole world. If we recognise this state of things then the awareness of the deepest personal guilt is linked with that of the universality of our deed. We cannot take refuge behind carrying the guilty burden of an empirical and temporal first sin, for this would mean falling back upon the biological concept of the race. But we are to connect our individually general deed with the universal guilt. And it is clear that this leads not to an unburdening but to renewed burdening. Every act is at once an individual act, and one in which mankind's general sin is brought to life again. In this way we have established the universality of sin as necessarily given along with and in individual sin.

From this recognition of the bond between the individual and the race there emerges what has been called the experience of common sinfulness. 'I am a man of unclean lips, and I dwell in the midst of a people of unclean lips,' Isaiah cries, as, in the utmost loneliness, he confronts the holiness of God. In speaking thus he is not divesting himself of his personal guilt, but rather positing it together with the awareness that in him the sin of the whole people comes to life, and that his sin stands in the closest connection with it. The experience of ethical solidarity and the recognition that one is the *peccator pessimus* belong together. But the experience does not in any way constitute sociality; but sociality is present before and apart from it. It is necessary to bear this carefully in mind (see below on 'Experiencing the Church', 194ff.). The experience of ethical solidarity is built upon the uncompromising singularity of the person, so that even in the awareness of the closest belonging together the ontic and ethical separateness of individual persons on account of sin can never cease, nor fade from the consciousness. There is no over-leaping the limits of the I. Here we once again meet the I-Thou relation presented above (realised in the guilty sense), the 'aboli-tion' of which is possible only in the concept of the church. We now add, however, to complete the picture, that it is not only the Thou which is essential to the I, but the race too. The 'experience' of the *peccatorum communio* in its relation to the basic ontic re-lationships paves the way for the experience of the church, as we shall later present it.

Further, the I which has become a person experiences the bond only with other individual I's which have become persons, and it is only to these I's that the concept of community can be applied. All others belong only in possibility to community. (Note how the basic outlines of the concept of the church are already emerging.) With these considerations all empirical objectification of the universality of sin is rejected, and we have consciously turned aside from the Augustinian doctrine of original sin.

The defence of the idea of original sin recently suggested by Max Scheler is based on the proper recognition that our ethical concepts do not keep pace with our social insights, but are one-sidedly individualistic. Guilt, he says, is necessarily connected with autonomous personal action, but not with concrete indi-viduality. It is perfectly possible for a person to act guiltily without being individually guilty. The basis for this view is the Platonic conception of good and evil as substantial entities, with the consequent weakened concept of autonomy. For Christian thinking good and evil are qualities of the will, and this destroys Scheler's argument. I think we have shown that nevertheless we are not driven to think in sheerly individualistic terms.

But since we are bound to accept some kind of historical spread of sin, we must now face the question of the nature of this empirical spread. First, we must say that basically nothing can be known about this. Sin is on every occasion an unfathomable and inexcusable contradiction of God, arising out of the free will. The psychological motivation of sin can be analysed right up to the deed, but the deed itself is something entirely new, done in freedom, and psychologically inexplicable. All explanations whether in the psychic or the mental realm are historicisings, excuses, weakenings of the fact of sin. If we remember this, then we avoid fundamental error, and can at the same time recognise the relative justification of our question. At least we must try to analyse the motivation of sin up to the actual doing of it. We look for these motives not in sexuality, as is done in traditional teaching, but in spirituality bound up in sociality. The original community of love, as the repose of wills in mutual action, is destroyed when one will exchanges the movement of love for an egocentric movement. And it is of the nature of the situation that the one who sees everyone around him abandoning the unbroken community and adopting an egocentric direction should himself take the same direction, for he sees that his own movement towards community is empty, and without response. This begins in the smallest circle and extends ever farther, so that one can say that the reason for general egoism is to be found in sociality.[6]

Is this development identical with the shift from community to society? Clearly not. For in practice both community and society continue, though no longer in their purity, but in 'relativity'. There is now no community without sin, but on the other hand a 'society' is not just a 'sinning community'. A 'contract' as such is not evil (see above). It is only evil when it

THE COMMUNION OF SAINTS

consciously exploits or destroys the other. Nor is the will to self-preservation as such evil. Therefore sin in the community is not the newly-added individual will to self-preservation—which in fact makes community possible—but the sin is the will to affirm in principle oneself and not the other as a value, and to acknowledge the other only in relation to oneself. But it will be objected that this is precisely the nature of a society. Not so. A society is not built upon self-seeking, but on the instinct to self-preservation; and thus it is no more built upon the evil will than a community is. By a relative life of community we mean that the community is a necessary form of human activity in general, and that it is not completely bound to the ethical content of the will. Even when the will takes an evil direction there is still community, though it is hollow. In contrast to a society the value of the common life, without defined purposes, is acknowledged, though the individuals in this community are fundamentally separated and isolated from one another. But the evil will at work in a society turns it into an institution for the systematic exploitation of its members. It would be misguided to try to understand the real nature of communities and societies in terms of this state of affairs. For we see here the degeneration of their real nature through sin. A solution of this problem can only be found in the Christian concept of community.

B. ETHICAL COLLECTIVE PERSONS

If the subject of sin is at once the individual and the race, what is the form of sociological unity suitable for the mankind of Adam? This reintroduces the question of the ethical personality of collective persons which we previously left open and which determines whether there is any meaning in the idea of a collective person. Is it possible to regard the collective person as an ethical person, that is, place it in the concrete situation of being addressed by a Thou? If so, then we shall have proved that it is a centre of action.

The meaning and reality of such a call can be comprehended

only by one who, as a part of an empirical community, has experienced it. It is the Israelite concept of the people of God, which arose solely through being thus challenged by God, by the prophets, by the course of political history and by alien peoples. The call is to the collective person, and not to the individual. It is the people that is to do penance as the people of God. It was the people, and not the individuals, who had sinned. So it was also the people who must be comforted (Isa. 40.1). When peoples are called, God's will is seen shaping history, just as when the individual is called, he experiences his history. There is a will of God for the people, just as there is for the individual. When a people conscientiously submits to God's will and goes to war, to fulfil its history, its mission in the world, thus entering completely into the ambiguity of human sinful action, it knows that it is summoned by God, that history is to be made; here war is no longer murder. God does not only have eyes for the nation; he has a purpose for every smallest community, for every friendship, every marriage, every family. And in this same sense he has a purpose for the church too. It is not only individual Germans and individual Christians who are guilty; Germany and the church are guilty too. Here the contrition and justification of individuals is of no avail; Germany and the church themselves must repent and be justified. The community which is from God to God, which bears within it an eschatological meaning—this community stands in God's sight, and does not dissolve into the fate of the many. It has been willed and created, and has fallen into guilt; it must seek repentance, it must believe in and experience grace at the limits of time. It is clear that this can happen only 'in' the individual. Only thus can the hearing of the call be concretely comprehended, and yet it is not the individuals, but the collective person (*Gesamtheit*) who, in the individuals, hears, repents and believes. The centre of action lies in the collective person. Thus the collective guilt of a community is something else than guilt as a social phenomenon in the community. The 'people' is to repent, but it is not a question of the number who repent, and in practice it will never be the whole people, the whole church, but God can so regard it 'as if' the whole people has repented. 'For the sake of ten I will not destroy it' (Gen. 18.32). He can see the whole people in a few individuals, just as he saw and reconciled the whole of mankind in one man. Here the problem of vicarious action arises, which we deal with later. When the collective person is addressed ('He who has an ear, let him hear what the Spirit says to the churches'—Rev. 2 and 3), the conscience of each individual person is addressed. Each person, however, has only one conscience, which is valid for him both as a member of the collective person, and as an individual. For there are not two strata in man, one social and one private; a man is structurally a unity, and it is only the directional intentions which can be in conflict in him. He must know himself and make decisions as an inner unity, must not therefore blindly subject himself to the concrete claims of the collective person, but struggle through to an integrated decision of the will. Only upon such integrated persons is the ethical community built. Our conception of collective guilt is thus not that of a fault deriving from certain contents or parts of the soul; but the concrete form of collective guilt is the total guilt of the integrated person.

These insights now have to be applied to the concept of mankind. Mankind is the universal community comprising all communities. The participation in its life as a community is authenticated by the affirmation of life lived in fellowship with others. For this always exists within the collective human person. It too, like every person, is capable of receiving the ethical call, as it can be heard for the whole of mankind in the story of Jesus Christ. The collective human person has a heart. The individual authenticates his participation in this in its ethical aspect, that is, by every act of repentance and recognition of guilt. The collective person's heart beats at the point where the individual recognises himself both as an individual and as the race, and bows to God's demand. Here is the seat of its moral unity; it has in reality one conscience, in so far as every man is Adam. It is a structural peculiarity of the mankind of Adam that it breaks up into many isolated individuals, even though it is united as mankind, which has sinned as a whole; it is 'Adam', a collective person, which can be superseded only by the collective person, 'Christ existing as the church'. The sign of belonging to the old mankind, to the first Adam, lies in sin, and the individual's awareness of guilt reveals to him his connection with all those who have sinned; in recognising that he belongs to the mankind of Adam, the individual places himself within the *peccatorum communio*. 'The mankind of sin' is one, even though it consists throughout of individuals; it is a collective person and yet subject to endless fragmentation; it is Adam, as every individual is both himself and Adam. This duality is its nature, annulled only by the unity of the new mankind in Christ.

CHAPTER V

Sanctorum Communio

A. BASIC PRINCIPLES

1. *Conclusion of the discussion in the concept of the church: retrospect and prospect*

So far our whole theological inquiry has not only had the discussion of the *sanctorum communio* as its aim; but it has been possible at all, and significant, only in the light of the *sanctorum communio*.[1] Only through the *sanctorum communio* can we justify the introduction of philosophical discussions into the framework of theology. It is not that in the idea of the *sanctorum communio* all that has been said about the *peccatorum communio* has no substance; it is rather precisely in the *sanctorum communio* that the significance of the *peccatorum communio* first becomes immediate. It is true that the man who has been justified, who belongs to the church of God, has 'died to sin'; 'no one who abides in Christ sins'; 'the old has passed away, behold, the new has come'; 'for as in Adam all die, so also in Christ shall all be made alive'—but the life of those who are justified, namely, the new life, is 'hid in God', and 'I do not do what I want, but I do the very thing I hate.' *Nullum umquam extitisse pii hominis opus, quod si severo dei judicio examinaretur, non esset damnabile.*[2] The reality of sin has remained in the church of God too; so Adam, the *peccatorum communio*, is really superseded by Christ only eschatologically, namely ἐπ᾽ ἐλπιδι (*in spe*[3]); so long as sin persists, the whole of sinful mankind persists in every man. Thus everything we have so far discussed is gathered together in the idea of the church, in which it culminates and is overcome.

Until now we have been pursuing two, or rather three, different lines of thought, which we now have to bring together in our minds; or better, whose union, which is already present in the reality of the church, we now have to explore. On the one hand there was the line of thought about men being basically related to one another by ontic personal relationships. On the other hand there was the discovery of the human spirit's pre-volitional sociality, and the consequent investigation of the forms of empirical real community relationships, which always require volitional social acts to authenticate themselves as personal social relationships. The basic ontic-ethical relationships in the state of sin not only form the basis for all personal social relationships, but are requisite, even, for their empirical formation. When they are changed, or re-created, in the concept of the church, the concrete form of the community must also change; indeed it is this which makes the development of a special empirical form of community possible and necessary. We recognise certain basic forms as in accordance with creation, and consequently the question now arises, to what extent the form of the church enters into them, and whether in it we shall be able to find the synthesis of them all. This, however, can be dealt with only later.

Since even when the basic ethical relationships are changed sin remains, which means that the old ontic relationships are not radically annulled, every empirical formation will necessarily be subject to the ambiguity inherent in all human actions. What is unprecedentedly new, however, is that the new basic relationships have their own form; that the meaning of these relationships is that they produce such a form. In this we can perceive a special will of God which it is not open to us to belie by condemning everything that has taken on a form as the handiwork of man. It is in the necessary bond between the basic relationships and the empirical form of community as a special form that the nature of the church, formally speaking, resides.

There are basically two ways of misunderstanding the church, one historicising and the other religious. In the first, the church is confused with the religious community; in the second, with the kingdom of God. In the first, the character of reality which is possessed by the new fundamental relationships based on God is overlooked in favour of the 'religious motives' which in fact lead to empirical community (the urge to do missionary work, the need to impart one's faith, etc.). This outlook, however, receives its plain judgment in the words of John: 'You did not choose me, but I chose you' (John 15.16). The second misunderstanding springs from not taking seriously the fact that man is bound by history; that is, historicity is either deified as an object, as in Roman Catholicism, or it is simply evaluated as accidental, subject to the law of sin and death. This, however, is not to accept but to circumvent God's will, which is to reveal in the church as he did in Christ everything which he reveals by concealing it in the guise of historical events. To put it differently: the 'seriousness' which is so much talked about is carried so far that it loses its real character and becomes formalistic. The first misunderstanding is almost unavoidable in the study of the church from the historical or sociological point of view; but it is equally at home in the religio-romantic circles of the Youth Movement. The second is met with in theology. Both are dangerous, for both can be nourished by solemn and earnest religious feeling. In neither, however, is there any grasp of the reality of the church, which is at once a historical community and established by God. Thus the lines of thought we have pursued so far are justified and blended in the concept of the church. Upon the new basic ontic relationships there rests a communal being which, viewed from outside, cannot be characterised other than as a 'religious community'. Now it is certainly possible for us to confine ourselves to the empirical phenomenon 'church' *qua* 'religious community' or religious society, to analyse it as a 'corporation subject to the law applying to public bodies' and describe it in terms of sociological morphology. In this case all theological discussion of the subject would be superfluous. Or on the other hand—this is the second possibility—we can take the church's claim to be God's church seriously, when it regards the fact of Christ, or the 'Word', as constitutive. This means, further, that we must look at the new basic social relationships which are here presupposed, and which in the deepest sense make possible a social formation like the church. In this case one of our premises will of course no longer be susceptible of further justification, namely, that we take the claim of the church seriously, that is, not as historically comprehensible, but as having its basis in the reality of God and his revelation. We do not want to bring standards for judging the church from outside; the church can be fully understood only from within itself, from within its own claim; only thus can we suitably acquire critical standards for judging it.

Here, however, we apparently fall into logical inconsistencies from the very outset. We said we were taking the church's claim to be the church of God seriously, but in the first place, this, of course, is not to say that we may accept this claim untested. The question is only as to what criteria we should take to test the assertion. In principle the way is indeed open for the discovery of outside criteria, that is, for deducing the correctness of the proposition from outside. This way does not in principle take us farther than the category of possibility. Proceeding from this, however, one necessarily arrives at the concept of religious community. The concept of the church is possible only in the sphere of reality based on God; that is, it is not deducible. The reality of the church is a reality of revelation, part of whose nature it is to be either believed or denied. So if we want to find an adequate criterion for justifying the church's claim that it is the church of God, this is possible only if we place ourselves within it, if we submit in faith to its claim. Belief, of course, is not a possible method of arriving at scientific knowledge, but as the belief which accepts the claim made in revelation, it is the given premise for positive theological knowledge. It would be completely wrong, too, to 'establish' from the belief in Christ the belief in the church as a conceptual necessity. What is conceptually necessary is not for that reason real. Rather there is no relation to Christ in which the relation to the church is not necessarily presupposed. Thus logically the church presupposes its basis within itself; it can be judged only through itself, like all revelations. It presupposes what is to be found. Before one can begin to talk about the church there must be knowledge and acknowledgment of its reality. This is precisely what proves that it is a reality which has been revealed not to those outside, but to the man who believes its claim. Only the man who is already in the church can admit that these theological methods are justified; but in them he will have abandoned the objective outside position. It is this very thing which provides the logical stumbling-block for the entire question of the church. People ask whether the religious community—which is then also called the church—necessarily has its basis in the Christian religion, or whether the attitude of the religion itself is individualistic; they go to much trouble to derive the power to form communities from a concept of the 'Holy', to show by means of Christian ethics that men are ethically dependent upon one another, to arrive at a sociological category from the nature of revealed religion. But they never seek the point of departure in the recognition of the church of God as a reality which has been revealed, and so it is certain from the outset that the concept of the church is something they will never arrive at. Further, it is impossible to prove by means of a universal concept of religion the necessity of the concept of religious community. Two outstanding examples, taken from the most recent Protestant and Roman Catholic works on religious philosophy, may help to illustrate this.

Max Scheler,[4] in his *Wertethik*, develops a system for placing values in order of rank. The value accorded highest place is the religious one of the 'Holy'. Now there are certain *a priori* laws within this order of values, one of which can be expressed in the proposition: 'The higher the values, the less they are divisible.' If several persons wish to partake of a pleasure of the senses, then the value of the sense-object, of a loaf of bread, for instance, is divided among the number of persons. Half a loaf has half the value of a whole loaf. But with works of art, for instance, the situation is quite different. Works of art are in principle indivisible. The most pronounced contrast, however, is offered by the value of the Holy, which 'is in principle proper to every being', but which by its very nature does not even allow of any material bearer. As the sense value divides the partakers, so the function of the spiritual value is to unite, in a superlative sense.

The deduction is very illuminating, but the thought behind it is thoroughly formalistic. It is certainly true of a sense pleasure that the pleasure can only entirely profit one man; but what does Scheler mean by 'to unite'? Clearly the possibility of simultaneously assembling several persons round one object. For he cannot be thinking either of bringing several persons together empirically, or of community in the strict sense, since both ideas would clearly be wrong here. (Cf. the phenomenon of the mass and egocentric mysticism.) The thought that by its nature the Spiritual or the Holy presents such a possibility sooner than do the things of the senses is correct, but devoid of content. For one could just as well say that the value of the Unholy or Diabolical as a spiritual value was of incomparable unifying power. Likewise Scheler would be unable to demonstrate any difference in principle between the unifying effect of the Holy and that, for instance, of the Beautiful or Good. The correctness of the deduction lies in the perception that the immaterial value has an essential unity setting it above all material things, but that unity only potentially guarantees a certain wider partaking of that value. It is the applied logical proposition: 'The smaller the content, the greater the compass of a concept.' The flaw in Scheler's argument lies in the fact that in the idea of the Holy he proceeds from a metaphysical concept of value which in its absoluteness remains for ever inaccessible to us, instead of arguing, as he might have done, from the historically positive revelation of the Holy in Christ, the 'material bearer of the value', and arriving from the factors determining the content of revelation (which are not only a 'symbol') at the reality of community as established by the Holy. It is only upon the ground of concrete revelation that we can overcome the empty concept and potentiality and arrive at the real community relationships, which are present in virtue of the 'historical' reality of the Holy.[5]

This, it seems, is exactly what Heinrich Scholz[6] was trying to do. Proceeding from the idea of revelation he seeks to break through indirectly to the concept of community. First, he says, religion is one of the ponderables of the human spirit, and secondly it is not *a priori*, but revelation, these being mutually exclusive concepts. From this it follows that education in religion is necessary. Education in revealed religion is possible, however, only upon the ground of a tradition, which is in turn unthinkable without a community. We first dispute the idea that the categories of *a priori* and revelation are completely opposed in the sense in which Scholz uses the concept of revelation, namely as synonymous with the consciousness of revelation. Further, we must ask what educating someone in revelation is supposed to mean. Clearly only the subject-matter of religious knowledge can be imparted. But this does not seem to be specific education in or for religion, and the bearer of such an education, the community preserving the tradition, is not as such qualified as a specifically religious community, let alone as a church. It is just as true of science that it bears within it such 'sociological categories'; basically Scholz does not tell us anything more than that religion can be handed on to others (and even this he cannot show to be something necessary in principle—one has only to think of mysticism), and to this extent exercises certain social effects. This, however, does not tell us anything new, nor even anything essentially relating to religion. It is something historically self-evident.

Our problem was to decide to what extent the reality of God's revelation in Jesus Christ also postulated the reality of the revelation of the church. We see a decisive difference between the community as the guardian of the Christian tradition and the Christian church. Scholz should at least have asked why religion is handed down, whether such a phenomenon means more with religion than with science, whether community was inherent in the intention of his general concept of religion, or whether it lay in the accidental inclination of men. Scheler thought too formally; Scholz seeks to think more concretely, but falls into the opposite error of historicising and becoming too empirical. He himself admits that he does not derive the concept of community directly from the nature of religion, and is in doubt as to whether such a derivation is at all possible. There is in fact only one religion from which the concept of community is essentially inseparable, and that is the Christian religion. Thus in my view the two interpretations just described do not demonstrate the nature and necessity of religious community, let alone the necessity of the church. This does not mean that we repudiate the problem of the connection between religion and community as such, which belongs to the philosophy of religion. But in order to master it we must make more distinctions.

The general concept of religion has no social intentions. The idea of the Holy in its general sense as a religious category is not fulfilled in relation to society, but in the soul's solitariness with God. The mystic too has a religion. If it is nevertheless a fact that religion is for the most part social in character, this is primarily accounted for by various psychological factors of a more or less accidental nature (e.g. the need to communicate—Schleiermacher, the receptive-active nature of man—Seeberg). These factors indicate that religious community is possible, but not that it is necessary. This leads us back from the general idea of religion to its concrete form, which for us means the concept of the church. Here, however, a universal necessity for the communal form of the church cannot be proved. In what follows we shall briefly discuss this. We must note, however, that this problem can be treated not in terms of the church, but of the philosophy of religion, which means that only the basic ideas can be discussed

First, we must consider the general connection between religion and community, the concept of religious community, and secondly a typology of religious communities. Our first thesis is that, from the standpoint of its genesis, the concept of religion as a whole is taken from social life: if man were not a social being he would not have any religion.

All man's spiritual life has at least a mediate basis in society, and this holds true also for religion. The I-Thou relation of God and man, or God and community, which is as old as religion itself, is psychologically conceivable only in terms of social experience.[7] There is no religious content which does not have its counterpart in the purely social process: from total dependence to free action, from rebellion to conquest, from repentance to reconciliation, from mistrust to the most complete trust, from insolence to reverence (*pietas*), from the greatest possible distance from God to the utmost absorption in him—demanding and obeying, giving and receiving, everything has its place. Everything spiritual presupposes community, which means that even the original community cannot be derived from the spirit. But this original and archetypal connection of religion and community does not imply any social and communal intention in religion. Certainly the communal intention is directed to God, and without this there would be no religion. Religion must be defined here as the touching of the human will by the divine, and the overcoming of the former by the latter with resultant free action.[8] Religious community would then be a community which makes itself the object of divine action, and is itself active in communal terms. From this it is clear that in religion an intention directed to religious community is not established in principle, and this must be so: for the value of the Holy is not fulfilled, like that of righteousness or love or equality, and so on, in social terms, but also in solitary communion with God. The mystics too had their religion. So our second finding is that in the general concept of religion social community is not given, though made possible—community, that is, in the twofold sense, both in its empirical form and in its collective basis. These two concepts of community must be strictly distinguished in what follows.

But it is a fact that religion is a social matter. It may be uncertain whether in its first beginnings religion is a slow dawning of 'another' in the most primitive stirrings (horror, fear, longing, sexual desire) in the individual's soul, or whether the biological social form of the family, the *gens*, is experienced as the subject of religion. But it is certain that where we find worship of divine or demonic beings, even in the crudest style, it is carried on by a community, which so to speak 'keeps' this private god, and from which it expects protection for its communal life.

And it is also certain that in the cultic life there arise very early, alongside the acts of the individual (the paterfamilias, the sorcerer, the priest) communal practices, in dance and song and prayer[9] (the latter being either a chaotic mass prayer or a series of responses from the congregation). To this sphere there also must be added the sacred meals,[10] the sexual orgies of the fertility cults, and sacred prostitution, and indeed the orgy, 'the social form of ecstasy', can be regarded as the primal form of religious community.[11] Thus with these considerations the earliest beginnings of religion are closely bound up with social life. On the one hand the subject of religion may be seen as basically in the community, with the individual as a member of it, and on the other hand the community as a whole is religiously active.

But if, as we have shown, there is no essential connection between religion and community, nevertheless most concrete religious forms must have some affinity with the concept of community in the two senses.

What is the nature of this affinity?

We recognise four different modes of relation between religion and community. First, a radical rejection of outward and inward community, as is characteristic of mysticism. Second, there are free religious communities, which are held together by purely rational and purposive elements, by some common religious practice which is the means for attaining a specific goal. Such communities are individualistic cultic societies, and have the character of an association (see below). Distinct from these, there are, third, religious groupings based on physical communities. In this category the family, the tribe, etc., are so firmly regarded as the subject of religion that the individual takes part in the religions of the cult only as a part of the whole; and here we have a definite inner collectivism. To this group there also belong the historically conditioned religious communities. The people of Israel, who are also the 'children' of Israel, combine both types. It is true that in such communities the collectivist basis can be destroyed, and become individualist. Such an instance would belong to the second type. Fourthly, there are free communities which are held together by divine services, without which each individual would wither away religiously, and which see the essential significance of religion as fulfilled in the communal element.

From this analysis we may discern some motives which lead

to the formation of empirical communities. Utilitarian considerations, including the pattern of needs (need for communication and so on), the power of a thought or of an experience which has a concrete communal intention, all lead to religious groupings; physical and historical connections are regulated and sanctioned by religion. From this we see that the motives for empirical grouping are various and accidental. It is impossible to show an objective or a psychological necessity for the connection between religion and community. Whether we take Schleiermacher's idea of the individual's need to communicate, or Seeberg's idea of the receptive-active nature of human spirituality, we must conclude that first there is no sign of a psychological necessity of community, and secondly a community which rested only on its members' need to communicate is a purely individualistic association. A collectivist basis and a corresponding motivation for empirical grouping is to be found only in actual religions, but the general concept of religion knows nothing of specifically social intentions. It is only when we look at actual religions that we may see some relation with community. Now it is not the task of the sociology of religion to study the arising of religious communities, just as no genetic problem is essentially sociological. The task of the sociology of religion is rather to investigate the general structure of religious communities. This is not our task here. We can only indicate briefly that such an investigation would deal with the two basic types of community, the free charismatic community characterised by the 'sorcerer', and the normative uncharismatic type characterised by the priest, both being overcome by the third type, the prophetic, with its specifically religious form of community.[12]

In recognising that we can understand what a community is only from a study of the concrete religious form, we are thrown back upon the problem of the church. It is possible to discern certain communal intentions from a study of the actual contents of Christian faith, as these are found in empirical groupings. But in this way we cannot reach the concept of the church. (Schleiermacher even thought that he could reach the concept of the church from the general concept of religion). This can only be done when the Christian revelation is believed, that is, taken seriously. The Christian concept of the church is reached only by way of the concept of revelation. But once the claim of the church has been accepted, it is as superfluous as it is impossible to prove its general necessity. The situation is the same as with the Christological attempts to prove the necessity of redemption, after its reality has been comprehended. Only by first believingly making the meaning of redemption one's own can one clearly see what makes this reality necessary. Only from reality can we deduce necessity in dogmatics. This is basic to the concept of revelation.

When works on dogmatics end by presenting the concept of the church as necessarily following from the Protestant faith, this simply indicates the inner connection between the reality of the church and the whole reality of revelation. Only if the concept of God is seen to be incomprehensible unless it is joined to the concept of the church, can the latter be 'derived' from the former, for technical reasons of presentation. It would be a good thing, in order to establish clearly the inner logic of the structure of dogmatics, to begin the subject, for once, not with the doctrine of God but with the doctrine of the church.

In order that we may stand on firm ground in the positive presentation which follows, we now give a short outline of the New Testament teaching on the church, in particular as a social phenomenon.

2. *A brief outline of the New Testament view of the church*

We can only give a general outline. The New Testament has two different concepts of the church, that of Jerusalem and that of Paul.[13] The former, the Jewish-Christian, is the basis for the Roman Catholic view, the latter, the Gentile Christian, is the basis for the Lutheran view. On the first view, there was in the church 'from the beginning a proper hierarchy, a divinely established order, a divine church law, a church as an institution, into which the individuals were taken up. A clearly defined group, the "apostles", that is, James and the Twelve, possessed a lasting divine pre-eminence, unattainable by any others, and were therefore marked out for the leadership.'[14] Paul overcame this view of the church on the basis of his understanding of the gospel. We give a brief account of his views. ἐκκλησία[15] is the Septuagint translation for 'ēdhā, and in Paul also for qāhāl, which elsewhere is translated by συναγωγή. The concept ἐκκλησία originally signified gathering, the congregation of the people, and is not essentially different from συναγωγή. Later, συναγωγή signified the individual Jewish congregation, while ἐκκλησία signified the religious community as such. The Jews retained ἐκκλησία to describe themselves. The Christian adoption of this term was to this extent a happy usage, that it was already to be found in Greek, though exclusively in the sense of a political assembly. The Christian congregation, ecclesia, is not limited by national or political boundaries, it is universal; though still a 'people', it forms, along with heathen and Jews, the 'third race.'[16] To help the Greeks to understand this, Paul speaks of the ἐκκλησία τοῦ θεοῦ,[17] though mostly in order to describe the whole Christian people (I Cor. 10.32—15.9; Gal. 1.13). But Paul also uses ecclesia for the local congregation (I Cor. 1.2, II Cor. 1.1, I Thess. 2.14, Gal. 1.2, and in the plural I Cor. 16.1, etc.). His reasons are not only linguistic, they are also theological. The local church is the concrete form of the whole church of God (I Cor. 1.2). But it is also itself the church of God. It is 'the form in which the whole church appears in one place.' The whole church is real only in the local church. By ecclesia, therefore, Paul always thinks of what God has established on earth, even when he speaks of the local church. The church exists[18] by the work of Christ and the work of the Holy Spirit, which have to be distinguished. The church has been chosen by Christ from eternity (Eph. 1.4ff., II Thess. 2.13, John 15.16 in the Diatessaron). The new mankind lives in him, it has been created by his death (Eph. 2.15). It is the second, the new Adam (I Cor. 15.45). Thus mankind is really redeemed in him, for he gave himself for the church (Eph. 5.25), and the building-up of the church means exclusively the actualising of what has been accomplished in Christ. In the church Christ is the foundation (I Cor. 3.11, Rom. 15.20), the corner-stone (Eph. 2.20ff. I Pet. 2.4), he is the beginner of a new mankind (I Cor. 15.27), the first-born among many brothers (Rom. 8.19, I Cor. 15.20, Col. 1.15, 18, Heb. 1.6, Rev. 1.5). On the other hand, the church is the Body of Christ, and men are members of this Body (I Cor. 12.2ff, Rom. 12.4ff. Eph. 1.23, 4.15f., Col. 1.18) or of Christ himself (I Cor. 6.15, Rom. 6.13, 19). There are thus two different ways in which Christ is shown as being related to the church, but they are dogmatically logical. There follow descriptions of Christ as the Head of the Body, as the Head of the church (Eph. 1.22, 4.15, 5.23, Col. 1.18, 2.19). Finally, the idea of Christ as the Head leads to the thought of marriage, where the man is the head of the woman, and the relation of Christ to the church is described as analogous to the Old Testament image of Jahveh and Israel as married to one another (Eph. 5.23ff.). Christ's relation to the church is twofold: he is the creator of its whole life, which rests on him, the master-builder of the church, and he is also really present at all times in his church, for the church is his body, he rules over it as the head does over the body. The body, again, is ruled throughout by the Holy Spirit (I Cor. 12.13, Eph. 2.18, 4.4), and here again we have to distinguish between the Spirit of Christ and the Holy Spirit, which are not identical in their power.[19] What Christ is for the whole church, the Holy Spirit is for the individual. The Holy Spirit impels the individual to Christ, he brings Christ to them (Rom. 8.14, Eph. 2.22), he gives them community (II Cor. 13.3, Phil. 2.1),[20] that is, his power extends to man's social life, and makes use of man's social bonds and social will, whereas the Spirit of Christ is directed towards the historical nature of human life together.

If we now look at the church not in terms of how it is built up, but as a unified reality, then the image of the body of Christ must dominate. What does this really mean? In the church Christ is at work as with an instrument. He is present in it; as the Holy Spirit is with the individual, so Christ makes himself present in the congregation of the saints.[21] If we take the thought of the body seriously, then it means that this 'image' identifies Christ and the church, as Paul himself clearly does (I Cor. 12.12, 6.5); for where my body is, there too am I.[22] Thus when the church is split, Paul can ask 'Is Christ divided?' (I Cor. 1.13). From this conviction that Christ himself is the church there arises the idea of an organic life in the church, in accordance with the will of Christ, from this image of a living organism. It is clear that both ideas conflict with the reality of sinfulness, and that there is need of systematic work at this point. Thus Christ is really present only in the church. The church is in him and he is in the church (I Cor. 1.30, 3.16, II Cor. 6.16, 13.5, Col. 3.9, 2.17), and 'to be in Christ' is the same as 'to be in the church'.[23]

This touches on another idea. Schmidt quite rightly places alongside the image of the body of Christ the idea of the total personality of the church. The church has become a person in so far as it is in Christ (Gal. 3.28). In Col. 3.11 it is even said that Christ is 'all things' in the church, that is, once more Christ and the church are identified (similarly Eph. 1.23).[24] All the references to 'putting on the new man' (Col. 3.10, Eph. 4.24) belong to this range of ideas. So also 'putting on the Lord Jesus Christ' (Rom. 13.14, Gal. 3.27), and the words about 'the new creature' (II Cor. 5.7, Gal. 6.15), and Eph. 2.15, 4.13. Yet one thing is still not clear—just why the plain identification of Christ and the ecclesia is so seldom made (I Cor. 1.13, 12.12, 6.15, Col. 3.11, Rom. 13.14), and why quite often the total personality of the church and Christ are seen as being in some kind of relation and yet not as identical. Schmidt's interpretation by means of Paul's mysticism is not satisfactory.[25] The total person of the church can only be conceived of in Christ, that is, in his person. But Paul does not wish to make this complete identification because Christ for him is also with God. He has gone to heaven (Eph. 4.8ff., I Thess. 4.16, I Cor. 15.23). We await his coming (Phil. 3.20). Paul did not raise this dogmatic problem. Nor do Schmidt, Kattenbusch etc. discuss it.

The problem becomes more complicated when we add, as we must, the idea of *pneuma*. For clearly the Holy Spirit is personally at work in the creation of the church. He gives community (see above) and is also the principle of unity (I Cor. 12.4ff., especially vv. 11-13, Eph. 4.4, though this is not very clear in Paul: for the body as such is also a unity). The church is the body of Christ, but only under the gathering and uniting influence of the Holy Spirit. So once more the identification of Christ and the church is made difficult, and yet it has to be made, and it is made.

The social significance of Christ is decisive. He is only present in the church, that is, where the Christian community is united by preaching and the Lord's Supper for brotherly love. The real presence of Christ is also decisive. The relation of this presence to the problem of the Word and of preaching is only indicated by Paul. The sole content of the church is in any case the revelation of God in Christ. He is present to the church in his Word, by which the community is constituted ever anew. The church is the presence of Christ, as Christ is the presence of God.

The dogmatic difficulties that arise here must be discussed later. There can be no thought of a second incarnation of Christ (say in an individual man, see below), but rather we must think of a revelatory form in which 'Christ exists as the church.' Only then can we grasp that Paul can speak in the indicative: 'You are the body of Christ' (I Cor. 3.16, 6.19, 12.2, II Cor. 6.16, Eph. 5.30). What is meant is the actual local church, in whose midst there lives a fornicator (I Cor. 5.6), and this is the body of Christ. Christ is present to this visible community. It is the basic error in pietism and in religious socialism to look on the primitive community as 'pure'. There has in fact never been a kingdom of God on earth, of which one could have said 'lo, here it is' (Luke 17.21). The church is and was and remains an *ecclesia militans* in history, not *triumphans*. The theological significance of Paul's indicative does not consist in its description of empirical facts—even considered well-meaningly as somewhat idealised—but in the hard contradiction of the actuality and reality of human holiness.[26] Every misunderstanding of the early Christian idea has led from early times to a sectarian ideal of holiness in the establishing of the kingdom of God on earth.

In the body of Christ there prevails a communal life in accordance with the laws of organic life (I Cor. 1.12). The body is attached to the head, and the whole is held together by joints; but the bond of the community is love (Eph. 4.16 and Col. 2.19). The Pauline idea of organism is neither the Roman Catholic nor the biological, nor is it the organological view of a philosophy of the state. In all these views the actual whole is superior in value to the individual, the individual becomes a part of a whole body and loses his own being. Paul is speaking of the church of God, which as such is the revelatory reality of God, and the individual is really only a part of this, but a part as a whole, as one who is chosen by God in the community. But the church can in principle make no absolute claim over the individual; this would involve the Roman Catholic view of the church. So by this organic view Paul means on the one hand all belonging to the body of Christ, who is the unity of all members, and on the other hand he means the belonging to the community of God, in which alone the individual can live. But from this there follows the demand, or rather there follows as a matter of course, that one co-operates in the whole. It is not the empirical church as such which is the organism—the empirical sociological view of organism is untenable sociologically, if it tries to be more than a partial image, and superfluous[27] if it does not try to be more—but the community of God. The organism of the community is the function of the Spirit of Christ, that is, it is the body of Christ in the sense we have already described, of the body as a collective person. We may now understand how Paul can say that we are the body which is ruled by the head. 'Body' is always a functional concept (see below), and on the other hand where Christ rules human wills he is himself present. He is the 'body', he is 'Christ existing as the church'.

From all this it follows that the sociological structure of the church in the New Testament view involves a multitude of persons, a community and a unity, all belonging together, analogous to the structure of communities of will.

The church is God's new purpose for men. His will is always directed towards actual historical man, and therefore has its beginning in history. At some point in history it must become visible and comprehensible. But since the primal community, in which God speaks and the Word becomes deed and history through men, is rent asunder, now God himself must speak and act, and because his Word is always deed this means that he simultaneously accomplishes a new creation of men. Thus his will is at the same time fulfilled, that is, revealed. So just as the church has its beginning in Christ, so it is fulfilled in him. He is the corner-stone and foundation of the building, and the fullness of the church is his body. He is the first-born among many brethren, and yet all are one in him—Eph. 1.4f.: 'According as he hath chosen us in him before the foundation of the world, that we should be holy and without blame before him in love; having predestinated us unto the adoption of children by Jesus Christ to himself . . . (verse 11) in whom also we have obtained an inheritance, being predestinated according to the purpose of him who worketh all things after the counsel of his own will' (cf. II Tim. 1.9, John 15.16—Diatessaron). Note the use of ἐν throughout;[28] 'not merely by him but in him are we reconciled; hence also rightly to discern his Person and his history is the right discernment of our reconciliation.' If we, the members of the Christian church, are to believe that God in Christ has reconciled us, the Christian church, with himself, then in the Mediator of our reconciliation there must be combined not merely the love of God that reconciles, but at the same time the humanity that is to be reconciled, the humanity of the new Adam.[29]

If the church consummated in Christ is to build itself up in time, the will of God must constantly be realised anew, no longer acting as a general principle for all men, but in the personal appropriation of individual men; and this appropriation is possible only upon the ground of God's action in Christ, and pre-supposes both the being of mankind in the church (which is consummated in Christ) and the bringing of the individual into the church, that is, into the humanity of Christ, by the act of appropriation. The refractoriness of the ideas of revelation and time, consummation and becoming, cannot be overcome logically. Revelation enters into time, not only apparently but in reality, and in doing so bursts the time-form asunder. If, however, we sought for this reason to understand revelation only as a beginning (potentiality) and not as at the same time con-summation (reality), we should be depriving God's revelation of its decisive quality: the fact that his Word has become history.

In order to carry out the temporal building of the church as his community, God reveals himself as the Holy Spirit. The will of God which brings individual human beings together in the church, maintains it, and is effectual only within it, is the Holy Spirit; and only by being personally appropriated by the Holy Spirit, by standing in the actual church, do we experience our election in the Church, which is based on Christ.

Thus our study falls naturally into the following parts: first, we have to inquire into the consummated church established in Christ through God's action, the church of God; or, as we expressed it earlier, into the life-principle of the new basic relationships of social existence. We have therefore to discuss the analogy with the basic relationships established in Adam, and their abolition. The new relationships are completely estab-lished in Christ, not ideally but in reality. Mankind is new in Christ, that is, new when seen in the light of eternity, but it also becomes new in time. Thus the second part will be the study of the action of the Holy Spirit as the will of God for the historical actualisation of the church of Jesus Christ. Only we must take strict note that the opposition here is not between actualisation by the Holy Spirit and the potentiality in Christ, but between the actualisation by the Holy Spirit and the reality in the revelation in Christ. That is the basis for the whole understand-ing of the problem of the church. The 'possibility' that the church will not be made actual by the Holy Spirit simply no longer exists. But it is the church which is completely established in Christ as a reality which is necessarily made actual. It is a great temptation to apply here the category of potentiality in Christ. But this category destroys the character of redemption as real; the reconciliation and justification of the world is, with regard to revelation, really based on Christ—for the faith which, admittedly, is possible only within the actualised church. The church is not first made real by assuming empirical form, when the Holy Spirit does his work; but the reality of the church of the Holy Spirit is one which is founded on revelation, and it is a matter merely of believing in that revealed reality in its empirical form. As Christ and the new mankind now necessarily belong together, so the Holy Spirit too is to be seen as effectual only within this mankind. This makes evident the misunderstanding which consists in regarding the objective action of the Spirit as independent of the church. The Holy Spirit is solely in the church and the church is solely in the Spirit. *Ubi enim ecclesia ibi et Spiritus; et ubi Spiritus Dei, illic ecclesia et omnis gratia.*[30] And yet Troeltsch thought it necessary to maintain that in the Protestant conception of the church it was not a question of the congregation, but solely of the Word, that is, of the objective action of the Holy Spirit; that where the Word is, there the church is, even in the complete absence of hearers. This is a complete misunderstanding of the Protestant tenet of the significance of the Word, of which we have yet to speak.

It will then, thirdly, be necessary to determine the relation between the Holy Spirit ruling over the church and the human spirit of the community which the action of the Holy Spirit brings about. This raises the problem of the empirical church. In this connection the difference between the Idealist and the Christian concept of objective spirit will become plain.

1. *The church established in and through Christ—its realisation*

The reality of sin, we found, places the individual in the utmost loneliness, in a state of radical separation from God and man. It places him in the isolated position of one who confesses that he committed the 'first' sin, that in him the whole of mankind fell. But at the same time it brings him both objectively and subjectively into the closest bond with the rest of mankind, precisely through the guilt involved, which, while it cannot, it is true, take on empirical form as a bond of guilt, is nevertheless experienced in every concrete bond. Now since in the individual act of guilt it is precisely the humanity of man which is affirmed, mankind itself must be regarded as a community. As such it is at the same time a collective person, which, however, has the same nature as each of its members. In Christ this tension between being isolated and being bound to others is really abolished. The thread between God and man which the first Adam severed is joined anew by God, by his revealing his love in Christ. He no longer demands and summons, approaching mankind purely as Thou; but gives himself as an I, opening his heart. The church is grounded in the revelation of the heart of God. But as, when the primal communion with God was rent asunder, human community was rent too, so likewise when God restores the communion of mankind with himself, the community of men with each other is also re-established, in accordance with our proposition about the essential connection between man's communion with God and with his fellow-man.

In Christ mankind is really drawn into communion with God, just as in Adam mankind fell. And yet in the one Adam there are many Adams; but there is only one Christ. For Adam is 'man', but Christ is the Lord of his new mankind. Thus each man becomes guilty through his own strength and guilt, because he himself is Adam; but each man is reconciled without his own strength and merit, because he himself is not Christ. Whereas the old mankind consists of countless isolated units of Adams which are conceived as a unified entity only through each individual, the new mankind is completely drawn together into the one single historical point, into Jesus Christ, and only in him is it comprehended as a whole; for in him as the foundation and body of the building of his church the work of God is accomplished and consummated. And in this work Christ has a function which sheds clear light on the difference in principle between Adam and Christ; his function is vicarious (this we shall discuss more fully later). Adam's action is not deliberately vicarious but is on the contrary extremely egocentric. The fact that its effect looks very similar to that of a deliberately vicarious action must not deceive us as to its completely different basis from that of the action of Christ. With the old mankind it is as if mankind falls anew each time one man incurs guilt, whereas in Christ mankind is placed—and this is the very essence of real vicarious action—once and for all in communion with God.

As history begins with death, which is the wages of sin (Rom. 6.23), so life lived in love breaks the continuity of history, not empirically but in reality. Death can indeed still fully separate past and future for our eyes, but it cannot any longer separate them for the life lived in the love of Christ. That is why the principle of vicarious action can become fundamental for the church of God in and through Christ. Not 'solidarity',[31] which is never possible between Christ and man, but vicarious action, is the life-principle of the new mankind. I know, certainly, that I am in a state of solidarity with the other man's guilt, but my dealings with him take place on the basis of the life-principle of vicarious action.

Since now Christ bears within him the new life-principle of his church, he is at the same time established as the Lord of the church, that is, his relation to it is that with a 'community' and that of a 'ruler'.

But because the whole of the new mankind is really established in Jesus Christ, he represents the whole history of mankind in his historical life. His history is qualified by the fact that in it the mankind of Adam is transformed into the mankind of Christ, by the fact that, as Jesus Christ's human body became the resurrection-body, so the *corpus Adae* became the *corpus Christi*. Each equally leads through death and resurrection; the human body, the *corpus Adae*, must be broken, so that the resurrection-body, the *corpus Christi*, might be created. The history of Jesus Christ is, however, closed to us without his Word. Only if we take both together shall we be able to read mankind's past and future in that history.

Jesus Christ places his life under the law (Gal. 4.4), he sets himself within God's community of Israel. The clearest evidence for this is his baptism (Matt. 3.15). What was God's community of Israel? It was the people which God had chosen as a collective person; it was constituted by God's law. For Israel God's law is the right hearing of the call. The law and the call belong together. The fulfilment of the law is the obedient realisation of the call. Because the people is called as a collective person, the fulfilment of the law is the fulfilment of God's call to be a people of God, his holy community. That is why communion is intended in the idea of the call as it is in that of the law. To play off the call against the law is to distort the meaning of the law, and thus not to fulfil it. This shatters the community, which is constituted by the genuine correlation of call and law. When a man dominates the law, it becomes a claim of each individual upon the God who calls him. But then the law reveals its living quality by becoming, for the man who thus misuses it, a wrathful power, showing him the incurable rift in the community, and completely isolating him. That is in brief the history of the community of Israel.

Christ, in setting himself within this community, does not declare himself to be at one with it, but vicariously fulfils the law for all men through love, thereby overcoming the Jewish conception of the law. Whereas until then it was only the wilful transgressor of the law who was excluded from the community, Jesus now declares that essentially the whole community has fallen away from God; hence, far from being itself God's community, it is part of the mankind of Adam, and must be reconciled with God, that is, remoulded into a new community. Whereas until then each man had been isolated in the community in his relation to the law, now the person of Christ is to bring together all individuals in himself and stand vicariously for them before God. The transformation of mankind into a new community is possible only if men are aware of the deficiency of the old. To create this awareness Jesus calls to repentance; that is, he reveals God's ultimate claim and, in so doing, makes man's past and present subject to the reality of this claim. Man, when he recognises his guilt, feels his solitariness before God; he begins to perceive the state in which objectively he has long been living, his state of isolation. Thus the old community of God, which had its standard and constitutive strength in the law, is broken. The law does not establish communion, but loneliness—by reason, of course, of man's guilt, for the law is holy and good, and was intended to be the standard and form of life of a holy people of God. The law can be spiritually fulfilled only through the Spirit, that is, in an integral will to obey God in complete love. Once man recognises that he lacks the strength for this, the way is prepared for Jesus's gift, for the message of love and of God's reign in his Kingdom. Thus from the utmost isolation concrete community arises; for in the preaching of the love of God we hear of the communion which God has entered into with each and every man who in his utter loneliness knows that he is separated from God and his fellow-man, and who believes this message. It was not fitting, however, that Jesus should create the church of God anew during his lifetime. His love had to become complete by his fulfilling the law, that is, the claim of God and man, unto death. The revealed fellowship of love had to be shattered once again by the free act of him who had founded it, though this was not done before Jesus, at the last hour, had encircled it with a close bond. This took place at the Last Supper. Jesus says: 'As I break this bread, so to-morrow my body will be broken, and as you all eat and are filled from the one loaf, so too you will all be saved and brought together in me alone.' The Lord of the church gives his disciples communion with him, and thus with one another. This has been regarded as the scene representing the founding of the church (Kattenbusch), and with some reason. Jesus has now openly expressed his will to found the church; but dogmatically the moment of the formation of the church is to be sought in another event.

The service of the law leads Jesus to the cross, leads him into the most profound loneliness which the curse of the law brings upon man. When he is taken captive all the disciples forsake him, and upon the cross he is quite alone. The community seems to be shattered. This has its theological significance, and is not simply to be dismissed as the result of the disciples' weakness or disloyalty. It is a happening with an objective meaning; things had to fall out thus—so that 'all might be fulfilled', one should like to add. In Jesus's death upon the cross God's judgment and wrath go forth upon the whole selfishness of mankind, which had misinterpreted the law. This misinterpretation has brought God's Son to the cross. At this the burden assumes immeasurable proportions, and each individual is Adam, is himself wholly guilty; here each man stands alone before God: here all hope is gone, for the community existed only so long as men knew Jesus to be living. Jesus himself, however, in going to the cross, in surrendering to the law and taking upon himself the curse of the law for us, had apparently admitted that the world was right. The old 'community of God' seemed to have triumphed. That was why Jesus died in loneliness, because he was made to be sin for us, accursed through the law for us; and that was why the disciples, for whom the present was without a future, were also doomed to loneliness.[32] For us, to whom Easter forms part of the past with all the rest, Jesus's death is conceivable only in the light of the triumph of love over the law, the triumph of life over death. The death of Jesus as something absolutely present is no longer given us, so that for us there has arisen the paradoxical reality of a church of the cross containing within it the contradiction of utmost loneliness and closest fellowship. And this is the specifically Christian community. But it is only through the Easter message that there is a church of the cross: in Christ's resurrection his death is revealed as the death of death, and thereby the limit upon history imposed by death is removed, the human body has become the resurrection-body, the mankind of Adam the church of Christ. The church as an empirical church could indeed be created only by the Holy Spirit. In the resurrection it is 'created' only so far as it has now run the course of its dialectical history. It has been made real, but not actual. In the resurrection the heart of God has pierced through guilt and death and has truly conquered his new mankind, subjected man to his lordship.

It is true, the empirical community could not yet be the church made actual, for Christ had not yet ascended. The time between the resurrection and the ascension and the time after Pentecost are different in that in the first case the church lived in Christ as its Lord and life-principle, whereas in the second Christ lives in the church. Previously the church 'represented' Christ, but now it has him as revelation, as Spirit. Thus the day of the founding of the church made actual remains Pentecost; as human community first became such when it became spiritual community of will, and as the human spirit is operative only in sociality, so the church originates with the pouring out of the Holy Spirit, and so too the Holy Spirit is the Spirit of the church of Christ. But where the Spirit is operative only in the church, this church cannot be derived simply from individual spirits. Hence for systematic sociology the problem of the church cannot consist in the question of the empirical gathering of its members and their psychological motivation, but only in showing in connection with the idea of spirit the essential structure of the social formation, in its acts of will and in its objective shape, in accordance with our earlier definition of sociology.

The relation of Christ to the church can now be stated as follows: essentially Jesus Christ was no more a founder of the Christian religious community than he was the founder of a religion. The credit for both these things belongs to the primitive church, that is, to the apostles. That is why the question whether Christ founded a church is so ambiguous. He brought, established and proclaimed the reality of the new mankind. The circle of disciples about him was not a church; but they simply sketched out the church's inner dialectic. This was not a new religion seeking adherents, which is a picture drawn by a later time. But God established the reality of the church, of mankind pardoned in Jesus Christ. Not religion, but revelation, not a religious community, but the church: that is what the reality of Jesus Christ means. And yet there is a necessary connection between revelation and religion, as there is between religious community and the church. Nowadays that connection is often overlooked, and yet it is only because it exists that Paul can call Jesus the foundation, the corner-stone of the building of the church. As a pioneer and model Jesus is also the founder of a religious community, though not of the Christian church (for this only came into existence after Pentecost—Matt. 16.18 and the Lord's Supper give expression to this fact). And then after the resurrection Christ restores the shattered fellowship, in the case of Peter by appearing to him, as presumably the first to whom this happened (I Cor. 15.5), and perhaps expressly entrusting him with his new office (John 21.15f.), and then in the case of the Twelve by appearing in their midst (I Cor. 15.5; John 20.19). Thus Christ is the sole foundation upon which the edifice of the church rests, the reality from which the historical 'collective life' arose. Thus the relation of Jesus Christ to the Christian church is to be understood in a dual sense. 1. *The church is consummated in him and time is annulled.* 2. *Within time the church is to be built up on him as the foundation. He is the church's historical principle.* The vertical direction, time, belongs, as it were, to him.[33] These statements correspond to a truth long since known from the New Testament concerning the presence and the coming of the kingdom of God, but they are not identical with it, for the church is not identical with the kingdom of God, any more than the *iustus peccator* is actually perfected, although he is essentially perfected. The kingdom of God is a purely eschatological concept, which from the point of view of God is present every moment in the church, but for us remains an object of hope, whereas the church is an object of faith here and now. The church is identical with the kingdom of Christ, but the kingdom of Christ is the kingdom of God which has been realised in history since the coming of Christ.[34]

Upon what principle, then, does Christ's efficacy in relation to the new basic social conditions rest? The crucified and risen

Christ is recognised by the church as God's incarnate love for men, as his will for the renewing of the covenant, for the setting up of the divine lordship, and thus for community. Two things still oppose this: time and the will for evil. The second is self-evident. The first signifies that what has happened has happened. That is the burden of time, a burden we have had to bear so long as there have been death and guilt. If man is to have communion with God then both must somehow be removed. Man's sins must be forgiven, and what has happened must by God's decree be judged as not having happened. Now man's guilt cannot be regarded by the God of truth 'as if' it did not exist; it must truly be made 'unhappened', that is, eradicated. This cannot come about by a reversal of time, but by divine punishment and the recreation of the will for good. God does not 'overlook' sin; otherwise it would mean that he was not taking man's personal being seriously in its very guilt, in which case there could not be any recreation of the person, or of community. But God takes man's guilt seriously, and for that reason only the punishment and overcoming of the sin can avail. Both must be accomplished at a point in time, and they happen in a way valid for all time in Jesus Christ. He takes the punishment upon himself, obtains forgiveness for our sins and, to use Seeberg's expression, goes surety for man's renewal.[35] Thus Christ's vicarious action can be understood from the situation itself. In him concrete action within time and its being 'for all time' really coincide. There is vicarious action for guilt and punishment. Here the one demands the other, for 'punishment' does not mean to take the consequences of sin upon oneself, but to judge these consequences to be a 'punishment' for sin. The idea that the Passion of Jesus was in the nature of a punishment has frequently been disputed. Luther laid all possible stress upon this. It is conceivable that someone might take the consequences of sin upon himself even in the moral life of society. The unique quality of the Christian idea of acting vicariously is that this action is strictly vicarious with regard to guilt and punishment. Jesus, being himself innocent, takes the others' guilt and punishment upon himself, and as he dies as a criminal, he is accursed, for he bears the sins of the world and is punished for them; but on the felon's cross, vicarious love triumphs; obedience to God triumphs over guilt, and thereby guilt is in fact punished and overcome. Such, briefly, is our way of seeing Christ's vicarious action. It contains deep problems of social philosophy.

Can this Christian view of vicarious action with regard to guilt be upheld morally? The moral person clearly wishes to be responsible before God for his own good and evil actions. How can he lay his guilt upon another, and himself go free? Certainly the doctrine of vicarious atonement embraces a wider sphere than that of man's moral conduct, but man ought to let his guilt be taken from him, for he cannot carry it alone; he ought not to reject this gift of God. It is God's love which makes the gift, and only for this love's sake man ought to abandon his standpoint of moral self-responsibility, which—and this shows the necessity for vicarious action—counts for nothing in God's sight. Thus the idea of vicarious atonement is possible only so long as it rests upon an offer from God, that is, it is in force only in Christ and his church. It is not a moral possibility or standard, but solely the reality of the divine love for the church; it is not a moral but a theological concept.[36] Through the Christian principle of vicarious action the new mankind is brought and held together. In it the material particularity of the basic Christian relationships consists. To what extent this principle not only brings together the new mankind and Christ, but also links men with each other in fellowship, is something that will be discussed later. Thus much, however, is certain, that human community is established where communion with God is real.

Thus the Church is established in and through Christ in the three basic sociological relationships already known to us: his death isolates the individuals, each bears his own guilt, each has his own conscience; in the light of the resurrection the church of the cross is vindicated and sanctified as one in Christ. The new mankind is focused together in one point, in Jesus Christ; and as the love of God through Christ's vicarious action restores communion between God and man, so the human community too once again becomes a living reality in love.

2. *The Holy Spirit and the church of Jesus Christ—the actualisation of the essential church*

The church is established in reality in and through Christ—not in such a way that we can think of the church without Christ himself, but he himself 'is' the church. He does not represent it, for only what is not present can be represented. But in God's eyes the church is present in Christ. Christ did not make the church possible, but he realised it for eternity. If this is so, Christ must be accorded central significance in the temporal actualisation of the church. This place is given him through the Word, impelled by the Spirit, of the crucified and risen Lord of the church. The Spirit is capable of operating only through this Word. If there were an unmediated operation of the Spirit then the idea of the church would be individualistic, and thus be dissolved at its very source. In the Word, however, the most profound social relationships are established from the outset. The Word is socially determined not only in its origin, but equally in its aim. The linking of the Spirit with the Word expresses that the Word is intended for a plurality of hearers, and a visible sign is set up, by which the actualisation is to be brought about.

The Word, however, is qualified by being the Word of Christ himself, brought by the Spirit to the hearts of the hearers as an active force. Christ himself is in the Word; the Christ in whom the church is consummated seeks through his Spirit to win man's heart, in order to fit it into the actualised church of Christ. But in the Word of Christ the actualised church is also present, just as every Word of Christ comes from the church and exists only in it. If anyone should ask how the actualised church could be present at the time of the first preaching of the Word of Christ, before the individuals who were moved by that Word joined together to form a church, he would be forgetting the ideas we previously presented: that the Spirit is solely the Spirit of the church, of the community, and that there were thus no individuals moved by the Spirit before there was a community.

Communion with God exists only through Christ, but Christ is present only in his church, hence there is communion with God only in the church. This fact destroys every individualistic conception of the church. The individual and the church are related in the following way: the Holy Spirit operates solely in the church as the communion of saints; thus each man who is apprehended by the Spirit must already be a part of that communion. No one, on the other hand, whom the Spirit has not yet apprehended can be in the communion; whence it follows that the Spirit, by the same act whereby he moves the elect, who are called into the communion established by Christ, brings them into the actual church. Entry into the church forms the basis for faith, just as faith forms the basis for entry.[37]

The church does not come into being through people coming together (genetic sociology). But it is in being through the Spirit which is effective in the community. So it cannot be derived from individual wills. The individual will can at most express that the individual concerned belongs to the church. Thus the individual is possible only as a member of the church, and his membership of the church is not only a historical preparation for the higher individual life; but it is only in the church that personal life is possible. A man who is not in the church does not live in communion with Christ; but a man who is in Christ is in both the perfected and the actualised church. A man, however, is in Christ through the Word proclaimed by the church. Thus in the Word which comes to the individual both the perfected communion of saints and the communion of saints developing itself in time are equally present. For Christ and the Holy Spirit are active in the Word, and both are inseparably connected; the Holy Spirit has no other content than the fact of Christ. Christ is the measure and the goal of the Spirit's operation, and to this extent Christ himself also participates in the actual building of the church in time, though only in the action of the Holy Spirit.

The Word is active in three different ways; the Holy Spirit, that is, acts in a three-fold way upon his church, analogous to the three basic sociological relationships which we found were in force in the church established in Christ: as multiplicity of spirits, as community of spirit and as spiritual unity. These three forms are thus analogous also to the basic sociological data which we saw formed the essential structure of every community. Both analogies are of the greatest importance.

a. Multiplicity of spirits

The Holy Spirit of the church is directed as personal will towards personal wills. It approaches each person in that person's singularity, and leads him into 'loneliness'. The Holy Spirit makes the members of his community lonely not only by what he claims, but also by what he gives. Each one believes and experiences his justification and sanctification in loneliness, each one prays in loneliness, and each struggles through in loneliness to the certainty of his eternal election; each one 'possesses' the Holy Spirit, and in him also Christ, completely by himself. This loneliness, however, is none of faith's doing,[38] but is willed by God.[39] It is the individual's loneliness, which remains everywhere preserved, inherent in man's structure as a creature.

The recognition of the person's structural singularity as a creature and his ethical singularity finds expression in that idea of the church which takes as its point of departure the deepest individual Christian perception; namely, the predestinarian idea. From outside, the consequences of this idea seem to be the dissolving of the church into a plurality of single predestined persons. Scheler[40] is quite right in saying that from this viewpoint the primal 'way to God' is that of the inmost person's intercourse with him. This idea seems to contain a permanent dissolvent of the idea of the church, for clearly the individual person perceives himself as something ultimate in God's sight; all community seems to be shattered into its individual component parts, and it is solely to these that God's will seems to bear any relation.

Viewed logically, the concept of the *numerus praedestinatorum* can define the range of this individualistic dissolution of the concept of the church. But it has no content (it is the counterpart of our concept of mankind expressed by means of the concept of sin). On the other hand it is in fact impossible to define the church's range in any other way,[41] whence it follows that nothing essential about the concept of the church can be expressed by a definition with an individualistic starting-point.[42] The problem takes a completely different turn, however, if the idea of predestination is understood not from the human viewpoint, but as a way from God to man. Here too no doubt all the attention is directed towards the individual, but in so far as it is the Word about Christ which realises the predestination in man, the individual is intended and elected only as a member of the church. In this sense the idea of predestination is the necessary basis for any concept of the church; God sees the church of Christ and the individual in one act; thus he really sees the individual, and his election really extends to him. For this reason recent dogmatics recognises the concept of predestination as a necessary basis for the concept of the church,[43] and it was in fact already taken up by Luther.[44] Hence the predestination concept is only a part of the whole concept of the church, and is Christian and meaningful only in connection with this whole. It needs to be supplemented, and the supplement springs just as much from the action of the Holy Spirit as does the predestinarian concept itself.

b. Community of spirit

In the Word the Holy Spirit brings the love of God which has been revealed in Christ's crucifixion and resurrection to the hearts of men. He places them within the divine community. The church is based, however, on Christ himself. If Christ comes 'into' man through the Holy Spirit, then the church comes 'into' him too. But the Holy Spirit moves man in such a way that in putting Christ into his heart he (the Spirit) creates faith and love. The faith in Christ which the Spirit effects, however, involves faith in the church in which he reigns; but love, as the love or heart of Christ in man, is given to man as a new heart, as the will for good. Faith recognises and receives God's lordship; love makes the kingdom of God actual. Thus it is a question of love making concrete not the metaphysical but the moral social relationship, which we saw could be perceived in the sinful state only as a broken relationship, but one which could be shown actually to exist in the fact of moral personality and sin, having its basis, as a dogmatic testament, in the doctrine of the primal state. In every human socialisation there is an actualising of the metaphysical social relationships. What is peculiar to the actualising effect of the Holy Spirit is that it links both basic relationships. In every previous formation of a social unit the basic moral relationships remained broken. Here, by their renewal and actualisation, a concrete form of community is established. The man living in the fellowship of the I-Thou relation is given the certainty that he is loved, and through his faith in Christ receives the strength to be able to love in return, in that he, who in Christ is already in the church, is led into the church. He no longer sees the other members of the church essentially as a claim, but as a gift, as a revelation of his love, that is, of God's love, and of his heart, that is, of God's heart, so that the Thou is to the I no longer law but gospel, and hence an object of love. The fact that my claim is fulfilled for me by the other I who loves me—which means, in fact, by Christ—humbles me, frees me from the bonds of my I and lets me love the other—once again, indeed, in virtue of faith in Christ—lets me give and reveal myself entirely to him.

This makes it certain that new social relationships have been created, and that the rift of sin has been closed, but both things have come about through the revelation of the divine heart in Christ, through God's putting his heart, will and Spirit into man in order to realise his purpose for the formation of the church. Now we must try to grasp how 'love' can bear within itself this social significance, and what is evidently expressed in the Christian idea of *agape*. This will clarify the Christian concept of community, as it is given both in the relation of men with God, and in that of men among themselves.

It is remarkable how this decisive concept of Christian love[45]

gives rise to a great diversity of views and a consequent divergence
about this concept of community. It will be well to hold fast
to the New Testament, otherwise we shall scarcely avoid the
greatest danger, that namely of arguing from the humanitarian
standpoint, with its fatal confusion of *eros* and *agape*.

We have two infallible points of reference for what the New
Testament calls love: the first, defined positively, is the love of
God revealed in Christ, the second, defined negatively, is our love
of ourselves. Thus our point of departure must not be our love
for God or for men. Nor do the dangers of war, the sacrificial
death of our brethren or personal experiences of love shown to us,
tell us what love essentially is. Instead we know it solely from the
love of God which reveals itself in the cross of Christ, in our
justification and in the founding of the church, and from our
egoistic attitude towards ourselves. The former shows us love's
foundation, its depth and meaning, but the latter shows us the
hardness with which that love turns against ourselves. The moral
command to love is not specifically Christian, but the reality of
love is nevertheless present only in Christ and his church; thus
the Christian concept of love must have a special meaning. And
this supposition proves to be true.

1. *Christian love is not a human possibility.* It is nothing to do
with the humanitarian idea or feelings of liking, with eroticism or
sympathy.

2. *It is possible only through faith in Christ* and through the work
of the Holy Spirit. It has its basis in obedience to the Word of
Christ who, in ministering to our needs, demands that we should
make absolutely no claim upon God and our neighbour. But it
is only possible for us to be without any claim, to surrender our
own will in face of the divine will, if we have faith in Christ; if
we are far from him, all our love is self-love. Only through faith
in Christ do we understand our love as the love of God which has
been put into our hearts by the Holy Spirit, only thus do we see
our will as subdued by God and obedient to his will for our
neighbour.

3. *Love, as an act of the will, is purposive.* It is not mere baseless
inclination, but, bearing within it the strength imparted by the

complete absence of any claim, it is just as much a matter of rational reflection as of the empathy possible to human beings. The aim of love is exclusively determined by what God's will is for the other man. This will seeks to subject the other to his lordship. The means for accomplishing this are infinitely varied, and cannot be formulated as a set of principles. Each man is left, or rather it is his duty, to perceive them for himself. But it is the whole man who must give himself, with all his strength, to be a means for reaching this aim. This makes it seem as if we are caught up in general definitions of aim which can never be the conscious motive of active love. The good Samaritan does not help the man 'fallen among thieves' in order to realise through him the aim of subjection to God's lordship. He helps him because he sees that he is in distress. He positively helps his neighbour through love for him. Thus it is not true to say of Christian love that it loves, 'in everything it does, as it were the dormant or dawning possibility, that the others will become members of its own (the Christian) community, but does not love the reality of the Thou.'[46] But the reverse is true.

4. *Christian love loves the real neighbour*, not because of any pleasure it might take in his individuality, but because as a man he invokes the other man, that is, because he acts as a Thou and makes the other experience God's claim in this Thou. The other does not, however, love God in his 'neighbour', but loves the concrete Thou; he loves him by placing his own self, his entire will, at his service. In the earlier discussion of the basic moral relationships there was only the perception of the barrier, that is, the claim of our neighbour; love supplies the strength which makes possible the real fulfilment of this claim through the Spirit, that is, the 'overcoming' of the claim. Then does this love, which makes us love only our neighbour, have no definite aim? Does it arise simply from the moment? It does both. God wants from the man who loves him real love for his neighbour.[47] This love, however, is nothing else but the realisation of the aim of establishing God's lordship over men. Not that men through their active love can bring about God's lordship—this 'glance aside' would merely sap the power of the deed—but that God

uses the obedience exercised in our love of our neighbour to carry out his will. This, however, implies that.

5. *Christian love knows no limits.* It seeks the realisation of God's lordship absolutely everywhere. Its limits are only where God himself has set them. Man is forbidden to love where he knows that God has condemned. 'Even if I could make the whole world blessed in one day, if this was not God's will, I should not do it' (Luther). The hard saying in I John, 5.16 goes further than this, seeking to warn us against praying for someone God might have condemned. It sees human weakness and divine severity clashing and calls out a warning of danger. But man does not know where God condemns, and the command that we should love our neighbour, that is, obey, is given without any reservation so that his love is boundless.[48] Love of one's neighbour is man's will for God's will for the other man; God's will for the other man is characterised for us by the command that we should un- reservedly surrender our own will to our neighbour, and thus neither love him in God's place, nor love God in him, but set the other in our own self's place and love him instead of ourselves; '*homo diligit se ipsum perverse et solum quae perversitas non potest dirigi nisi loco suo ponat proximum.*'[49] This attitude, however, cannot be wrung from man, but is 'poured out by the Holy Spirit into our hearts'. It is a part of the intentional nature of love as will directed towards the other man in his concrete being, that it should seek to form community, that is, to kindle love in return. The entire Christological school which followed Abelard built unconsciously upon this insight. In recent times Scheler[50] has examined it in its various aspects and presented it in clarified form. While love certainly does not aim at receiving love in return, it nevertheless lies in love's intention to seek reciprocation. We must distinguish between spiritual communion, which is of necessity entered into between the one loving and the one loved (irrespective of the latter's attitude of mind) in order to make God's will work upon him—a communion both of understanding and expression—and the communion based on mutual love which love deliberately seeks. Most misunderstandings on the subject can be explained as the result of a confusion between the two,

as for instance in Schleiermacher's definition that 'love is the tendency to unite with others and to want to be in others.'[51] This definition still carries a vestige of egoism. The fact that love brings about a community based on love does not make this definition any more correct.[52]

Does all that we have said also hold good under the reality of God's love in Christ? God loves men; as this is so we would expect him to place himself at man's service as a means. But since his will is an end in itself, this gives rise to a seeming contradiction. The meaning of the fact of Christ is, however, in very fact 'that God organises his rule to be a means for achieving his own ends.'[53] It is in Christ that God loves men and makes a gift of his heart, and because he makes a gift of himself to sinful man he renews him at the same time, and thus makes the new community possible and real. This means that God's love wants community. Once again there is the threat of contradiction: we said in speaking of love of our neighbour that love surrenders itself completely, without any self-will. But surrender to the other man means obedience to God; in other words, it is based upon surrender to God's will. Hence God's love is both surrender and will for community. The question of the nature of God's communion with men, based on love, and of communion based on love in general, is linked with the problem of the Word. Man has communion with God only in the Word of Christ. But all conscious communion is communion of will. It is based upon the separateness of persons. Hence communion is never 'being at one', nor is it a final 'being One' in the sense of a mystical fusion; it is real only when the will is constantly creating it anew. It can be affirmed as an end in itself, or it can be organised solely for the achieving of an end. Communion based on love is based upon each person's complete surrender for his fellows. The fact that man can surrender himself completely to God constitutes God's complete surrender to man. God has a purpose for man; thus man can have a purpose for God: communion is an end in itself. God wants his way with man, and this is the only reason why he wants communion; and man wants God's will as the end of communion, so that it is even possible for man, in order that he might satisfy this will, not to will communion with God any more, that is, to will his damnation, if God so wills: communion is not an end in itself. But it is precisely in man's so willing that his communion with God becomes unshakeably firm, and the deepest reason for this is simply that God wills communion for its own sake, but this is the same as to say, for his sake. His will seeks communion, and the human will, surrendering itself completely, enters into communion precisely because it is God's surrender that makes this human surrender possible.

Now the new man who is drawn into communion with God is hidden not only from the world, but even from himself.[54] Man enters into communion with God only through faith, that is, through the Word. He does not 'behold' his 'new man' in the will for good, but believes his will is good, because God says so, that is, because Christ has fulfilled for him what he himself would never have been able to fulfil; such is the Protestant position, as opposed to the Roman Catholic view of the *signa praesentis gratiae*. The reality of the 'experience' of justification and sanctification, that is, the reality of man's being presented with a new will, is not disputed. The safeguarding of this reality, however, lies exclusively in the 'objective' event through the Word and the faith brought about by God. Thus we arrive at the result, important in principle, that there is communion with God for us only in faith, that it is not experienced like any spiritual communion based on friendship or shared experience. We believe that, through Christ, God has entered into a communion of love with man. And this faith is simply that the true faith brought about by God is present—that is why it cannot be an experiential proof that man has communion with God.[55]

From this, however, there follows the equally important further conclusion that my communion of love with my neighbour can subsist only in faith in God, God who in Christ fulfilled the law for me and loved his neighbour, and who draws me into the church, that is, into Christ's love and into fellowship with my neighbour. Only this faith allows me to understand what I do to the other man as love, and bids me believe in our communion as the Christian communion of love.

We must now ask whether the church in which God's love is at work is really 'communion'. It was the great conception of Augustine to represent the communion of saints, the core of the church, as the communion of loving beings who, stirred by God's Spirit, pour out love and grace. It is not the organised church and the ministry which give forgiveness of sins, but the communion of saints.[56] He who has received the sacraments must first be drawn into this spiritual stream of life; all that was promised to the church is promised to the communion of saints; it is the communion of saints that has the power of the keys, that can forgive sins; it alone endows all the undertakings of the official church with God's spirit. This provides the pattern for all thinking about the *sanctorum communio*. The Christian communion of love means that men should surrender themselves completely to each other, in obedience to God's will. This communion is possible only through the work of the Holy Spirit. When several persons wish to surrender themselves completely, the constitutive element in the concept of communion, namely, the affirmation of communion as an end in itself, is also present; and yet communion is not consciously intended; rather, the surrender of the I is an act willing the Thou, but this very act proves and establishes the new I in accordance with God's will. Thus it is precisely in several persons' complete surrender to each other that their new person becomes real and there arises a 'community of new persons'. Love finds communion without seeking it, or rather precisely because it does not seek it. Whoever loses his life will preserve it. Only thus does the surrender of the individual person to God's will for his neighbour really lead to the communion of saints, for whose realisation each man serves as God's instrument. Hence the Christian community of love shows a sociologically unique structure; in the mutual love of the saints 'communion' is in fact established as an end in itself. There is nevertheless a repetition here of the difficulty arising from the idea that communion is after all not an end in itself in so far as its sole aim is that God's will should be realised. But as it is precisely this communion of saints that the divine will purposes, the difficulty is resolved; the position therefore is not that this communion has a further aim outside itself—which, sociologically, would be possible—but that communion (in the broader sense) is in fact organised exclusively towards a specific end, namely, the achievement of God's will. But, as the community itself represents this realisation it is an end in itself.[57] This makes it a completely new structure sociologically.[58] In order to understand this fully we must note further that the communion of saints knows that it is organised on the basis of authority. It is communion only by virtue of the rule of the divine will within it. The paradoxical nature of this relationship of authority between God and man in revelation has its basis in the fact that God rules by serving; this is postulated in the concept of God's love. He commands, and, in commanding, he himself—and this distinguishes the relationship of authority from that of power, with its idea of the incomprehensible paradox of the divine revelation —puts the will to obey and the understanding of what is commanded into our hearts, he establishes, that is to say, man's communion with God and with his fellow-men. God's will to rule is his will to love his church. The ideas of God's lordship and kingdom are thus intimately connected, but are nevertheless to be distinguished logically and materially, and, as we can now add, sociologically. And if we speak here of 'communion'— as we have a perfect right to do—let it be said at once that later this idea of communion will have to yield to an even deeper understanding of the term (see p. 180).

We must now ask what the concrete acts are of the communion of saints acting as a community of love. The question shows that we are not concerned with the function of the church in general, with preaching, the sacraments, etc.—we shall speak of these in another connection—but solely with the social acts constituting the community of love, which tell us in more detail about the structure and nature of the Christian church.

Two groups of ideas summarise these acts:

1. the God-appointed structural 'togetherness' (*Miteinander*) of the church and each of its members;

2. the fact that the members act for one another (*Füreinander*), and the principle of vicarious action.

In fact, of course, it is only through each that the other is possible; each has its basis in the other.

The structure of the church is such that where one of its members is, it is there too, in its strength, in the strength, that is, of Christ and the Holy Spirit. It is conceived of as one life, in such a way that none of its members could be imagined as separated from it. But within the church each member is constrained by the Holy Spirit; again, it is within the church that he has his God-appointed place, and his will, moved by the Spirit. The man whose life is lived in love is Christ in respect of his neighbour —but, of course, always only in this respect. 'We are God through the love that makes us do good to our neighbour.'[59] Such a man can and should act like Christ. He should bear his neighbour's burdens and sufferings. 'You must take other men's want and infirmities to heart as if they were your own, and offer your means as if they were theirs, just as Christ does for you in the sacrament.'[60] Luther calls this 'being transformed into one another through love.'[61] Without in any way linking this with any mystical ideas about the vanishing of the frontiers between the concrete I and Thou,[62] Luther is simply saying that now I no longer want anything but the Thou, and the one loving me does not want anything else but me; and that there is a reversal—as it were, a transformation—of the attitudes imposed by sin. In this event I am bound to reach the point where the want, infirmities and sins of my neighbour afflict me as if they were my own, just as Christ was afflicted by our sins.[63] 'Behold, as you bear them all, so you are borne by them in turn, and all things are a good or an evil shared.'[64] 'Bear ye one another's burdens' (Gal. 6.2). What makes this state of being 'with one another' possible is not something willed by men; it is given only in the communion of saints, in a sense which is higher than men's profane state of being with one another; it belongs to the sociological structure of the church. In the *Tesseradecas*[65] Luther has given us his thoughts upon this in terms of incomparable beauty. My burden is borne by the others, their strength is my strength; when I falter and fail the faith of the church comes to my aid. And even when I come to die, I should be assured that not I, or at least not I alone, am dying, but that Christ and the communion of saints are suffering and dying with me. We go the way of suffering and death accompanied by the entire church.[66] 'If I should die, I am not alone in death; if I suffer they suffer with me'—Christ, that is—'with all the holy angels and the blessed in heaven, and godly men on earth.'[67] Let us set against this the famous words of Luther's sermon to the people of Wittenberg: 'We are each one of us summoned to death, and no man will die for another, but each wrestle with death on his own account, in his own person. We are fond of exhorting others, but at the moment of death each man must be prepared for his own self; I shall not then be with you, nor you with me.'[68] Might one of these assertions be nothing more than a daring hyperbole? We must try to understand how Luther wants to apply here the idea of the communion of saints. He is not trying to express the platitudinous and doubtful wisdom that a sorrow shared is a sorrow halved, a joy shared a joy doubled. He is seeking rather to establish the communion of saints as the basis and strength for all individual Christian life, in that God's will is related to the communion of saints, whereas it is related to the individual only if he is in this communion. The individual in death and suffering does in fact face God single and alone; his faith and prayer are achieved in this separateness and loneliness. The whole weight and seriousness of his relation with God is not taken from his shoulders. Yet in spite of all that, he still remains in the communion of saints, and no matter what strain or stress of life he may be in, it is with him. For where he is it is too if he belongs to it, since where it is he is also. It is thus that Luther can say that the communion of saints dies[69] and suffers 'with' him. He is not necessarily thinking that even one member of it knows that another member is suffering and dying, living in temptation and desire: but even without this knowledge, by virtue of its being the communion of saints, it is entirely present where even one of its members is. Of course Luther is also thinking of conscious active sharing of suffering, joy, guilt, affliction even unto death, and this empirical life of the communion of saints must be practised.[70] This, however, is only a consequence of its being; it does not first constitute it. Now where the communion of saints is, Christ is, and it is only with this foundation that all Luther's statements become possible. 'I am the head, I seek first to be the one who gives himself for you, I seek to share your suffering and misfortune and bear it for you, so that you too will in turn do likewise, for me and among yourselves, and let all those things be done in me and shared by me.'[71] That is the meaning of the sacrament of the Holy Body. The church could not bear anything if it were not itself borne by Christ; thus it is only in view of Christ's *meritum* that Luther finds it possible to speak of the *merita* of others, of those who help me. But just as Christ is always there when distress and death cause men to stand in loneliness before God, so too the church is always there. It is true that the loneliness imposed upon the individual by God is not removed; he is created as an individual, and he must live his own life and die his own death as an individual, as a person. But the loneliness of the basic moral relationship is overcome, in faith if not in sight, and the sinner's lonely state is also overcome; it is thus that the church is there. But where it is, there is also God's will and aim, and thus his communion with man is there also. Even if the individual does not feel anything of this, it is nevertheless really so,[72] so he should believe it, and as truly as he is a member of the church he will believe it.

In this state, established by Christ, of being 'with one another', which is shared by the church and its member, the being 'for one another' is also given. This active 'being for one another' can be defined from two standpoints: Christ is the measure and standard for our conduct (John 13.15, 34f.; I John 3.10), and our conduct is that of a member of the body of Christ, that is, of one equipped with the strength of Christ's love, in which each man can and will become Christ for his fellow-man (I Cor. 12.12; Rom. 12.4ff.; Eph. 4.4, 12ff.; Col. 3.15). Just as no man can live without the church, and each owes his life to it and now belongs to it, so his merits too are no longer his own, but belong to the church too. It is solely because the church lives as it were one life in Christ that the Christian can say that other men's chastity helps him in the temptations of his desires, that other men's fasting benefits him, and that his neighbour's prayers are offered for him. But with this are we now drawing suspiciously near the Roman Catholic doctrine of the *thesaurus*, which is accorded a central place in the whole recent Roman Catholic view of the *sanctorum communio?* Indeed we are, and we are approaching it quite consciously, as we are seeking, together with Luther, to make sure of preserving, in Protestant dogmatics, the sound core which is in danger of being lost. The decisive difference lies in the fact that we do not recognise any overflowing deserts in one man, which might then be used for another. The 'treasury of merit' can be nothing else but God's love which founded the church in Christ. The Roman Catholic doctrine of the *thesaurus* is a rationalisation, moralisation and humanisation of the irrational fact that man can never do more than he ought, and that God nevertheless lets each man 'enjoy'[73] the other in the church, which in turn is to be accounted for by the fact that Christ died for the church so that its members might lead one life, with one another and for one another.

Our being for one another now has to be actualised through the act of love. Three great possibilities for acting positively for one another are disclosed in the communion of saints: renunciatory, active work for our neighbour, prayers of intercession, and lastly the mutual granting of forgiveness of sins in God's name. With all of them it is a question of abandoning oneself 'for' one's neighbour, for his good, but with the readiness to do and bear everything in his stead, indeed if need be to sacrifice oneself for him, to act vicariously for him. Even if purely vicarious action is seldom actualised, the intention to achieve it is contained in every genuine act of love.

If a man devotes himself to renunciatory work for his neighbour then he clearly gives up any claim to happiness. We are required to intercede vicariously for the other man in everyday matters, required to give up any claim to goods or honour, even to the whole of life itself. Man is meant to be active in the church with all the strength he owes to it. The 'strong' man does not have his qualities for himself, so that he can tell himself that they raise him out of the church, but 'for the common good' (I Cor. 12.7). Every gift of a material, spiritual or religious kind fulfils its purpose only in the church. Love demands that we should sacrifice our own interest. But this may include sacrificing even communion with God itself. Here is manifested the love which of its own free will is ready to incur God's wrath for its brothers' sake, which even desires God's wrath if by this means they will be enabled to have communion with him, which takes its brothers' place as Christ took our place for us. The two great examples of this are Ex. 32.32 and Rom. 9.1ff. Moses wishes to be blotted out of the book of life with his people,[74] and Paul wishes that he himself were accursed and cut off from Christ, not in order to be condemned with his brethren, but to win communion with God for them; he wishes to be condemned in their stead. This is a paradox of love for God which it is difficult to resolve: Paul loves his people, but loves God above all else. Moses' conduct was heroic; he wanted to be accepted or rejected by God with his people; such a wish we can still rationally comprehend. Paul, however, wants to win, for the people whom he loves, communion with God, which he loves above all things, and curses himself away from communion with God and away from his people, taking upon himself his brethren's condemnation, precisely because he really loves both communion with God and his people, that is, because he is obedient to the command that he should surrender himself completely to his neighbour. But for this very reason in wishing to be banished from God he remains in the closest union with him. At the point where the most terrible conflict with God seems to rage, the deepest peace is established. Thus we should not see in this a moment of weakness on Paul's part, a statement which is 'religiously and morally impossible';[75] instead of being disobedience it is on the contrary a deed of the most profound obedience. This very deed, however, gives us a clear proof that love ultimately seeks not communion, but the 'other'; and also that the less it seeks communion the more surely it will find it.

Fundamentally this describes the kind of abyss into which the individual can be drawn by his prayer of intercession. The problem of the social structure consists in the question of how we must conceive of the relationship between those who are praying for one another, and here the universal basis must be sought in the fact that the church leads one life, and that the individual has communion with God only if he takes part in this life; that he does not face God alone but is in the communion of saints, where even the prayer which is most his own no longer belongs to him, but to the church that made him and through which he lives. 'No man is saved alone; he who is saved is saved in the church, as its member in unity with the other members. Does anyone believe?—he is in the community of faith. Does anyone love?—he is in the community of love. Does anyone pray?— he is in the community of prayer. Do not ask: "What prayer can benefit the living or the dead, since my prayer is not even sufficient for myself?" Since in any event you do not understand how to pray, what is the purpose of your praying for yourself? The spirit of love prays in you. . . . If you are a member of the church your prayer is necessary for all its members. . . . But the blood of the church is the prayer of intercession for one another.'[76]

Every intercession potentially draws the one for whom it is intended into the church; the ancient intercession 'for all men'[77] necessarily does this too. If there is no possibility of making the other man a member of the church, the intercession has no object; it is ungodly. Its limit, like the limit of love of one's neighbour, is that of God's love. The doubt as to whether intercession is meaningful vanishes before such considerations as Khomiakov presents, but it must be admitted that these considerations do not explain the miracle of the church. It is a mistaken individualism to rely only upon one's own prayer, as if God could not just as seriously consider an intercessory prayer as he does every other prayer; our thinking thus indicates that we conceive of prayer merely as a good work of the individual and lack understanding of the idea that in Christ the church leads one life. God's will is sovereign over prayer too, so prayer remains a 'waiting for God to draw near' (Nietzsche). The extent to which a man doubts the value of intercession is the extent to which he is still self-righteous. And yet it matters who prays; in the positive form of intercession there is a positive meaning. Intercession should be seen from two aspects; as a human deed and as the divine will. In the first the fact that the members of the church belong together is made manifest. A third person is drawn into my solitary relation with God, or rather, I move in intercession into the other man's place, when my prayer remains my own, but nevertheless springs from his distress and his need; I really enter into the other man, into his guilt and his distress; I am afflicted by his sins and his infirmity. It is not that I must by my gift of empathy feel his grief with him or after him. If we had to do this there would be no intercession for all mankind; then I could not pray for a man living completely shut off from the world. We must rid ourselves here of all psychological thinking. The sins of the unknown sailor, for whom intercession is made in the corporate prayer of the church, afflict me just as much as those of my closest friend; for the basis for the affliction is the recognition of our own responsibility for the world's guilt, or, what is the same thing, of our own guilt in the death of Christ. If this guilt is recognised, man can act upon men as a Christian in praying for them. In his intercession he can become a Christ for his neighbour. Thus in intercession a man does not receive the cold comfort that others are in the same state as himself, but, if God so wills and he himself accepts, his guilt is forgiven him and his sins are taken away (James 5.15f.; John 5.16f.). His guilt, however, is borne by the church— Christ. The words of the Psalm, 'Truly no man can ransom his brother, or give to God the price of his life, for the ransom of their life is costly and can never suffice,' are only conditionally correct.[78] Intercession, like every other form of prayer, cannot compel God, but if he himself gives the final sanction then a man can ransom his brother, by virtue of the church. This finally disposes of man's moral self-assurance in face of his fellow-man. As a Christian he cannot boast of his aloneness with God; his strength comes to him from the church, and he will never know how much his own prayer did and what the fervent intercession of people unknown to him contributed for him. He knows that he owes unending thanks not only to God but to the church which prayed, and is still praying, for him. If his moral self-assurance in face of God is first broken by Christ's vicarious love upon the cross, it dies completely when he considers the nature of intercession, that is, by the church.

If we now consider intercession from God's standpoint, it is seen to be the individual's organisation of himself to realise God's will for the other man, so that he may serve the realisation of God's rule in the church. Here is where the meaning and strength of the corporate prayer of the church resides, as Luther speaks of it in the sermon on good works.[79] In this corporate prayer God possesses his strongest means for organising the whole church towards his purpose. The church recognises itself in prayer as an instrument of his will and organises itself accordingly in active obedience. This provides the church with its chief impulse;[80] the devil fears a roof of thatch beneath which the church is at prayer more than he does a splendid church in which many masses are celebrated.[81] Thus it is of decisive significance for the church that it should give to corporate prayer its proper, central place. The church that leads one life must also have and practise one prayer. In this prayer it takes upon itself the burden of the many individuals who already or still belong to it, and bears it to God. In the church each man bears the other's burden, and it is in knowing that intercession is a means supplied by God for the realisation of his aim that we can recognise and practise it with meaning. In intercession, too, we confirm the nature of Christian love as making us act 'with', 'for' and finally 'in place of' our neighbour, thereby drawing him deeper and deeper into the church. Thus when a man is interceding for another in Jesus's name the whole church is praying with him, but praying as 'Christ existing as the church'. We thus modify Hegel's conception.

This has brought us already to the final problem, the one giving us the deepest insight into the miracle of the church. This miracle is that one man, by the prerogative of his priesthood, can forgive another his sins. It was Augustine who recognised that this could come about only in the communion of saints. The promise of

John 20.23 refers solely to this communion, for it is only in the communion of saints that the Spirit is to be found. No one can forgive sins but he who takes them upon himself, bears them and cancels them; thus Christ alone can do it. But this means that the church, as the *sanctorum communio*, can forgive sins. The individual can do it only if he is a member of the church, and as a member he should do it. He relieves the other's conscience of its guilt and lays it upon himself, but this he can do only by laying it in turn upon Christ. His action is thus possible only in the church. This does not mean that his action must be confined to a member of the church, but that it is possible only because the church exists. Luther revived Augustine's idea that the *sanctorum communio* bears its members' guilt. But later in the same sentence he says that it is Christ who bears it.[82] 'Thus in this sacrament (Holy Communion) is given us God's immeasurable grace and mercy, as we divest ourselves of all grief and temptation and lay it upon the church, and especially upon Christ . . . all my misfortune is now shared by Christ and the saints.'[83] The church is thus able to bear the guilt that none of its members can. It can bear more guilt than all its members together. This being so it must be a spiritual reality extending beyond the sum of all individuals. Not the sum of all the individuals, but the church as a totality is in Christ, is the 'Body of Christ', is 'Christ existing as the church'. It bears the guilt in experiencing forgiveness through the Word and seeing its guilt cancelled upon the cross. It lives in very fact solely by the Word; but since it lives from it, it has the Spirit; it is the bearer of the Word, its custodian and instrument. It has authority so far as it believes in the authority of the Word; it can take the individual's sin upon itself if it is built upon the Word of the cross and knows itself to be reconciled and justified by the cross of Jesus. It has itself died and risen with Christ and is now the *nova creatura*[84] in Christ. It is not only a means to an end but at the same time an end in itself; it is the presence of Christ himself, and that is why 'being in Christ' and 'being in the church' are one and the same thing, why the individual's guilt, when it is laid upon the church, is borne by Christ himself.

The new basic social relationships can now be briefly summarised. The basic moral relationships which were disrupted in the *corpus peccati* (Bernard) are renewed by the Holy Spirit. The community is constituted by the complete self-forgetfulness of love. The relationship between I and Thou is no longer essentially a demanding but a giving one. Each reveals his heart to the other, as a heart subdued by the will of God, even though in actual fact the former moral and social basic relationships between the I and Thou remain so long as conscience, law and the wrath of God exist, so long, that is, as we walk by faith and not by sight. The Christian comes into being and exists only in Christ's church. He is dependent upon it, that is, upon the other man. Each man sustains the other in active love, intercession and forgiveness of sins through complete vicarious action, which is possible only in the church of Christ, resting as it does in its entirety upon the principle of vicarious action, that is, upon the love of God. But all are sustained by the church, which consists in this action for one another of its members. The church and its members are structurally together, and act vicariously for each other, in the strength of the church. This constitutes the specific sociological character of community based on love. In all this the singularity and solitariness of each member are not abolished; he must constantly struggle on his own responsibility to pray and to achieve an attitude wholly determined by obedience. His guilt is either entirely his own or not his own at all; he cannot foist part of it on his neighbour. Either he still bears it, or he has laid it upon the church and that means that it is now borne by 'Christ existing as the church'. So we are led to the problem of the 'unity' of the church in which multiplicity and community of persons acquires its comprehensive meaning. The concept of the church as *numerus praedestinatorum* and as *sanctorum communio*—in the sense of community, which sociologically still needs more precise definition—has still to be made complete.

c. The spiritual unity of the church — the collective person

The spiritual unity of the church is a primal synthesis willed by God. It is not a relationship that has to be established, but one that is already posited (*iustitia passiva*), and remains invisible. It is not made possible by concord, similarity or affinity between souls, nor should it be confused with unity of mood. Instead it is real just where seemingly the most intractable outward oppositions prevail, where each man leads his quite individual life, and it is perhaps absent where it seems to prevail most. It can shine more brightly in the conflict between wills than in concord. When two people come into collision the result may very well be that they will be reminded of him who is One above them both, and in whom they are both one. It was where Jew and Greek came into conflict as a result of the completely different nature of their psychological structure, sensibility and outlook that unity was established by the divine will; 'There is neither Jew nor Greek, there is neither slave nor free, there is neither male nor female; for you are all one in Christ Jesus' (Gal. 3.28). He has created in himself one new man in place of two, so making peace (Eph. 2.15). But this peace is still a peace that passes all understanding. For the oppositions remain; they even become more acute. For in the community everyone is made to tune his individual perception to the highest pitch, to be completely in earnest about it. This is in accordance with the basic sociological laws of social vitality, but—to put it paradoxically—the greater the dissimilarity brought to light by the conflict the greater is the objective unity. The decisive passages in the New Testament do not say: one theology and one rite, one opinion upon all things both public and private, and one mode of conduct in life.[85] But they say: one body and one Spirit, one Lord, one faith, one baptism, one God and Father of us all (Eph. 4.4ff.; I Cor. 12.13; Rom. 12.5); varieties of gifts for all of us, but the same spirit, varieties of service, but the same Lord, varieties of working but the same God (I Cor. 12.4). It is not a question of 'oneness in the spirit', but of the 'unity of the spirit', as Luther puts it in his exposition of Eph. 4.3;[86] that is, the objective principle establishes the unity in sovereign fashion, unites the multiplicity of persons into one collective person, without abolishing individual persons and communion of persons. Rather, spiritual unity, community of spirit and multiplicity of spirits necessarily and factually belong together. This we have already shown in our discussion of the basic ideas of social philosophy.

The reason why Idealist philosophy did not realise this lies deep within its system; once again we note the basic lack of a concrete concept of the person.[87]

The picture is everywhere the same. The spirit is the one, is everlastingly identical, supra-personal and immanent in man. It destroys the concrete person and thus makes any concept of concrete community impossible, sacrificing this to the unity of immanent spirit. The Idealists have fallen victim to the perils of 'imagining, by means of a short-circuit, that community is unity'.[88] We acknowledge their unanimous emphasis upon the idea of 'community', their perception that individual life is real only within the life of a group. But we mean by 'group life' and 'real' something very different. For us, both are moral categories, whereas for the Idealists they are partly biological, partly metaphysical in nature.

The unity of the Christian church is not based upon the oneness of human spirits, but upon the unity of the divine spirit, and the two are not identical. In our discussion of the sociological type of community we showed that its ultimate unity was its being as a collective person. This knowledge must be applied to the Christian religious community, as well as to the concept of the church; in the first case the course of the presentation would be from below upwards, whereas with the concept of the church it runs from above downwards. The personal unity of the church is 'Christ existing as the church'. Paul could even say that Christ himself is the church.

A man is in Christ if he is in the church.[89] The unity of the church as a structure is established 'before' any knowing or willing on the part of its members; it is not an ideal, but a reality. It is a reality as truly as the church is the church of Christ and as truly as the Body of Christ never attains to perfect representation in history. In Christ all are one; there are no more distinctions; there is not even any more multiplicity. All men are one, 'one cake', as Luther puts it.[90] It is only all men together who can possess Christ entirely, and yet each man possesses him entirely too. This unity arises from the fact that Christ 'is the One beyond every other' (Barth). It must be believed, and it will always be invisible. This unity does not exist because the members in the body have the same intentions; but they have the same intentions only as members of Christ's body, if indeed they have any intentions at all; for they remain members even if they sin (cf. the indicative sense of I Cor. 6.15). And yet there is no divine will for men that is not realised in men, at least in its first beginnings; thus the objective unity subsisting in Christ is realised in the persons, and it is only in being thus realised that it is objective unity.

In Eph. 4.5 together with the 'one Lord' the 'one faith' is mentioned—the faith in which the Lord declares himself and in which he is present. The unity of faith is a unity 'without which no oneness, be it of the State, of time, person, work or any other thing whatsoever, makes a Christendom'.[91] Seen from below, it is the very constituent of the church's unity, and this leads to some important consequences about the necessity for a creed in the worship of the congregation. The Christian congregation can only assemble as a unity before God, and give practical proof by its faith of the spiritual unity of Christ's church—'Christ existing as the church'—which is established by God and beyond our sight. If it is the will of God that there is one Spirit, one Lord, one God, constituting the church (*constitutio—cives*, see pp. 184f.), then the creed is the congregation's affirmation of this constitution. Indeed, seen purely from without, it is this constitution itself in which the religious 'community' focuses its objective knowledge of its own foundation, meaning and purpose, and by which it is held together. It is another question altogether, which we shall not discuss, whether the Apostles' Creed does justice to this element of confession in the Christian congregation.

It is as the church standing in the unity of the Spirit, living from the one life, that it offers the great corporate prayer and bows to the prayer which, according to ancient tradition (Luke 11.11ff.), Christ gave his church, the Lord's Prayer.[92] It is one of the serious signs of our times that we must constantly feel how little the congregation understands that during divine service it is praying as a church. We must make every effort to see that our congregations learn to pray again. The prayer of the congregation, as Luther never wearied of saying, is one of the main sources of its strength, concentration and unification. We are accustomed to call the Christian church a community of faith. Sociologically at least this is a shortened form of speech. The Christian community rests solely upon the fact of faith, that is, upon the acceptance of the divine Spirit. But in its concrete determination as a 'community' it is not a community of faith, but one of love and of the Spirit. Faith is not identical with communion, any more than God's rule is identical with his kingdom. Faith is the acceptance of the divine rule as the will of God; it is subjection to divine truth. Love is the activation, brought about by the Spirit, of this faith. Faith, by its nature, is solely orientation upon God; between several believers, as far as it is purely a question of their being believers, there only exists unity of faith. Even though, in faith in God, faith in his rule in the church is also presupposed, this faith is nevertheless something which only indirectly contributes to the establishment of communion. It is possible only in the church, in the unity of the church; it is activation of this unity. Christian community in its full sense, however, is formed only by love acting in virtue of faith. Thus, opposing one another, we have unity of faith as an idea correlative to the idea of God's lordship, and communion based on love as an idea correlative to the idea of the kingdom of God. Both belong indissolubly together, but sociologically they should be distinguished. Concretely however, the positive unity of faith is sustained by communion based on love. Unity, in so far as it is not already present, must be fought for. But the weapon of the Christian church is love; thus Christian love will always press towards, and demand, unity. We must not, in our church, lose sight of Augustine's great conception that *caritas* is the bond of church unity. But this idea presupposes unity based on God, and it is only upon the basis of this unity that human action is meaningful.

Nowadays there is much talk of unification of the churches.[93] But we must not forget that unification from below is not the same as unity from above, and that the wish for unification should be realised, first of all, in the smaller and even the smallest congregation. The way to unification, however, follows a course fraught with the most difficult obstacles; for the stronger the wish the more pronounced will be the individual opposition. There will indeed be a basic aim to serve as a relative unity upon which we shall be able to build. And this may also be assumed of a church in which it cannot be formulated, but where the will is at work to give it conceptual expression. In spite of the recognition that we shall never be able to attain an absolute oneness corresponding to the unity of the Spirit, the will for the greatest possible realisation of this oneness will be alive in the church, and will take comfort from Jesus's prayer: 'that they may all be one, even as thou, Father, art in me and I in thee' (John 17.21). And it will be to the glory of the church, by its oneness, to glorify Jesus before all the world (v. 23).

There is a sharp distinction between all this and the Idealist concept of unity. 1. The immanent unity of spirit is only the incipient actualisation of the transcendental unity really accomplished in Christ. 2. It is impossible to equate the spirit of a religious community with the Holy Spirit of the church. 3. The man moved by the Spirit becomes and remains a full person precisely upon the complete actualisation of the immanent unity. Even where all are one in Christ it would be wrong to imagine that the personality willed by God is effaced; we must rather imagine it as reaching its finest perfection at this very point. The unity is a complete one, but it is fraught with tension, a fact which points to an eschatological solution that is hidden from us (see below, 'The Church and Eschatology').

The absolutely fundamental indissolubility of personal being brings us to a problem which makes the peculiarity of the social structure of the church even clearer, the problem, namely, of equality. The concept of equality[94] presupposes a plurality of persons, similarly placed in reference to a certain value, be it of a material or spiritual kind. 'Equality before the law' does not tell us anything about the content of the relationship between men, but refers purely to the value 'law'. Similarly the Christian idea of equality says nothing about interpersonal relationships, but places all men within the sight of God, in that it states first the absolute distance separating the creature from the Creator, and even more so that separating the sinner from the Holy One: the equality of men consists in their universal sinfulness (Rom. 3.23), that means also in their universal need of redemption, and their equal share in God's grace. This is disclosed in Christ's death upon the cross. It is not the person who counts in God's eyes, but the heart (Acts 10.34, 15.8, Gal. 2.6, and elsewhere). In God's eyes there is no longer either Jew nor Gentile, nor does either have a prior claim. No one has any claim at all and each must live by grace; that is their equality.[95] Can we then say that the church of God is built upon ultimately equal beings? So far as the relation of each one of them to God is concerned, we certainly can. This formal equality extends to all of them. In the concrete situation which arises in life, however, when man is addressed by God and placed by him in this situation, each man as a person is completely unlike every other. But does not the equality of all persons nevertheless seem to be the more fundamental thing, whereas time and space, as the *principia individuationis*, show merely negligible differentiations? This is not so, since equality before God cannot be proved or demonstrated, nor is it manifest as 'similarity'. It rests ultimately upon the fact that God is always the same. Equality has nothing to do with affinity between souls, where the one man has only to look within himself to know the other; but it is only visible to God, and completely invisible to us, because we are dissimilar. But this equality is most plainly preached by the cross of Christ, in which the same judgment and the same grace is pronounced for the whole world. It has its basis in the spiritual unity of the church, which is beyond our sight, and we have here only the dialectical relation of multiplicity and unity repeating itself. The concept of equality, thus understood, does not allow of any schematising, but rather includes all men's concrete dissimilarity; in the Christian sense it is quite possible, even required, that there should be the strong and the weak, the honourable and dishonourable, those who morally and religiously have a higher value, and those who have a lower one, quite apart from obvious social inequalities. But it is this very idea of invisible equality before God that sets a limit to our recognition of these inequalities. This equality is to be realised within the frame of what is possible, in that strength and weakness, honour and disgrace, morality and immorality, piety and impiety are there for one another, but never for themselves alone. Thus the idea of equality leads us again into the idea of community. This duality of the idea of equality is also expressed in Luther's doctrine of the priesthood of all believers. The equality upon the basis of which every Christian is a priest is invisible, and becomes 'visible' only for faith—but can never be deduced without it!—through the unity of the gift in Word and sacrament. As the whole church rests upon the unity in Christ, upon the fact of 'Christ existing as the church', so all Christian community rests upon the equality of all which is based on God. This can be said only when the view is from above. But the priesthood of all believers signifies the affirmation of the concrete dissimilarities of the individual believers, in that the individuals are drawn into mutual service whereby the one proves himself a priest for the other. Thus all we have already said about the community of spirit applies here to. If this is borne in mind the possible connection between the priesthood of all believers and patriarchalism immediately becomes evident. The Christian conception of equality does not make everybody equal, but simply and solely recognises the actual facts in which Pauline patriarchalism, for instance, finds its justification. This is the difference in principle between the Christian idea of equality and all socialist or Idealist ideas of equality. And that in turn directs us back to the Christian concept of spiritual unity, as represented in a theological concept of the church.[96]

My purpose so far has been to represent the church as consisting of unity, community and singularity, and to represent these three factors, which are based on the Spirit, in their relation to one another, thus contributing to the doctrine of the social structure of the church as the *sanctorum communio*.

3. *The empirical form of the church*

a. The objective spirit of the church and the Holy Spirit

The church of Jesus Christ actualised by the Holy Spirit is at the present moment really the church. The communion of saints represented by it is 'in the midst of us'. This proposition gives rise to a twofold question about the empirical church. There is the question of 'history and the communion of saints', and the question of the *communio peccatorum* within the *sanctorum communio*.

The empirical church is the organised 'institution' of salvation, having as its focus the cultus with preaching and sacrament, or, in sociological terms, the 'assembly' of the members. It is legally constituted, and links the bestowal of its benefits with the orders of divine service it lays down. It accepts all who submit to these orders, and hence has no guarantee for the inner disposition of its members, but, from the moment it is sanctioned by public opinion and perhaps has even become a political power in the state, it must necessarily reckon with the fact that it will have 'dead members' within it. It is the 'historical result of the work of Jesus Christ' (Seeberg), and as such represents the objective spirit of the church in its development and being, in transmitted forms and embodiments and in present vitality and effectiveness. The objective spirit, as we saw, is the new spiritual principle springing from socialisation. The autonomous effectiveness of its will regulates and guides the wills of those partaking of and forming it. It is embodied in certain forms and thereby visibly authenticates its own life. Again, it acts in two directions, that is, it has an intention both in time and in space; it seeks to be effective both in the historical and in the social sphere. It is the bearer of historical tradition, and its action and effects are to include more and more individuals in its scope. It seems as if this sociological structure in the empirical church should now be studied and analysed as presenting the religious type of community among many types of community. And yet if we did this we should entirely distort the matter. The empirical church is not identical with a religious community. Rather, as a concrete historical community, in spite of the relativity of its forms, its imperfect and unpretentious appearance, the empirical church is the Body of Christ, the presence of Christ on earth, for it has his Word. It is possible to understand the empirical church only by looking down from above, or by looking out from the inside, and not otherwise. Once this fact has been grasped it is of course in principle possible once more to define the church as a religious community, always bearing in mind that it is really based on God. Thus if we now apply to the church what we said about the objective spirit, we have the claim of the objective spirit of the church to be the bearer of the historical work of Jesus Christ and of the social action of the Holy Spirit.[97]

The historical church claims that it possesses the Holy Spirit and is the effective custodian of the Word of God and of the sacrament. This brings us to the first question, the great body of thought on the problem of the relation of the Spirit of Christ and the Holy Spirit of the *sanctorum communio* to the objective spirit of the empirical church.

The *sanctorum communio* moved by the Holy Spirit has continually to be actualised in a struggle against two sources of resistance: human imperfection and sin. To equate the two, giving imperfection the weight of sin, or evaluating sin merely as imperfection, is to avoid the seriousness of the Christian concept of sin, and leads either to regarding the church's sociologically empirical form as sin, or, in the manner of Kant,[98] to viewing the empirical church only as a manifestation of the non-real, ideal church of the future or as unattainable in this world. Neither attitude does justice to the empirical church's historical importance. The first is wrong because Christ entered into history[99] so that the church is his presence in history. The history of the church is the hidden centre of world history, and not the history of one educational institution among many. For the church is Christ existing as the church. No matter how dubious its empirical form may be, it remains the church so long as Christ is present in his Word. Thereby we acknowledge that God has willed the church's historical life, in the sense that it is intended to perfect itself. The Body of Christ is just as much a real presence in history as it is the standard for its own history. This brings us once again to what was said at the beginning of our inquiry, about the normative character of basic ontic relationships. In the sphere of Christian ethics it is not what ought to be that effects what is, but what is effects what ought to be.

This shows us the easily perceptible flaw in Kant's concept of the church. The church is not only ideally present, but really present in history. And yet the church is not only imperfect, but also sinful. Kant, who with his concept of 'radical evil' had expressed a perception (of Lutheran provenance) leading beyond the whole of Idealistic philosophy, did not utilise it in his concept of the church. The members of the kingdom of virtue are indeed imperfect, but good. Luther's idea of the *iustus peccator* was something Kant did not understand.

1. The decisive thing for the Lutheran concept of the church is that the *sanctorum communio* remains as it always has been, a community of sinners. This is the chief reason why Hegel's theory of spirit is unacceptable. The absolute Spirit does not simply enter into the subjective spirits and gather them in the objective spirit;[100] but the Christian church is the church of the Word, that is, of faith. Present sanctification is only a preliminary sign of the last things; here we still walk by faith; that is to say, here we see only our sins, and believe in our sanctity.[101] The 'Word' is the rock upon which the Idealists' spirit-monism founders, for the Word signifies that there is still sin, that the absolute Spirit must fight for its authority, that the church remains a church of sinners. These ideas have been brought

home to us by modern Luther studies, and also by the most recent trend in theology. We shall now include them in the picture we have sketched of the *sanctorum communio*.

The difficulty in determining the relation between the objective spirit and the Holy Spirit springs from the concept of the community of love. The idea that the individual and the community are purely instruments of the Holy Spirit is shown to be an illusion. Communion with God, and likewise human communion, are continually being broken and renewed. Man does not constantly live a genuine organic life of fellowship. The *peccatorum communio* lives on in the *sanctorum communio*. The mankind of Adam is still in actuality there, even if in reality it has been overcome. Justified man does not get beyond the earliest beginnings of the new life. So he still experiences the other man as 'Thou', in the sense of alien, making claims. Only in faith in the communion of saints is this overcome. Thus the communion of saints represents only the beginnings of the new life; it is eschatological and proleptic, in which the Thou reveals itself to the I as an I, as heart, as love, as Christ.

Thus although the *sanctorum communio* is continually falling, coming into existence anew, passing and coming into existence once more, a state which we saw was part of the nature of every moral person, this movement of repentance and faith is fulfilled at one fixed point: it is by the Word that the church is broken, to become the church of the cross, and by the Word it is 'built up' to become the church of Easter. The communion of saints as the communion of penitent sinners is held together by the unity of the Body of Christ. As in every other community, so in the church, penance is done by each man for his own sins and for those of the collective person of the community. Is this collective person 'Christ existing as the church', the Body of Christ? It can be only in so far as God himself is at work in the penance. It is not the communion of sinners, but the sanctity even of this community that is 'Christ existing as the church'. The fact that as the communion of sinners it is nevertheless the communion of saints, or rather, in this world, is never saintly without being sinful, is Christ's presence in it; it is precisely as such, as a communion saintly in its sinfulness, that it is 'Christ existing as the church'. If it were argued that it is the individual and not the church's objective spirit that is sinful, this would be right to the extent that in the church the general direction of the wills in principle becomes a new one. This is not to say that when the empirical church is active as a 'whole' what it does is an act of the Holy Spirit. This would conform with Hegel's theory, and to assume it would be to do away with the monadic image of society as we presented it. A church council is no holier than one man alone. Thus into the objective spirit of each particular time, apart from human imperfection, much evil will will have flowed too, and frequently Augustine's words have seemed to be confirmed that 'the church has often been only in one individual, or in one family.'[102] Sin has to be taken up into the concept of the objective spirit. Thus the fact of guilt makes it clear that the objective spirit of the collective person of the church cannot be identified with the Holy Spirit. There is, however, a further equally clear reason for this.

2. The empirical church lives in history. As the spirit of one man as a member of the church might have a particular task at a particular time, so the objective spirit of the church, fashioned according to the given situation, is different in every age. It receives its stamp from historical circumstances. The fact that the objective spirit is within history necessarily implies the fallibility and imperfection of its knowledge and will. In the objective spirit embodied in the church of each particular age in the past, the individual, accidental and imperfect nature of this spirit is made manifest. These qualities make it impossible to identify the objective spirit with the spirit of Christ or the Holy Spirit.

3. Perhaps many who are not predestined also affect the objective spirit of the church, both helping and hindering it. This is probably the most compelling proof that the objective spirit and the Holy Spirit cannot be identified with one another. For those who are not predestined do not belong to the church, and yet the Holy Spirit, through the objective spirit, can use them too as instruments of his creative activity. They remain of course purely instruments, and are never the object of the Spirit's

work. The distinction between the objective spirit and the Holy Spirit has thus become quite plain. And yet we must assume that there is a connection between them.

Through all the church's sinfulness, its historical contingency and fallibility, the historical tendency of the Spirit of Christ is at work in the form of the objective spirit, and the Holy Spirit uses this too as the bearer of his concentrating and sustaining social actions, notwithstanding all the sinfulness and imperfection of the individuals and of the whole. This happens in accordance with what was said earlier about the time-factor and the space-factor in the rule of Christ and the Holy Spirit. It is solely by the Word, however, that each assures the church of his presence. Here it is clear that in the building of the empirical church Christ and the Holy Spirit make use of historical forms of objective spiritual life. Hence the objective spirit of the church will have its special functions in this service, as we shall see later.

Opposing one another, then, we have on the one hand the endlessly changing, imperfect, sinful objective human spirit, and on the other hand the Holy Spirit and 'Christ existing as the church', the Holy Spirit everlastingly one, and perfect, bearing the objective human spirit. The objective human spirit is a prey to the historical ambiguity of all profane communities, of all so-called ideal social groups, vain, extravagant and mendacious. Nevertheless it claims with certainty that it is the church of Christ, that it has its place in spite of everything within a church built and sustained by the Holy Spirit. It is a certainty which, precisely by reason of the church's similarity to other 'religious communities', often threatens to come to naught. Confronting one another there are the purely historical collective persons of the church and the person of Christ as God's presence in the church; the 'religious community' of men and the community of the Spirit; and in so far as the former, in spite of all appearances to the contrary, and with a full awareness of its position, believes that it is identical with the latter, it believes in the church, in the communion of saints (see below on 'Believing in the Church'). Thus there cannot be any question of establishing by historical means that the two are identical. The identity is 'invisible' and can be seen only in the Last Things, and yet it already has its actual beginning now. The objective spirit is the bearer and instrument of the Spirit of the church of Christ, it has certain visible forms, which the Holy Spirit has created out of himself and infused into the objective spirit. Thus the Holy Spirit working through it is the guarantor for the efficacy of these forms, which are in fact the preaching of the Word and the administration of the sacraments. But the objective spirit does not bear these as a man bears a sack on his back; rather it is itself sanctified by the burden; it bears it in its heart, that is of course only in so far as the Holy Spirit is himself doing the bearing in it, for the objective spirit is not the Holy Spirit. But the objective spirit is at once an instrument and an end in itself, in accordance with our earlier definition of the community of love. It is the object and the means of operation of the Holy Spirit, and it is both these things in the manner of the blending of Holy Spirit and objective human spirit described earlier—which clearly shows the impossibility of the two being identical.

b. The logical relation between the empirical and the essential church

Our discussion of the relation of objective spirit to the Holy Spirit and the Spirit of Christ has determined the material relation between the empirical form of the church and its form in the spirit. Does this still allow us to speak of a church? Can the empirical and the essential church be reduced logically and sociologically to a single concept?

This question first of all puts the concept of the essential church into correct relation with the concept of the kingdom of God.[103]

1. Both by their nature comprise only those who are pre-destined (the problem of the *donum perseverantiae* requires a separate dogmatic inquiry on its own account, and has no great significance here).

2. The material content of each is identical, namely the sub-

jection of mankind to God's will for his rule over men and for their redemption.[104] The purpose of God's rule over man is the kingdom. But whereas all the predestined are included in the kingdom, the church includes only those elected in Christ (Eph. 1.4; I Peter 1.20). Thus the former exists from eternity to eternity; the latter has its beginning in history. To talk of a church of the Old Testament would be meaningful only if this were understood as meaning the community of those awaiting Christ.[105] But such a description would be misleading, and would unnecessarily burden the concept of the church. 'The church is the kingdom of God, but in the form ordained for the time between Jesus's ascension and second coming.'[106] 'The church is the kingdom of God realising itself on earth under the constitution of the New Covenant.'[107] In its visible historical form it comprises many more members than the kingdom of God, but in its essence not a single member more. (Rather, many members fewer. This in opposition to Hofmann,[108] for instance, is our assumption for the time since Christ as well). We prefer to call the church the kingdom of Christ (see above).[109]

This kingdom of Christ or the church, is, however, present to us in concrete historical form, and present in such a way that it must reckon with having many nominal members. It is present, in other words, as a national church (*Volkskirche*) and not as a 'gathered' church (*Freiwilligkeitskirche*). How can a church that, as a human community, is by its very nature a community of wills, at the same time be a national church? Such is the sociological formulation of the problem of the empirical church. The solution is to be found by reflecting upon the nature of the 'Word'. The *sanctorum communio*, with the preaching of the Word which it bears and by which it is borne, extends beyond itself and addresses all those who might belong to it, and this is part of its nature. From this it does not of course follow that the 'dead' members also belong to the Body of Christ.[110] The second reason is that here on earth there is no way of telling the wheat from the chaff; this is something that will be revealed only on the Day of Judgment, and is now being secretly prepared. At the same time the *sanctorum communio*, as it extends beyond itself, presses back

151

upon the 'real' church, to realise what is possible. The *sanctorum communio*, which by its nature presents itself as a national church, equally demands the gathered church, and continually establishes itself as such; that is, the *sanctorum communio* sustains the others, as it were, in whom the possibility of becoming 'effective' members of the church is dormant, by virtue of the Word which constitutes it and which it preaches. A man can be assumed to be a possible member, however, as long as he has made no conscious retraction, and even this the church will not necessarily consider as final, so that it can never be demonstrably impossible for him to become a member. The logical and sociological unity of the gathered and national, essential and empirical, 'invisible' and 'visible' church[111] is thus established through the Word, and this is a genuinely Lutheran perception. Now for the church there is a point in time when it may not be a national church any longer, and this point is reached when it can no longer see in its national form any way of fighting its way through to becoming a gathered church. But such a step would in the event spring from church politics and not from dogmatics. It does, however, show that the church's essential character is that of a gathered church. It is nevertheless in its historical national form that the church's chief strength resides. This is overlooked by those who scorn the church's historicity. True love for the church will help to bear and love its impurity and imperfection too; for it is in fact this empirical church which nurtures God's holy treasure, his community. There have been many presumptuous attempts at purifying the church[112] from the formation of the perfectionist sects of the early church to those of the Anabaptists and Pietists; there has been the Enlightenment and Kant's secularised notion of the kingdom of God, then the beginnings of the socialist expectation of the kingdom of God as represented by Saint Simon, which led *via* Tolstoy to the religious and social Youth Movement of our day—everywhere the attempt to have the kingdom of God present not only to faith but to sight, not shrouded in the particularities of a Christian church, but clearly manifested in the morality and sanctity of persons, in the ideal regulating of all historical and social problems. But of the fact that God's revelation is really proceeding in history, that is, in a hidden way; that this world is still a world of sin and death, that is, historical, and that its history is sanctified by the fact that God made it and entered into it, and used it as a means to his end—of all this the apprehension is lacking, and so too is the love which is alone capable of seeing it. No matter how much in earnest those who despise the historicity of our church may be, their efforts are the merest trifling if they fail to hold fast to the realities God intends should be taken seriously. The church is meant to let the tares grow in its garden, for where else can it find the criterion of knowing and judging which of its members are tares? Thus it will perhaps lovingly tend many a budding life that will later become pernicious to it, but it will never condemn and judge, but remain aware of the limits of its historicity.

Luther's love for the church and deep dogmatic insight into the significance of its historical nature made it very hard for him to tear himself away from the church of Rome. We should not allow resentment and dogmatic frivolity to deprive us out of hand of our historical Protestant church.

We spoke of 'the' empirical church. Does this phenomenon exist at all? For those who view it historically the church consists of many individual local churches and a single organisation comprising them. Can the individual local churches be brought together into a unity? The 'empirical church' appears to be an abstraction, or alternatively a statistical collective unit made up of the individual local churches, if one does not wish to see these as merged and lost in the organisation. The question is whether the meaning of the idea of the empirical church is completely contained in the idea of such a collective unit. In answering this question we shall discover more information about the structure of the *sanctorum communio*.

The New Testament calls individual local churches the 'Body of Christ', just as, on the other hand, it sees in them 'the realisation in a specific place of the one church of God',[113] and just as all those who cleave to Christ are one body with him. Thus the New Testament supplies only the problem, and not the answer. Luther

laid full emphasis upon the individual congregation and yet said:
'No one says: I believe in the Holy Ghost, one Holy Church of
Rome and the communion of Roman Catholics; which makes
it clear that the Holy Church is not tied to Rome, but extends
throughout the world. . . .'[114] Zwingli, after adopting Wycliffe's
notion of the church, and linking with it the Swiss idea of the
Kilchhöre (the local church) coined the idea of the 'universal
church' as the church embracing all individual churches.[115]
This corresponds to our idea of the empirical church and had its
origin in the recognition that the many individual congregations
do not exist side by side as separate units, but are there to be
gathered together into a real unity. This is a reality corresponding to what is simply the empirical church, namely the totality
of all the congregations (*Gesamtgemeinde*). This conclusion is a
necessary one, for only thus does God's whole historical will for
redemption become plain. In this totality as the 'sum' of all the
places at which the gospel is proclaimed, there is the 'same
spirit', the one Word. It is one Body, real community, *sanctorum
communio*. The reality of the fact that all the individual congregations belong together has always been more strongly emphasised by Roman Catholicism than by us. The Roman Catholic
Church has of course historicised it. We do not say that the
empirical universal church (Council or General Synod) is more
than the local church; that would be completely un-Protestant.[116]
But the Body of Christ is Rome and Corinth, Wittenberg, Geneva
and Stockholm, and the members of all the individual churches
all belong to the totality as the *sanctorum communio*.[117]

Is the Body of Christ as a whole then primarily present in the
universal church, so that all individual local churches are only
members of the Body? The New Testament says nothing of the
kind, and the question has no value for dogmatics because it
understands the concept 'Body of Christ' simply in the organic
physical sense, whereas in fact this concept describes the presence
of Christ and the work of the Spirit in his church, the concept of
body here being not one of form but of function with regard to
the work of Christ (see above on the 'body' of the collective
person). Christ is fully present in each individual, and is yet

One, and is again not fully present in any one person, being fully possessed only by all men together.[118] Thus each individual local church is the Body of Christ, and yet there is only One Body, and again only the universal church can actualise all the relationships in the Body of Christ. If the idea of the Body of Christ were applicable only to the individual local church, then difficulties would immediately arise concerning the question of this as the smallest sociological unit in the idea of the church, and doubtless the community of two people, placed under his Word and sustained by him, as, for instance, in marriage, would have to be considered as such a unit, so that, to be exact, the idea of the individual local church would have to be applied to it as well, and so the Body of Christ would also be present 'where two or three are gathered together'. But since where the Body of Christ is the *sanctorum communio* is, this makes marriage the smallest sociological unit of the *sanctorum communio*. In fact it can be present in marriage to the highest degree. Just as every collective person stands without knowing or willing it in another more comprehensive one, so the smallest sociological unit of the *sanctorum communio* necessarily extends beyond itself and stands in the midst of the 'whole' Body of Christ, of which it is simply the individual realisation. It is wrong, on the other hand, according to the fundamental principles of social philosophy already established, either to imagine that individual local churches have priority and that the whole body is atomistic in its structure, or to assume the opposite.

c. Sociological forms and functions of the empirical church

i. *The worshipping congregation.* A Christian church, as an individual local church or a house-church, is held together by the fact that its members are gathered round the Word. The Word represents the unity of the essential and the empirical church, of the Holy Spirit and objective spirit, which is to say that the concrete function of the empirical church is the divine service of preaching the Word and of administering the sacraments. Preaching is the 'ministry' of the church, so there must also be a congregation. The one implies the other. This has been axiomatic from the earliest Christian times right up to the age of pietism and orthodoxy. It was only when life began to be conceived of in individualistic terms that the necessity for a congregation ceased to be regarded as reflecting the natural course of things and came to be thought of as psychological, the question of the significance of the congregation then being raised in terms of its use and necessity for the individual. The question itself reveals a basic lack of understanding of the idea of the church. Thus a long recital of the reasons why it is inwardly and outwardly advantageous or morally necessary for the individual to go to church would not be any answer to it at all. In replying thus we should from the outset be foregoing our rights to our own basic position. The question is unable to deal with the facts of the matter. The only idea that can be put forward as a basis is that of the church itself; this does not mean that there is no basis for the significance of the congregation—it is not simply something that has established itself as a tradition in the course of time, as one might suppose—but simply that the basis must be sought upon a completely different plane. Preaching is an activity of the church divinely ordained for the church. I belong to the church, so I go to the gatherings of the congregation; such is the prosaic reasoning of the members of the congregation. Their presence is not the result of any calculation of expediency, nor an act of dutifulness, but something 'organically' self-evident. Max Weber rightly emphasises how important the gatherings of the congregation were in primitive Christianity (in contrast to its significance in the time of the prophets of Israel).[119] Only in the congregation is the Spirit at work; there he dispenses his *charismata*. The idea of a Christian who does not attach himself to the congregation is unthinkable. The church united by the one Word congregates again and again to hear it, or conversely the Word creating the church continually calls it together anew in a concrete congregation; for it is a Word that is preached, in accordance with God's will and that of the church, through which he realises this will.

This answer, it is true, does not satisfy the questioning individualist. Cannot each church member read the Bible on his own and profess his belief in the church, the invisible communion of 'consciences', or 'souls', in private? What purpose is served by the dreary flatness of public congregation, where you risk having to face a narrow-minded preacher alongside spiritless faces?

There is no doubt that those living far from the congregation can also belong to the *sanctorum communio*—I am thinking of invalids, castaways, etc.—which means we cannot say that for the individual the congregation is 'necessary to salvation'. Nevertheless, the significance for the church of gathering together is fully maintained. These people too have received their faith through concrete contacts with others, through the preaching of the word (Rom. 10.17). Every other case it is possible to think of in this connection proves that it is possible in principle for God to subdue men to his lordship without the mediation of the actual congregation. But this is something that falls beyond the scope of our aims. For us the preaching of the empirical church is the 'Word of God' we can hear. And this must be applied in the narrower sense to the historical, congregational form of the empirical church. The congregation of the faithful remains our Mother. Thus the question why, from the psychological point of view, we hold fast to the congregation is synonymous with the question why we love our mother, and the answer—if answer is needed—is gratitude. The decisive factor, however, is that the Christian feels he has never outgrown this place of his spiritual birth, so that he is prompted to seek the congregation not only out of gratitude for the gift he has received, but also because he prays that he might ever receive it, and forever be born anew (John 3.3; II Cor. 4.16). He knows that there God's Word is preached according to his will, and that there too the church of God is to be found (Matt. 18.20). But no matter how isolated he may be he knows that he is one of the Good Shepherd's flock, attached to the historical fellowship of the church, the congregation, from which he received his past and present life, and in which alone he can truly live. In the congregation the church stands surety for God—in accordance with God's will—and it is here that God stands surety for his presence in the church. Thus the actual congregation has a significance all its own. First, it makes it apparent that the church is 'visible', a community of men, body and soul; not kinship of soul, or a community based on like feeling, but a community of love between whole men. That is the historical importance of the congregation. Its historicity, is, however, the cause of both its defects and its strength, which fructify the personal life. The defects are, in the first place, all the unedifying factors of which we should find it just as easy to speak as do the individualists. Secondly, we know that we remain individuals, Greeks, Jews, Pietists, Liberals, etc., and that each man is completely enmeshed in the concrete circumstances of his life. It is precisely from this, however, that the strength of the congregation derives. My neighbour, the man living beside me completely immersed in his own affliction, quite different from me, a stranger—he too is clearly willed by God. The unity of the divine Word rises sovereign above the utter dissimilarity of the individual members of the congregation, and the perception that the one man cannot have anything in common with the other, the completely alien, unknown 'Thou', that there is a gulf between them extending to the very ground of their being, makes it evident that here only the hand of God can intervene, that only the love given to our heart by God can sustain communion. Thus one man reminds the other of the God who wishes them both to be in the same church. In the other man in his actuality there is revealed to me the power and the glory of the kingdom of God, and the congregation becomes the fountainhead for the prayerful profession of belief in God and his church.

In the congregation, moreover, I do not, as if I were communing alone with the Word, speak and hear at the same time. But there is someone else speaking, and this gives me an incomparable certainty. Someone completely strange to me is proclaiming God's grace and forgiveness to me, not as an experience, but as God's will. He helps me to grasp in concrete form that the church and its Lord are guarantors for my certainty that I shall receive grace. The fact that there is someone else promising me grace makes me certain of the church, and rules out any danger or possibility that I might be lost in illusions. The certainty of faith arises not only from solitariness, but also from the congregation.

To summarise: The congregation is willed by God, and is the means whereby he makes use of the social connection between men to spread his rule over men. This will of God is realised, through the objective spirit of the church, in the setting-up of ordered worship. The worshipping congregation is an essential part of the church. Such is the objective picture. Subjectively the individual's constant link with the congregation arises from his recognition of God's will to speak in the empirical church, from his awareness of belonging to the community whose office is to preach the Word, and which is itself the object of the preaching. There is an organic link between the congregation and the individual, brought about by the gratitude of the latter to the mother who gave him his life, and by his love for her, along with the confidence that she will constantly bestow her gifts upon him. Lastly, there is his firm hope that in the congregation he will again and again, in concrete form, receive the assurance that he is in the church of God and lives in his grace.

Hitherto the meaning we have given to the word 'congregation' has been the general one of a worshipping congregation, whether worshipping publicly or privately. Both represent the *sanctorum communio*, and have the same value. And yet it must be stressed that the first is more necessary than the second. The local church is a piece of the world organised purely out of the *sanctorum communio;* it is not, as the house-church, for instance, merely a renewal in the Spirit of a form already given. Thus the difference is that in the first the objective spirit of the church must always be active in a productive and constructive way, finding new forms and preserving old ones, whereas in the second there is no objective spirit of the church as such, but one coinciding with the spirit of the household. Thus the local church will always serve as a pattern for the house-church. The former is moreover indispensable for the further reason that for all its insufficiency it ensures a relatively uniform doctrine. The decisive reason, however, is that the local church is independent of all family and political connections. It is as such that it is the 'historical result of the work of Jesus'; whereas house-churches must be regarded as but the consequences of the work of the local churches. As such the local church is intended to become universal, and has a commission which transcends all nationality. As such it makes effective the concrete community which is of its essence, since both Jew and Greek and bond and free belong to it; and as such it is not only in the world, but against the world as an objectively spiritual power with a moral will and the courage to fight. Thus the congregation represents the will of God and performs the task of the church not only as between the church and God but as between it and the world. It is demonstrative action 'pointing' to the power of the objective spirit of the church, which is sustained by the will of God; 'that they may become perfectly one, so that the world may know that thou hast sent me, and hast loved them even as thou hast loved me' (John 17.23).

For house-churches to increase at the expense of the local church community is a retrograde step, a proof of a lack of spiritual productiveness in the local church, and a flight from the seriousness of the historical situation. Both kinds of congregation should grow hand in hand. The impulse to community should not sap the life-blood of the public church, but contribute to it.

At the start we established that the congregation and the ministry go together. We must now examine the meaning of the Protestant ministry, and investigate the sociological forms of the various congregations, as these forms are given by the ministry.

ii. *The Sanctorum Communio as bearer of the ministry.* The church is 'Christ existing as the community'; Christ's presence consists in the Word of justification. But since where Christ is his church is, the Word of justification gives reality to the church, which means that it demands a coming together of the faithful. These are thoughts which have already been worked out.

The Word is the Word the church preaches. Not the Bible,

then? Yes, the Bible too, but only in the church. So it is the church that first makes the Bible into the 'Word'? Certainly,[120] in so far, that is, as the church was first created and is maintained by the Word. The question as to what came first, the Word or the church, is meaningless, because the Word as inspired by the Spirit exists only when men hear it, so that the church makes the Word just as the Word makes the church into the church. The Bible is the Word only in the church, that is, in the *sanctorum communio*. The Word is concretely present in the church as the Word of Scripture and of preaching—essentially as the latter. There is no distinction between these in themselves, since so long as they are not inspired by the Spirit they remain the word of man. The Spirit has not united himself in substance with the word of the Bible. Thus effective preaching is possible only in the *sanctorum communio*. The promise that the Word shall be fruitful applies (Isa. 55.11) to the preaching carried out within the *sanctorum communio*. *Praedicatio verbi divini est verbum divinum*.[121] This is not self-evident, for preaching is obviously a product of the objective spirit of the church. And it is meant to be so, because it does not just repeat, but says new things, does not recount from the past, but addresses the present;[122] no member of the church can evade the objective spirit. To attempt to flee is useless; flight only makes the situation more confused. 'Serve the time' (Rom. 12.11) is preaching's great motto.[123] The objective spirit, burdened as it is with so much contingency, imperfection and sinfulness, nevertheless has the promise that it can preach the Word of God; it becomes the bearer of the social action of the Holy Spirit. Anyone who really hears the Word in preaching sees the clash between the objective spirit (especially perhaps that of 'theology') and the Holy Spirit in its most striking aspect, but he sees too that it is the Holy Spirit's wish to take his course through the objective spirit of the church. The basis of all this is the reality of the *sanctorum communio*, for it is to the *sanctorum communio* that the Word is given, as both creating it and as the instrument of its activity. Where it is present the Word is not ineffective.

But who, then, is permitted to preach? Surely it can only be someone belonging to the *sanctorum communio*? And yet how is man to know what God alone knows? 'The Lord knows those who are his.' This seems to be the rock upon which the church, and its task and its hope with it, must founder. There seems to be only one way left open. If the person is perhaps not holy, it must be the office that is holy; the consequence is—the Roman Catholic idea of the priest and his ministry. But this will not do either, for nothing is holy but God's holy will and our will, if it is touched by the divine one. Now it may be supposed that there are preachers active at all times who, at the time of their preaching at least, do not belong to the *sanctorum communio*. Is the preaching of these men really condemned to bear no fruit? Luther took comfort from the idea that the spirit bloweth where it listeth, and that being able to preach effectively, that is, possessing this *charisma* from the Holy Spirit, was something quite different from actually having the Holy Spirit within one as a justifying and sanctifying force. Even Judas may have been a most powerful preacher.[124] Since therefore the Protestant Church believes the words of Isa. 55.11, and even more because it has a knowledge of the freedom of the Holy Spirit and of the charismatic significance of preaching, it is able to accord preaching a central place in its divine service without recourse to the Roman Catholic idea of the ministry or any sectarian ideas of the holiness of the person. If our starting-point is that preaching has the purpose of working on subjective spirits, subduing them to God's lordship and making them members of the *sanctorum communio*, that it is testimony to Christ, and not to one's own faith, then its effectiveness is mediated by the objective spirit, for it is plain that a purpose can be achieved without the man who is pleading its cause being inwardly connected with it. He is rather the point through which two powers pass: that of the objective spirit of the church and that of the Holy Spirit. Likewise a preacher can bear witness to the objective spirit that is alive in the church without himself partaking of the Spirit of Christ that gives rise to it. To summarise: even if the man who preaches does not belong to the *sanctorum communio*, and will never belong to it, the fact that he uses and must use the forms developed by the objective spirit means that the Holy Spirit can employ even him as an instrument of his activity. Objective spirit subsists not only in forms that have become fixed, but in like degree in the living force of public opinion, in theology, for instance, in interest in certain problems, in strong volitional impulses for some particular practical undertaking, etc., so that there is no qualitative distinction in this respect between preaching and the administration of the sacraments. These are the reasons why the *sanctorum communio* is in fact able to found an 'office' of preaching and of administration of the sacraments that is as such entirely sustained by it and is yet completely independent of it from the point of view of the persons performing these functions. (This has nothing in common with the idea of the ministry as presented by Stahl, Kliefoth, etc.) On the other hand no exception can be taken to the formula of the Confession of Augsburg VII, '*congregatio sanctorum, in qua.*' Its meaning is that preaching is possible only in the *sanctorum communio;* that is, that it is based upon it.[125] The office depends upon the church; this makes the according of any special position to the bearer of the office impossible. In the Protestant Church there is no theurgy, and no magical authority interested in the office, or in individuals bearing this office. The idea of the priesthood of all believers is only another way of expressing this principle. The fact of the church that has only one Head, Christ, preserves us from the idea of an ecclesiastical this-worldly head, which, as Luther justly explains, cannot exist, since he would not know those whom he was governing.[126]

When the Protestant idea of the ministry is thus grasped and justified, in connection with the objective spirit, there is a deeper understanding of the organised local church, which is held together by the orderly gathering for the administration of the Word and sacraments. It is therefore clear that the empirical church, the ministry and the congregation, go together, and that God's way with his holy people is through the midst of history.

iii. *The sociological context of the acts of the ministerial office and the congregation, the three concentric circles.* We have now to establish the significance of preaching and the sacraments in the Protestant sense for the congregation in which they take place. It is important to begin with a brief analysis of the sense-experiences in relation to their sociological character. We indicate only the basic matters which are important for our purpose. These are the matters of hearing and touching, which are presupposed in preaching and the sacraments. Hearing is the mediator of the most profound and differentiated spiritual perceptions and feelings, indicated by 'word' and 'music' (Schopenhauer described music as a pure idea). Every acoustic 'sign' demands man's spiritual attention. There arises a system of relationships of understanding to what gives the sign. Spiritual self-activity is aroused among the individuals. They find themselves involved in a spiritual traffic, whether of agreement or disagreement, with the speaker. The entire spiritual person of the man is involved. In contrast to this the experience of the tactile—in which we include 'tasting'—is exhausted in the sense-experience itself. There is no essential connection between the sense-experience and the spiritual significance, but only a symbolic and unreal connection. The word is not a symbol, but a 'sign'. The word means something in itself, whereas the contact of touch means nothing 'in itself', but can become the bearer of the 'symbol' of meaning. The word is an adequate expression of a meaning, whereas touch has to be somehow explained if it is to be understood. In his sense of touch man knows with his body, which experiences the contact, that he is quite alone, and what happens is related to him alone. With the spoken word, on the other hand, it is clear to him in an objective way that a number of men can be gathered round it. So when preaching is put at the centre of the Protestant service, this emphasises that the preaching creates a community composed of individual hearers who are to some extent intellectually active members. It is not that a mass is caught up in a cultic spectacle by some magic contact, but each individual is addressed, both in a general intellectual sense in the challenge to think about what is said and to enter into the intellectual context which is presented, and in an ethical sense in being placed before the decision 'for or against'. The Protestant congregation is a congregation in which ethical personalism is at work. It can never become a 'mass'.

What is the sociological relation of the congregation to the preacher? Is he drawn into their fellowship as one questioner among others? Or is he the bearer of unconditioned truth, and is he their teacher, answering their questions? Should the sermon be a dialogue or a monologue? Is the question-and-answer method of the catechism theologically as well as pedagogically significant? In answering this question, which is so important sociologically, and has been frequently discussed, there has been a great deal of one-sided argument. It is characteristic of the preacher that he simultaneously questions and proclaims. He must ask along with the congregation, and form a 'Socratic' community—otherwise he could not give any reply. But he can reply, and he must, because he knows God's utterance in Christ. He is there in the pulpit to proclaim the truth, to be a teacher, and to let the hearers know. In sociological terms, in the sermon God's claim of authority is made plain to his congregation. The congregation is the society of authority. But the preacher himself does not have this authority—this belongs to the Word which he speaks. Jesus in his preaching combined personal and objective authority, but not so the preacher. The preacher himself is a member of the fallible and sinful congregation, and thus we have sociologically a twofold character in the congregation where preaching takes place. It is a pre-supposition of a Christian congregation that it comes together as a questioner, and at the same time it is the strength of the congregation that each individual learns of the knowledge and the truth that belong to the congregation, and in so learning possesses the truth, that is, in faith. Here too it is true of this knowledge of faith that it is possessed only in a constant question about the truth and a constant winning anew of this knowledge. Question and answer go together, not because there is in fact no answer (as Barth says[127]) but because the actual answer can only be grasped in faith.

In brief, the congregation in which preaching takes place is ethical and personalist, it is a community of men who ask questions and who know, it is a community which bows before God's claim of authority.

What then is the situation with the congregation gathered for the administration of the sacraments? The Roman Catholic concept of grace produces a magical concept of the sacraments; infant baptism must be understood as having the same significance as adult baptism. This means, however, that the Roman Catholic congregation gathered for the sacraments is the 'mass', which formally corresponds to the idea of the *massa perditionis*, but is now united in a positive direction. Original sin, regarded as a natural fate, is set aside by the natural physical infusion of grace. But sociologically the 'mass' is the concept correlative to a physical *dynamis*. Is there also a Protestant congregation composed of the 'mass'? Tillich, prompted by the proper feeling that the 'Spirit' turns away from the masses, made an attempt to discover an immediate relationship between the two[128] by seeing the sanctity of the mass in the fact that, as something unformed, it might be an object for the revelation of the formative Absolute. But this has nothing to do with Christian theology. We know only the sanctity of the church of God, which is bound up with the Word in Christ and formed by it. The Word is taken up only by personal appropriation, so that the church presses out of the mass. But what Tillich was trying to point out is nevertheless important. The church must enter into a discussion with the mass; it must hear when the masses are calling for community, as in the Youth Movement and in sport, for instance; and it must then not neglect to make its Word of the *sanctorum communio* heard in their midst. The basic rule, however, is that the mass must be adjusted to the Christian idea, and not the other way round.

The Protestant idea of the sacraments is necessarily connected with the Word, and this rules out the idea of the mass. Sacraments are acts of the church, and like preaching they unite within them the objective spirit of the church and the Holy Spirit operating through it.

Protestant and Roman Catholic baptism are both infant baptism. But since the children do not themselves have faith, not even as *fides directa*, and yet the sacrament nevertheless requires faith, what plays the part, for the child, of the one who receives the sacrament in faith can only be the objective spirit of the congregation. This takes the child up within it in faith through baptism, but since, where one member of the church is there the whole church is, in this child it is the whole church that is believing. Thus on the one hand baptism is effective divine action by the gift of grace, through which the child is placed in the church of Christ. But at the same time it involves the stipulation that the child should remain in the Christian church. Hence the church as the communion of saints carries its children, like a mother, as its most treasured possession; it is only by virtue of its 'community life' that it can do this; if it were a mere 'association' the act of baptism would be meaningless. So the meaning of infant baptism is limited at the point where the church cannot seriously consider 'carrying' the child any longer, where the church is inwardly broken and it is certain that the child being baptised is coming into contact with the church for the first and last time. The church should be open to all, but in being open to all it should be conscious of its responsibility. The only reason for its doors being closed can be its responsibility to God; in this, however, there must be a prompt recognition of the fact whenever a church has ceased to be a national church and has become a mission church.[129] The interpretation of baptism as an act of the church is opposed to the idea of a Protestant 'mass'. Baptism embraces the whole circle of the empirical church, in that the church is defined by it. (The question whether all who have been baptised belong to the body of Christ we discussed earlier.)[130]

If infant baptism embraces all those who are possible members of the church, the sacrament of Holy Communion[131] gathers together all who earnestly wish to subject their will to God's lordship in the kingdom of Christ. The sacrament of Holy Communion is given to the *sanctorum communio* as an act symbolic of the active divine will for communion, and, like the Word, is real only 'in' the *sanctorum communio* (*in qua*); that is, it is part of the organising activity of the church and is of the greatest significance for its sociological structure, and it is only in it that its effectiveness, like that of the Word, is assured.

Holy Communion is, first, God's gift to every individual. Its sensory nature cannot be ignored. It means that the sacrament demands a personal decision with the same distinctness with which it urges itself upon a man, and is equally distinct in its promise of a gift. The fact that it involves actual physical touch convinces the individual that its gift and the task whose fulfilment it expects from him are assigned to him personally (not only to his spiritual, but to his bodily person).

Holy Communion is, secondly, and to a much greater extent, a gift to the church. Christ's spiritual presence is not only symbolised, but really given. Christ comes alive in the faithful as the church; the gift, that is to say, is twofold: Christ makes a gift of himself, of communion with him, that is, he gives me the benefit of his vicarious Passion and he makes a gift of the church, that is, he causes it to become new and thus gives the church to the church itself. He presents each of us with the rights and duties of priestly action towards our neighbour, and likewise gives each of us our life in the church. It is his gift that enables one man to sustain the other, and be sustained in return. In giving himself he gives us the duty and the strength to act in brotherly love. In that he is present, in that the church is Christ's body, brotherly love is there too; it does not merely follow, even though in point of time this might appear to be the case; the presence of Christ means communion with God through Christ, and the effective reality of the church as bearer of the individual members. Christ's priestly action is the basis for ours. I John 3.16 clearly states this, as does I Cor. 11.26: 'For as often as you eat this bread and drink the cup, you proclaim[132] the Lord's death. . . .' Just as the performance of the act combines both, so the connection is also materially present. Holy Communion is the ultimate source of all we said above about the community of spirits.[133] Luther, in the works we quoted at that point, has given clear expression to the gift and miracle of the church which takes place in the sacrament.

But the sociological significance of the action in the sacrament is not complete unless it is recognised in its third aspect as a human action before God. A congregation of people professing its faith places itself before God, and symbolising what has been done for it, meets in the most intimate fellowship to eat of the same bread and drink of the same cup. This free gathering to eat from the table of the altar is not free but obedient symbolism, which means that divine action is assured. This obedient symbolising on the part of a congregation gathered of its own free will is what distinguishes it from the congregation where preaching takes place. The decision brought about by preaching now becomes a visible action, a profession of faith not only in God's grace, but in his holy church. Thus the congregation where preaching takes place is a necessary presupposition of the congregation in which the sacrament is celebrated, and the latter, as a fellowship of those professing their faith, is by its very nature smaller than the former. It is therefore not the case, as is often supposed, that the congregation for the sacrament brings the church into existence. It is the preaching of the Word which does this; the decisive factor is that the church now bears witness in a way visible to all, acting obediently and symbolically, and that God acknowledges it as such in visible fashion.

Two present-day problems demand attention. First, there is talk of 'the church within the church',[134] the members of which meet regularly within the framework of the local church upon certain occasions, either within or outside the church, especially for the sacrament, taking as their warrant Luther's famous Preface to the German Mass, of 1526. Luther speaks in this of the setting-up of small gatherings of a private kind for the purpose of worship, for prayer, Bible-reading and the celebration of Communion, the members being subject to church discipline and interdict, for those who 'want to be Christians in earnest'.[135] Luther expressed similar ideas as early as 1522.[136] On both occasions it is plain that he is not speaking of a *sanctorum communio* visibly represented in such acts, but of serious-minded Christians, so that the idea of a 'church within the church' is not identical with the 'true church'. This, however, is the great danger that must almost inevitably be latent in such an idea. The church within the church is not separable from the empirical church community, and is itself such a community. If the separatist attitude is nevertheless adopted, the result is the establishment of factions. It is thus advisable to proceed cautiously with the idea of the 'church within the church', as also with the thing itself, which religiously is just as momentous as it is perilous. The congregation for the sacrament is the empirical church, and nothing else, not the *sanctorum communio* in pure form.

Secondly, it has been deplored that communion services in the big towns suffer from the participants not knowing one another; the idea of brotherly fellowship is said to lose some of its force and the services some of their personal warmth. On the other hand we must ask: is not just such a congregation as this an overpowering sermon on the significance and reality, transcending all human community, of the communion of saints? Is not the profession of the church and of brotherly love at its most unequivocal precisely when there are such complete safeguards against its being confused in any way with any kind of human fellow-feeling? Does not this kind of communion, in which Jew remains Jew, Greek Greek, worker worker and capitalist capitalist, and yet all are the Body of Christ, much better preserve the reality of the *sanctorum communio* than one in which the hard fact of human differences is veiled in deceptive mildness? Where there is a real profession of the communion of saints the strangeness and seeming coldness can but fan the flame of the true fire of Christ, but where the idea of the *sanctorum communio* has not been grasped and professed, personal warmth can serve only to disguise the absence of the essential thing, but cannot replace it. Such then is the special fruitfulness of Communion services in big towns, and the minister at such services should speak of it in his sermon too. It is only because the type of sermon still used for such occasions did not originate in the age of the big cities, because the sociological phenomenon of the big city is not understood, and because the minister who serves the city-dwellers does not make himself one of them, that these sermons are usually so devastatingly irrelevant.

To summarise: the sociological principle by which the whole

church is built up is the Word. Upon the Word the church 'builds itself up', intensively and extensively. Christ is the foundation upon which and in accordance with which the building up (οἰκοδομή) of the church is carried out (I Cor. 3; Eph. 2.20). And thus it grows into a 'holy temple in the Lord' (Eph. 2.21) 'with a growth that is from God' (Col. 2.19) 'until we all attain . . . to a mature manhood, to the measure of the stature of the fulness of Christ' (Eph. 4.13), and all this so that we grow up into him 'who is the head, into Christ'. The whole process of building goes from Christ to Christ, its point of unity being the Word. Whereas baptism characterises the congregation's wish to spread God's lordship as widely as possible (that is, it characterises for us the fact of the national church), the congregation gathered for preaching is composed of those personally placed before the decision of accepting or rejecting the divine gift; it is both a national and gathered church. At the Lord's Supper the church presents itself purely as a gathered church, as a confessing congregation, and is required and acknowledged as such by God. But it does not represent the pure *sanctorum communio;* it is the smallest of the three concentric, sociologically distinct circles, and is both the source of the church's effectiveness and the focal point of all its life. This two-sidedness makes for its vitality, which is the vitality of the church in being at once the point at which God is aiming, and his instrument.

iv. *The sociological problem of the care of souls.* On the basis of the empirical and historical church the relation of one member to another now takes a new turn. We have to look at the problem of the care of souls, which is sociologically unique.

The position of anyone engaged in the care of souls (which of course means every Christian brother) with regard to the church-member is twofold. On the one hand he is a member of the church of Christ, and is thus endowed with every priestly right and duty. On the other hand he is just 'another believer', who cannot basically say anything of decisive import about me. Thus in Protestantism the care of souls has two aspects, the 'priestly' and the 'counselling'. The meaning and content of the first is clear from the idea of the church already described.[137]

The idea of the counsellor, however, presents us with a new problem. What can be the significance for the Christian of the fact—thus runs the question as generally put—that he sees before him another man who is also a believer? Of what help to the individual, who has to rely upon himself, is the 'cloud of witnesses' (Heb. 12.1), of what help is the example and model, the history of the church, and tradition? For the Protestant all these questions are basically identical. Not only is Christ *exemplum* as well as *donum* for men, but equally one man is these things for the other. When a man stands before God every model, every example, every tradition to which he might make appeal vanishes; each man must decide alone what he has to do. How is it that Luther continually emphasises the necessity for one man to seek 'counsel'[138] from the other when faced by important decisions, as also did Kierkegaard, who has spoken as no other has done of man's solitary state?[139] Both men kept their eyes open to the concrete historical and social relationships within which man is placed. Man, in fact, is surrounded by models, and should therefore use them, not transferring to them the responsibility for his own deeds, but receiving reports from them upon the basis of which he then freely decides. God has made it possible for man to seek counsel from others; it would be presumptuous folly on his part not to make use of God's offer. Having a history behind him that testifies against him must give pause to the individual who is not without conscience. That was what made the struggle against Rome so difficult for Luther. Man is meant to use every possibility that might help him to arrive at a correct decision. Such is God's will. And the history of the church, the 'counsel of our neighbour', in short the fact that man lives in society, is of the utmost significance. The two kinds of pastoral care must therefore be strictly distinguished. The first represents one man's absolute significance for the other, deriving from the idea of the church. The second concerns one man's relative significance for the other, deriving from man's historicity. To overlook this distinction is to misunderstand the whole Protestant idea of the church. It shows once more the difference between the church and a religious community.

It is not easy to see how we may get this pastoral care in the church today. At any rate it will only be possible on a proper understanding of the Protestant view of the church. The first kind is particularly impossible if there is no understanding of the presence of Christ in the church. On the other hand, the contact between members in mutual pastoral care can give concrete actuality to the idea of the church. If there were the possibility of regular private confession, this would perhaps help; but of course only if the church were ready to give the congregation clear teaching about the real nature of the church.

d. Authority and freedom in the empirical church

The church rests upon the Word.[140] The Word is the absolute authority present in the church. It is indeed present only in the word of the church, that is, in represented, relative authority, but it is still the norm directing the church, in accordance with which the church also 'directs itself'. The absolute authority of the Word demands absolute obedience, that is, absolute freedom, whereas corresponding to the relative authority of the church we have relative obedience, that is, relative freedom. The only irksome element in this formulation is the concept of the relative authority of the church and the relative subjection and freedom of the individual facing it. This seems un-Protestant, a threat to freedom of conscience. And yet it is precisely the acknowledgment of the theological necessity for the idea of the church's relative authority that makes the boundary between the gospel of the Reformation and fanaticism in all its forms. We hear the Word of God in the word of the church, and this qualifies the church's authority. The fact that the church has the burden of the Word laid upon it forces it into the responsible situation not only of having to preach but also of having to speak authoritatively, especially upon all points connected with preserving the purity of the Word, its preaching: upon the creed, dogmatics, exegesis, the order of public worship, and so on:—there actually were Presbyteries once, at which these things were discussed, at which theology was practised! The church is further called to speak authoritatively upon its attitude to contemporary events and to the world at large, but this, of course, only after it has spoken clearly and unequivocally about the primary things: otherwise everything else will be lost in thin air. But even in cases where the church is not able to speak authoritatively it may still have recourse to qualified silence essentially different from ignoring things and passing them over without qualification. But once the church has spoken authoritatively, upon, let us say, what it considers to be valid Protestant dogmatics, then I as a dogmatist—and every Protestant Christian is a dogmatist—have only a relative freedom in respect to this matter, within the framework of what the church has said, or conversely, I am relatively bound in my ideas on dogmatics, my confession of faith, and so on. I owe relative obedience to the church; it has the right to demand from me a *sacrificium intellectus* and perhaps upon occasion even a *sacrificium conscientiae*. Only when I am faced not by my detached understanding, my unruly feeling and experience, but really by the absolute authority of the Word of God demanding my absolute obedience and absolute subjection does my relative freedom become absolute; at this point my relative subjection to the church can be destroyed if it stands in the way of my absolute subjection to the Word. If this were not so the principle of social equilibrium, which is also justified theologically, would be invalidated; but this would be to demolish the Christian idea of the church, and we should be back with the Roman Catholic conception of the church and of authority. The councils and synods have relative authority and should most vigorously and emphatically assert it, and plainly and clearly say what their standpoint is towards the Bible, dogma, the creed and doctrine, and then there will no longer be cause for them to lament the world's indifference. But the church must know that its authority is still a derived and reflected authority. The actual moment when the individual church member feels constrained to rebel against this authority, is a matter for God alone; in any case the only valid motive for turning against the authority of the church would be a perfect obedience rooted in the closest attachment to the church and to the Word in it; it can never be an act of irresponsible wilfulness.

e. The church as an independent sociological type, and its place in the order of sociological types

We now have to fit the picture we have drawn of the church into our earlier definitions of the nature of sociological relationships. It is not a genetic question, but the problem of the church's essential nature.

We said that in the concept of the church there is a collision between two lines of thought; between the idea that the church is founded by God, and that nevertheless, like every other kind of community, it is an empirical community. This adds to the difficulty of determining the church's sociological type. It seems, however, that it can be seen as such a type.

1. The picture of the church as an organised type of social grouping makes it seem possible to class it sociologically as a 'society'. A society, according to our definition, is based upon a multiplicity of atomistic wills. It is constructed as a means directed towards an end. The entry into a society must be a formal one. What constitutes the society is the contract. It is possible to construe the sociological type 'church' according to two types of social groups; that of an institution and that of an association.[141] The sociological difference between the two is that the institution is essentially independent of people coming to it, whereas the association, if its members disperse, is by its very nature disbanded. If the church were constructed according to the latter type, it would appear to be an association of those interested in religion, pursuing their interest in regular meetings, in exactly the same way as a music club, for instance, comes together regularly for concerts.[142] The church then caters for the free enjoyment of each individual. The act of confirmation publicly testifies that the person being confirmed is really

interested, or is at least willing to submit to the rules of the association. If of course he loses interest in the object of the association, he can always declare that he is withdrawing and is then exempted from paying the 'club subscription' (in the form of church taxes). The association is disbanded upon agreement by all its members. If we feel tempted to ask how the theory that the church is an association can be reconciled with the church community's idea that it is an organ of God's authoritative purpose, we are given an answer in which this claim is reduced to a merely relative one by a comparison with that of other religious communities, so this will get us nowhere. The idea of the church as a construction of this kind seems to be illuminating. But sociologically it leaves a great many loose ends. (a.) What meaning can be ascribed to the acceptance of infants into an association? However fanatical he might be, no chess-player would dream of making his child a member of a chess-club. (b.) Every organised association is private, and can refuse admission. The meetings of the church, on the other hand, are in principle open, and accessible to all. There is no exclusion from the church.[143] (c.) The forms of the objective spirit of an association are conventional, practical, and propagandist; those of the church are symbolic and full of meaning. Those of the association are dispensed with as soon as their practical usefulness is over; in the church there are dying forms that are deliberately maintained.[144] The association is as such traditionless; the church is not.

But the theory that the church is an association, if it is already discredited by the church's external organisation, is completely demolished when we come to consider the doctrine of the church. This surely need not be outlined again. A glance at the Christian view of sin, grace, Christ, the Holy Spirit and the church shows the complete inapplicability of the idea of an association to the concept of the church.

The difficulties alluded to above can—so it seems at least—be overcome by the idea put forward by Max Weber[145] and Troeltsch[146] that the church is an institution,[147] a 'trusteeship'. The church, they say, is essentially not a community of persons, but an institution. In it a certain efficacious gift is promised to those fulfilling the requirements for its attainment. A parallel would be the university, for instance, where the condition for receiving the gift is the payment of money, but for its effective reception specific co-operation. Similarly, each member is enrolled and made subject to a tax, in the institution of the church, but is guaranteed eternal salvation if he makes regular use of the means of grace and submits to the institution's rules, its commands and punishments. It is possible, useful, and indeed required, to subject children too to the rules of the institution, in order that they may become partakers of salvation as soon as possible. The demands made upon the greater number of those who come to the institution are small. Baptism, confirmation, withdrawal, the church dues, the meaning of the gatherings of the congregation and in specific circumstances also the objective-spiritual forms can in fact be interpreted as institutional, so it seems as if Weber and Troeltsch are right. The critical point with regard to their theory is reached only when one inquires into the authority upon which the institution is based. If it is asserted, as in Roman Catholicism, that it is simply divinely based, then the purely institutional character of the church is preserved and demonstrated, and Weber's and Troeltsch's definition, applied to the organised phenomenon of the Roman Catholic church, is sociologically correct. In it the spirit, the institution and the ministry belong together without necessary reference to the congregation. From the point of view of dogmatic teaching, however, there are many obvious contradictions. It is impossible to interpret the basic social relationships atomistically, if they claim a Christian foundation. This fact has never been lost sight of by the Roman Catholic Church itself. In spite of the dissimilarity of their structure Catholicism affirms both the institution and the community[148] side by side, as is already made clear in the writings of Augustine. The Protestant 'institution' is not set up by God over the congregation but is an act of the congregation itself, since the ministry too belongs to it and may be conceived of only in connection with it. This, however, disposes of the idea that the Protestant Church is an institution in the true sociological sense, since, first, there is no Protestant institution without a congregation, as there is in Catholicism, and secondly the gifts it promises are those God gave to a community of persons, to his church, in confiding to it the Word of preaching, through which he also sustains the church. The idea of an association is more correct here, since it at least sees the church as composed of persons, and it is no accident that it sprang up —doubtless in connection with the study of Protestant sects— upon Protestant soil. The whole interpretation of the organisational forms of the Protestant Church as being those of an institution must therefore be dismissed as erroneous.

2. It is only by beginning with the church as a community of persons[149] that the Protestant forms of baptism, confirmation, withdrawal, gatherings of the congregation and church rules (taxation procedures) can be understood; only from this standpoint can one understand the structure of the objective spirit of the church, as it is embodied in fixed forms. This is what we have now to show. At the same time, the defect in the theory of the church as an association, and the insufficiency of the sociological concept of community will become clear.

Only a community, not a society, is capable of carrying children (see p. 57 above). Infant baptism in an association is nonsensical.

The association theory sees confirmation, or reception as a communicant, as the moment of entry into the association. Since we too see in Communion the first open act of profession, it would seem that we are in agreement with that theory, but only to someone confusing the problems of genesis with those of essence; a mistake which is at the root of Troeltsch's entire distinction between church and sect. All genuine community, as community of will, presupposes the free act of affirmation of the community—there are no 'organic' communities, in the sense of purely vegetable growth, which could be described as human— and this is true above all of the community of the church. Thus it is the object of the social act of will that is the decisive factor. If this is really only the enjoyment of being uplifted by preaching, etc., then the association theory is quite right. But this is not the root of the matter. The object of the affirmation is the church, in which I come under God's lordship, to which I am grateful for having baptised and instructed me, and the value of whose fellowship I recognise—and this view of the matter puts the association theory out of joint. This is not, however, the whole significance of the object which is affirmed, as will soon become clear.

Just as the Christian church, when it accepts members, does not impose any other condition but the affirming act of will, so its only condition for the exclusion of one of its members is the denying act of will. The Christian community has no right to dispose of the individual member. With an association it is different: just as upon entry the prospective member must fulfil certain conditions (respectability as a citizen, payment of money, etc.), so the loss of these attributes entails exclusion, no matter how much the person concerned may wish to continue in his membership. The community of the church by its very nature and on principle does not practise any exclusion. Protestant excommunication[150], if it existed, would not be exclusion from the community, but the temporary removal of the person concerned from special proceedings of the community. The deepest reason for this is God's wish that the church should be a historical church. This is the third argument against the theory that the church is an association.

Nor can the legal forms of the church be interpreted as being those of a society; rather the church must maintain itself, and it is for that reason that its members pay their dues, just as in a family everyone contributes to its maintenance. All the matters thus regulated by law originated in the will of the community itself. They serve only to make its own life possible.

Finally, the reflection that the church, like every other genuine community, is an ethical collective person must be a conclusive proof for the sociologist that the church is a community. The church has its own guilt, just as a marriage has. It is called and judged as a whole by God, and is one of many collective persons, even if it is bigger and more powerful than most. Its uniqueness does, it is true, first appear when it is conceived of as the community and church of God, based upon and brought into being by the Spirit, as which it is 'Christ existing as the church', Christ's presence. The association theory as well as the institution idea fail to cope with the Protestant understanding of the Spirit and the church, the former in that it does not take the problem of the reality of the Spirit into consideration at all, and the latter in that it severs the essential connection between the Spirit and the church, thus entirely losing its sociological interest.

We shall now show, by reference to the concept of objective spirit, the inadequacy of the pure concept of community as a sociological category for interpreting the church.

The structure of the objective spirit, in the forms in which it is embodied, is clearly that of a community, a way of acting, that is to say, which is filled with symbolic meaning. Its essential expression is in the cultus. It is true that when we consider the proper activities of the church, preaching and the administering of the sacraments, we hesitate to describe them as purely representative, although such a description, from the point of view of their forms, would be possible and quite logical. The congregation gathered round the Word and the sacraments is certainly the representation of the church, both before itself and before God. The means of grace then appear as the adequate forms of expression of the church. We have already seen that this is only a part of the matter, and that the administration of the Word and of the sacraments must also be something effective and purposive. In line with this idea, we see in the structure of the church a certain antinomy, which we also saw in the concept of a community of love. It is not enough to interpret the church as a community; it is indeed a community, but a community concretely defined as a community of spirit. And this not only modifies and specifies the general concept of 'community', but also postulates a new antinomy in the basic relationship into which we must inquire.

We must now correct and limit the whole sociological construction placed upon the church by considering the theological character of the concept of the church. We are speaking not of religious community, but of the empirical church as the *sanctorum communio* present in its actual embodiment as community of spirit, extending beyond all community possible to man. A community of spirit is not the same thing as a communion between souls; rather, it affirms the community's transcendental foundation and thus attests that its nature is that of an objective authority-group, and not of a power-group—a view towards which dialectical theology seems to incline—which would exclude all community. This clearly means that the church is organised towards a certain aim, namely the achieving of the will of God. But the will of God is aimed at the church itself, as a community of spirit, so that it is both a purposive society and an end in itself, in accordance with our perception that the church is both an instrument and an end in itself. God, as he seeks to make his will prevail, gives himself to the hearts of men and creates community, that is, he provides himself as the means to his own end.

This mutual co-inherence must neither be distorted into a picture in which there is a community which has in addition an aim, nor into the idea that there is a society with an aim which becomes a community—both of which cases would be possible sociologically. But in the idea of the church the one element does in fact mingle with the other in such a way that every attempt to separate them genetically completely destroys the sense.

The objection that acts of the will cannot simultaneously be of the nature of a community and of the nature of a society, otherwise the distinction between the two would have no object, can be countered only if both acts are comprised and surmounted in a new and different act; and this in fact comes about in the act of love wrought by the Spirit in which the community of spirit consists. I organise my relationship to the other man so that it has one sole aim: the will of God is fulfilled in my love of my neighbour; now the fact that the Holy Spirit loves in me makes me certain that when I organise my relationship to the other man so that it has an aim, this aim is the relationship itself. Only the Holy Spirit in me is capable of linking the two together; his effect is that, in wishing to be obedient to God alone, that is, in having a pure aim, which as such lies outside the community, I completely surrender my will, so that at the same time I really love my neighbour. The Holy Spirit unites in himself the claim for lordship, the will for an aim and the will for a meaning in drawing the person into his own course, and is thus himself at once master and servant. The act specially characterising the conduct of the church is that of love wrought by the Spirit as manifested in all the different kinds of activities described earlier. Christian love is primarily not identical with the 'will for a meaning', it is not directed towards the acknowledgment of the value of the community, but towards the acknowledgment of the divine will for the other, and thus towards the divinely-willed value of the other. We have already shown that it is in complete surrender that one finds the fellowship of the Holy Spirit ('He who loses his life . . .'). It would therefore be wrong to say that the specifically sociological action of the Christian church is that of a community in the ideal and typical sense. Its action is beyond that of a community and that of a society and it combines both. And yet it is really a community, the community of spirit and of love. Here we go beyond the sociological type of 'community', we see it as one-sided. All empirical action by the church should be judged from the standpoint of the twofoldness and unity of the will for community and the will for achieving God's purpose; it is from this standpoint too, that is, that we must develop the theory of the objective spirit of the church.

The only sociological category that could possibly be compared to the church, and even then only approximately, is, so far as I can see, the original patriarchal structure of the family, which, indeed, is imitated by smaller groups of Christians. The father's will is that his children and servants should live in community, and obedience to the father consists in preserving this community. That is why the image of the family occurs so frequently in the Christian vocabulary, and has given us the most usual New Testament name which Christians call each other, namely 'brother'. Paul's saying (Eph. 3.15) that all fatherhood on earth has its name from the divine fatherhood is very significant. That is why, since the earliest Christian times, the idea of patriarchalism has featured so prominently. The treatment it received in the Middle Ages was admittedly also connected with the class structure and cultural developments of that time, but in any event it did exploit and revive one of Christianity's earliest sociological perceptions. Troeltsch has given a powerful exposition of this idea.[151] It does in fact seem that the structure of the patriarchal system is similar to that of the church, and yet it provides no possibility for the pure combination in one organisation of the aim of obedience and of the real community-relationship. Either it is the one or the other; but effective co-inherence is achieved only through the action of the Spirit himself, so that the church can also be characterised as a family moved by the spirit. The reason for the church's unique sociological structure is found in the idea of the Spirit, that is, in the reality of its being based upon the Spirit, which means that the understanding of this uniqueness can only be theological and not morphological and sociological. Viewed as a religious community the church, like most organised social groups, is but an impure case deriving from an ideal type. We saw that the church can be regarded sociologically as a community, and our view remains that this solution is more correct than any other. The religious community has, it is true, no sociological structure *sui generis;* only the empirical church based upon the Spirit has this. In it community, society and authority-groups are intermingled in real and most intimate fashion. As this structure becomes effective only through the Spirit, we speak of it as a community of the spirit. But we must reiterate that all community exists in faith in the Word so long as we do not live by sight, but only in a world of eschatological signs. Love as the community's life-principle overcomes the social attitude of people to one another. In point of content the structure is based upon the Christian idea of revelation. The divine will to rule over men by love seeks to build a kingdom of persons for itself. Love is the kingdom's aim, love seeks to rule and conquer; but the kingdom itself is intended to be the victory of God's love, and thus it is an end in itself as the kingdom of the loving community; that is, God's love serves to realise the kingdom and reigns in it. Basically this reveals once more the unique involvement of God's rule[152] and

God's kingdom. We met with the same ideas in the antithesis of the church as an instrument and as an end in itself, which was also repeated in the action of the church. In preaching, the church makes itself the instrument of its own constant edification. It confronts itself in preaching as a social grouping simply and solely organised towards the will of God. Thus the goal of God's will is simply the communion of saints. In the means of grace, just as in the organised forms of church discipline and doctrine, God's will for lordship is reflected—after the prescript of Matt. 16.18—not in the persons exercising them, but in the functions as sustained by the *sanctorum communio*. Mosheim knew that in a kingdom one must distinguish between the *cives* and the *constitutio*.[153] This is a fruitful sociological insight. Although Christ has reserved the *iura maiestatis regni sui sibi soli* the *ordinatio* and *gubernatio* are nevertheless present in the church too. The idea of extending the *constitutio* to the means of grace, as we have done, in order to see in them an expression of God's rule over the church, was not familiar to Mosheim. For us the church's entire claim to authority derives solely from the authority of the Word. Thus the idea of the priesthood of all believers remains the principle upon which the church is built. No empirical body 'in itself' has a claim to authority over the church. Every claim derives its authority from the Word. It seems to me that the necessary conclusion is that the church should become independent, that is, be disestablished; but we must leave this question here.

Thus the objective spirit too, as the will directed towards an end, strives upon the one hand continually and in an ever-wider compass to subject individual spirits to itself and hence to the rule of God, and it is impelled to do this by the unqualified will to rule of God, who uses it as the means to his end. It is in this boundless will for subjection that the missionary idea has its foundation. God is one, and his kingdom shall be the whole world; thus universality is set in the very heart of the Christian message. Missionary activity is God acting through the church. On the other hand the objective spirit is the representation of the community moved by the Holy Spirit and is itself will for community, precisely because it subjects itself to God's will for lordship. In its structure it is a *novum*, for it springs from its sources in order to achieve its purpose and yet at the same time represents itself as the community. Only from within can one understand this structure not as an impure sociological type, but as the *novum* of community of spirit.

To summarise: the church is a community *sui generis*, a community of spirit and of love. In it the basic sociological types, society, community and authority-group, are combined and surmounted. In all its effects the objective spirit of the community must be conceived of both as representative and as purposive. The relations of the members of the community are those of a community of spirit and not those of a society. The only element of a society is that objectively the church is constituted by a final aim. There is no need to repeat here all that has been said before about the church's multiplicity of spirits and spiritual unity.

i. *Church and Sect*. From this point the problem of church and sect can easily be resolved. We maintain that the sociological definition of the church is equally applicable to the sect, i.e., that sociologically there is ultimately no essential difference between the two. Thus we oppose Weber's and Troeltsch's now famous definition that 'the sect is a voluntary association of people exclusively qualified (ideally at least) religiously and ethically, into which one enters voluntarily provided one finds voluntary acceptance by proving one's religious quality.'[154] Again, 'The sect is a voluntary society, composed of strict and definite Christian believers bound to each other by the fact that all have experienced "the new birth". These "believers" live apart from the world, are limited to small groups, emphasise the law instead of grace and in varying degrees within their own circle set up the Christian order based on love; all this is done in preparation for and expectation of the coming Kingdom of God.'[155] Holl[156] has shown that this idea of the sect derives solely from Protestant sectarianism and is thus erroneous for this reason alone. To contrast it with the idea of the church seen as something instituted for salvation, into which one is born, which is open to all the world in adjusting its claims to the masses, makes it evident that Weber's and Troeltsch's view is based on a genetic analysis. The essential difference as they see it, is that the church progresses historically and organically, whereas the sect arises and subsists only through voluntary union. This distinction, however, if it is meant as one of principle, is inadequate both historically and sociologically, historically because in the second and third generation the great sects often become completely open national churches, and sociologically because it is an essential quality of the church community too that it should be a community of will. This Weber and Troeltsch do not recognise; had they done so they would have seen that the genetic approach was entirely misplaced. For the church too is only a church in so far as it comes to be effectively willed by persons, i.e., as a gathered church. The purely social act of will is, however, the same in both church and sect so long as it is oriented upon the Word of God, that is, so long as it is love wrought by the Spirit. The sect too, so long as it has the Word, is the church of Christ, and its community is the communion of saints. Its fundamental sociological elements are identical with those of the church. While the church's sociological organisation, as we have shown, is essentially adequate to the standard character of these basic ontic relationships and their consequences (infant baptism, the openness of the church, confessing congregations) the sect, by excessive and one-sided emphasis on certain insights (the sanctity of the person, conversion) very often produces one-sided results in the organisation of its basic sociological relations. These the national self-conscious church is bound to reject, they are not to be regarded as *adiaphora*. But so long as the sect is seen from the point of view of social acts of a Christian kind truly performed in it, we have no right to dispute in principle its essential identity with the church.[157]

In the distinction we made above between the Protestant and the Roman Catholic concepts of the church, which consisted in the fact that the former thinks of the Spirit as linked with the congregation, whereas the latter links it with the ministry, a

fundamental sociological difference is manifestly involved. But
we have to go further still. It is the miracle of the divine promise
that where the Word of God is preached it creates a congregation
for itself, wherever it may be. Thus we have to assume that in
the Roman Catholic Church too, where the Word is also preached
such a congregation is present, which falls into the same category
as those of the Protestant Church and the sects. The rock upon
which the Roman Catholic Church founders is not the Word but
'pure doctrine', and it is only from this standpoint that we are to
understand its sociological structure as an institutional church,
which is actually quite different from that of the Protestant
Church. No sociological structure is sacred in itself, and there is
no structure capable of completely obstructing the Word in its
course. That there should be an impulse to achieve pure doctrine
is just as obvious as the fact that no church can claim to possess it
absolutely. We must describe it as an error in the Confession of
Augsburg VII that it directly links the *recte docetur* with the
congregatio sanctorum. 'Pure doctrine' is not a condition for the
existence of the congregation of the saints (Isa. 55.11 says nothing
of this). That it always tends towards pure doctrine is certain,
but this tendency can remain ineffective through historical
circumstances. We are bound to recognise and believe in
principle, therefore, that the *sanctorum communio* is present both
in the Roman Catholic Church and in the sect. But we recognise
the Protestant Church as the 'true' one—which is not the same
thing as describing it as the 'essential' church—and think that in
it God has chosen for himself an especially pure instrument for
his work; which leads us further to believe that it is in a special
sense the lap of God's holy church.

One problem remains. If the church is essentially a gathered
church, what is its relation to national churches? 1. A national
church corresponds to the dogmatic meaning of the church as
offering the gospel to all; 2. but God's gracious will should be
specially recognised in a national church, in that as an organically
developed historical power it possesses greater firmness and lasting
power than the voluntary association: historically sterile periods
can be withstood by the national church, whereas the gathered

church is ruined by such a time. It is divine grace that we have a church which is deeply rooted in the history of the nation, which makes the divine will for us, given through the power of the church's historicity, relative independent of the momentary human situation.

Lastly, a national church is reproached for its conservatism, and certainly often not without reason. But conservatism is not only a significant power, but it is also justified on the Protestant view of history. Protestantism never rejects past history absolutely. Rather, it gives a relative value to history, to tradition. History cannot be absolutely holy, as in the Roman Catholic view, but it is nevertheless in some sense the will of God, even in its actual forms. That is why it was so hard for Luther to break with history, and to 'make' history himself. The conservatism of a Protestant national church is based on this relative evaluation of past history, and it is sceptical of all innovators. It makes the church old-fashioned, and it runs the risk of canonising the past. This very conservatism which preserves the good seed in superficial times becomes a danger to the church.

But this conservatism also provides the link with the sociological elements in the world, the constitution of the state, and the acknowledgment of the powers of the state in general. This acknowledgment is assured in principle by the idea of the priesthood of all believers. Within the sociological reference this means that since the time of Paul the church has justified patriarchialism. The dangers of conservatism are obvious, and the church has often succumbed to them, so that Troeltsch can even say, 'The churches are husks which gradually harden the kernel they were protecting.'[158]

Similarly the Christian evaluation of history gives rise to the principle of progress in the church. The church must be a church of the present day, it must take and prove all the forces that accrue to it from present-day life. Past history is in principle no more right than the present. As a modern Christian I have both the right and the duty to criticise history and give form to the gospel for the present. And every local congregation has this duty *vis-à-vis* the whole church. On the Protestant view this makes for a balance between the retarding and the progressive element. The sociological expression of the progressive element in the church is the idea of organism. The entire life of the community comes from co-operation of the members. Any concrete case of the rejection of something new, or the throwing off of a dead tradition, must be decided by the conscience of the church authorities. Their finest task is to make every possible power of renewal and vitality fruitful for the work of the church. To this task belongs the handing over of certain offices in the church to charismatically gifted personalities, whether in the exposition of Scripture or works of love or powers of organisation. Further, there should be a constant watchfulness over the interests of the young generation, and a prudent use of the situation where similar thoughts are stirring, and attentiveness to what is being said outside the church. Fundamentally it is in this lively attitude that the law of life for every community is fulfilled: a fighting movement all the time (such as the Roman Catholic church does not have—the institution and the people as a mass). Only when every door is open to this movement, and when on the other hand the retarding element is powerful enough to reject the useless and to deal critically with the fruitful, will there be a quickening mingling of proper conservatism and proper progress in the church.

Although both powers are at work in every national church and every gathered church, since they arise from the Protestant view of history and from historical life as a whole, although, further, there are national churches with a great will to progress, and gathered churches, certainly, which are crassly conservative, in general one can say that the national type of church tends more to the historical past and the gathered type of church more to the new and progressive. In view of all we have said, especially of the necessity of the national church from a dogmatic stand-point, we can now affirm that the national church and the gathered church belong together, and that it is all too obvious to-day that a national church, which is not continually pressing forward to be a confessing church, is in the greatest inner peril. There is a moment when the church dare not continue to be a national church, and this moment has come when the national church can no longer see how it can win through to being a gathered church (see above, on baptism and confirmation), but on the contrary is moving into complete petrifaction and emptiness in the use of its forms, with evil effects on the living members as well. We have to-day reached the point where such questions must be decided. We are more than ever grateful for the grace of the national church, but we are also more than ever keeping our eyes open for the danger of its complete degeneration.

To summarise, the *sanctorum communio*, the type of the Christian community of love, is bound to the Word of God, and to that alone. It is present, according to the promise of Isaiah 55.11, in every historical form in which the Word is preached. Weber's and Troeltsch's distinction between church and sect is historically and sociologically untenable. Even in the special sociological type of the Roman Catholic Church the *sanctorum communio* is believed in by virtue of the action of the Word. The effort to attain to the true church and to pure doctrine is essential.

f. The individual form of the objective spirit in the church of to-day

i. *Church and Proletariat.* 'What is the state of . . . the question concerning the significance of Christianity for the solution of the modern social problem? This is the problem of capitalist economics and the industrial proletariat created by it; the problem of gigantic bureaucratic and military states, and of immense increase in population leading to world politics and colonial policies; the problem of mechanised activity producing huge amounts of material, and mobilising and combining everything in world traffic, but also mechanising men and labour. We only need to formulate the question in this way to recognise that the most important answer is that this is a problem which is entirely new and unprecedented for Christian social work' (Troeltsch).[159]

We can no longer make the last of Troeltsch's assertions in his form, and yet we must recognise that for the church of to-day everything depends on its once more approaching the masses which have turned away from it, and moreover in such a way that the church brings the gospel into real contact with the present situation of the proletariat, in full attentiveness to how these masses look upon the gospel.

The objective spirit of the church in its present historical conditions has not yet shown much awareness of this problem. Christian social work has had some admirable achievements. But where is there to be found any objective discussion of the gospel, the church, and the proletariat? On my view it cannot be gainsaid that the future and the hope for our 'bourgeois' church lies in a renewal of its life-blood, which is only possible if the church succeeds in winning the proletariat. If the church does not see this, then it will spurn a moment of the most serious decision. Nor is it hard to see that the churchliness of the modern bourgeoisie is threadbare, and that its living power in the church is at an end. On the other hand it seems to me as if, despite outward opposition in the proletariat, there is no modern power which is basically more open to the Christian gospel than the proletariat. The living proletariat knows only one affliction, isolation, and cries out for one thing, community. These ideas are of course entangled and confined in class consciousness. Nevertheless they are seeking something more intensively than the bourgeoisie ever did. The church dare not let the proletariat proclaim 'human peace' without speaking its own word in this situation. It must not let the socialist youth movements speak of community without calling into their midst the word of the *sanctorum communio*. It must not shrug off the interest in sport shown by modern youth (not just the proletarians), but it must recognise that this too is a cry for community in discipline and struggle, and that here too the Word of the *sanctorum communio* could find attentive response. Certainly it will not be heard, and cannot be heard, in the way it often speaks to-day. For above all the gospel must deal with the present—and that means at this moment the proletarian mass—in a concrete way, 'serving the Lord' (Romans 12.11). But let there be no apotheosis of the proletariat! It is neither the bourgeois nor the proletarian which is right, but the gospel alone. Here there is neither Jew nor Greek. Nevertheless the gospel must be concretely proclaimed in history, and that is why it brings us today face to face with the problem of the proletariat. It is not very easy to offer a proof for something which is more instinctive than conceptual, in this case to prove that our modern church is 'bourgeois'. The best proof is that the proletariat has turned away from the church, whereas the bourgeois (the petty official, the artisan and the merchant) have remained. So the sermon is aimed at relatively secure people, living adequately in orderly family circumstances, relatively 'educated' and morally relatively solid. So the sermon meets the need for having something fine and educated and moral for the free hours of Sunday. Hence the all-too-familiar type of sermon which is called an 'address', in which proof is offered of the preacher's literary culture and the corresponding interest of the 'public'. The danger of the church's becoming a mere association is obvious. (In this context we also find the mischievous habit of individual artistic efforts, such as solos by a professional singer, in the framework of the service.) If I consider the pictures hanging in church halls and meeting-places, or the architectural styles of churches of recent decades, or the church music provided by Mendelssohn and others, I cannot help thinking that in none of these things is there the slightest understanding of the church's essential social nature. It would be an interesting task for a sociology of the church to make a historical examination of its artistic products; I believe one could perhaps get a better insight in this way than by any examination of the charitable works done by the church.

But we cannot pursue this matter. Is it mere accident that all this has come about? How can it be any different, when theological students have no duty to get into real touch and discussion with the present day, alongside their studies, and when they never hear actual criticism of their position in encounter with another group altogether, such as the proletariat? There can be no evangelical message without a knowledge of the present. But again, I seem to see possibilities opening up of real modern preaching. I believe that the attempt must be made to bring proletarians into the service of the church, and that the future of our church depends largely on our getting preachers from proletarian circles, in the first instance, of course, for the working-class congregations in the big cities. I also think that we should attract children from working-class families to go on in the Sunday schools to be teachers, and that schools should be established in which likely youngsters from working-class backgrounds should be prepared for service in the church. What all this would mean in detail, cannot be taken further here. If the need is recognised, then ways will be found. Serious consideration of the gospel, and open eyes for the present are the powers from which the living church will be born anew.

The church of the future will not be 'bourgeois'. We cannot tell what it will look like. What is certain is that it is not Thorwaldsen and Mendelssohn, but Dürer and Rembrandt and Bach who can make the serious message of the church known. We do not wish the proletarian spirit as such, nor compulsory socialist doctrine, but we want to take the church to the proletariat and out of the 'masses' we want to make 'congregations'. It is true that the Christian church will always be a community of individual persons, who know God in judgment and grace. There can be no deviation from this, just to please the masses. Tillich's ideas about the 'holiness of the masses'[160] have nothing to do with Christian theology. We know only of the holiness of the church of God, and we know that God has bound his church to his Word in Christ, and that this Word must be personally appropriated. We know of no 'absolute' revealing itself in the formlessness of the masses. We know of the actual historical will of God, and that we do not condemn the mass, but that we yield it to the power of the *deus absconditus*—hidden, namely, in his pity—to speak to us at this point his unknown Word. In this sense we must say, *extra ecclesiam nulla salus*. The masses must be pointed to the idea of the community of the church, not *vice versa*.

It is not that the idea of socialism corresponds sociologically to the idea of the Christian community, nor that socialisation means the coming of the kingdom of God to earth, as is often said by religious socialists. All the same there seems to us to be a certain 'affinity' between socialism and the Christian idea of community, which we must not neglect. What we have said earlier makes it clear that the socialist idea of equality is theologically and sociologically untenable; making men equal by force is not only bound to fail, it is also unchristian. The Christian community is based upon the innate inequality of persons, but nevertheless, as we have shown earlier, its basic principle is the priesthood of all believers. The free man remains free, and the servant remains a servant, and yet both are one in Christ.

The Christian community is also based upon the freedom of the individual. Enslavement by the majority is unchristian, because there is no earthly authority intervening between the individual and God which has supreme power over the individual. The community and the individual are maintained in equilibrium (we call to mind the monadic image). Socialism and individualism in the genuine sense go together. The distance which separates socialism and Christianity is clear, when we realise that in the last resort the Christian idea of community cannot be fulfilled in any political or economic organisation. Nevertheless we must take up the threads which are offered to us, and even if the confrontation and the discussion are hard, the church must dare to take this step into the life of the proletariat, the masses.

g. Faith in the Sanctorum Communio and 'experiencing the church'

The point of this question is three-fold:
1. to justify the method of our inquiry;
2. to elucidate the problem of 'church and religious community';
3. to avoid solemn pronouncements about 'experiencing the church' and to suggest a more dogmatic approach.

We have been speaking not of the experience of sin and grace but of their theological meaning and their social intentions. It was only thus that we were able to establish the reality of the basic relationships and arrive at a specifically Christian sociology;

otherwise it would have been impossible to form a concept of the church as opposed to that of religious community. We cannot deal here with the important problem as to how far faith and experience belong together. The important thing is that so far we have kept to faith not as an experience but in so far as it comprises realities. In so doing I think we have done justice to the special nature of theological method. Essentially the church can be understood only as a divine act, that is, in the utterance of faith; only upon this basis can it be understood as an 'experience'. Only faith comprehends the church as a community established by God. The so-called 'experience of the church' cannot in principle be distinguished from the experience of religious community; and yet there is a genuine experience of the church, just as there is an experience of justification. But far too often nowadays people forget that it is not the experience that makes the church. Supporters of the Youth Movement who speak of the church always fail to see the significance of the church's reality, that is, that it is established by God, and that it exists in principle 'before' any experience. The books of Erich Stange[161] and Paul le Seur[162] are especially characteristic of this. The church is not 'made' in great experiences of fellowship; it is not only historically but in point of faith too that everyone finds himself already in the church, when he becomes aware of it. We must re-awaken the perception that everyone who is moved by the Spirit stands in the church, and that this is something that is both a gift and a task. The loudly acclaimed 'will for the church' in its most recent forms is to be welcomed only in so far as it expresses not the will to make the church but the will of those concerned to recognise themselves, and be active, as the church moved by the Holy Spirit.

The fact that the 'will for the church' and the 'experience' of the church are for the most part confused with one another is very characteristic. We shall see at once why it is necessary to distinguish between them.

The confusion of community romanticism with the communion of saints is extremely dangerous. The communion of saints must always be recognised as something established by God, and of course as something we ourselves must will; but we ourselves can will it only if it is willed by God through us. It is thus willed by God 'before' all human will for community, and yet at the same time it is effective solely as will for community. This antinomy is overcome only by God's subjection of the human will to his own will. In actual fact this subjection always remains incipient, but God sees what has only begun as already consummated. This means that in speaking only of the present movement of will for community we have not exhausted God's action with us; it is rather that God's merciful judgment considers the new will of the church community, though constantly breaking down, to be something holy now, because he himself purposes to make it holy. God establishes the church in Christ as something which from that time on is in his view perfect at every moment. But to make it actual he uses the wills of men, who are thus both the means and the end. If a community of will is moved by the Spirit it is always *ipso facto* the church. The will for the church is necessary, but genuine only in connection with, or when arising from, faith in the church which is really present, already established by God. 'Experiencing the church' is something else. It is supposed to make it possible for us to experience the 'others' as members of the church of God. There are many weighty dogmatic considerations opposing this. 'We live by faith and not by sight.' None of us knows whether our neighbour has been elected, or has remained impenitent. He is completely nontransparent to us in all that he does. This means not only that nothing is known about a man's *donum perseverantiae*, but also that Christian actions can spring from a hypocritical, misguided heart, governed by false enthusiasm. Only the *opera*, and not the *persona, quae in manu Dei est* (Calvin), are perceptible; 'the Lord knows those who are his.' How then should it be possible for us really to experience the church, and not just religious community? The church is *impalpabilis, insensibilis;* as Luther says, it must be believed. Even when men reveal their hearts to one another in love no one of them can with certainty state whether the other belongs to the church. It is only through faith that the church can be grasped, and only faith can interpret the experience of communion that necessarily arises as evidence of the presence of the church. Man 'experiences' only the religious community, but knows in faith that this religious community is 'the church'. Even when two or three are gathered together in Christian community, and being one in Christ, profess their faith, they also believe in the church upon the strength of the promise (Isa. 55.11; Matt. 18.20) and their experience is only in faith an experience of the church.

But what does 'believing in the church' mean? We do not believe in an invisible church, nor in the kingdom of God existing in the church as *coetus electorum;* but we believe that God has made the actual empirical church, in which the Word and the sacraments are administered, into his community, that it is the Body of Christ, that is, the presence of Christ in the world, and that according to the promise God's Spirit becomes effective in it. We believe in the church as the church of God and as the communion of saints, of those, that is, who are sanctified by God, but within the historical form of the empirical church. Thus we believe in the means of grace within the empirical church and hence in the holy congregation created by them. We believe in the church as *una,* for it is 'Christ existing as the church', and Christ is the one Lord over those who are all one in him; as *sancta,* since the Holy Spirit is at work in it, and as *catholica,* since as the church of God its call is to the whole world, and it is present wherever God's Word is preached in the world. We believe in the church not as an unattainable ideal, or one which has still to be attained, but as a present reality.[163] What distinguishes Christian thinking from all idealist theories of community is that the Christian community is the church of God in every moment of history and it knows it will never attain perfection within the development of history. It will remain impure so long as history exists, and yet in this its actual form it is God's church.[164]

If we now ask at what point faith most purely 'experiences the church', then the answer is that this certainly does not come about in the communities built upon a romantic feeling of solidarity between kindred spirits, but rather when there is nothing but the church community linking the individuals concerned, where Jew and Greek, Pietist and Liberal come into conflict and nevertheless profess their faith in unity, nevertheless come together for Holy Communion and intercede for one another in prayer; it is precisely in the commonplace surroundings of every day that the church is believed and experienced; it is not in moments of spiritual exaltation, but in the monotony and severity of daily life, and in the regular worship of God that we come to understand the church's full significance. All else merely veils the true state of things. The impulses to community in the Youth Movement were great, but even when the attempt was made, they have not been able to contribute much to the experience of the church. We cannot be too sober about this. Until people understand what the church is, and that in accordance with its nature we believe in it in spite of, or rather because of, all its visible manifestations, it is not only dangerous but thoroughly unscrupulous and a complete confusion of the Protestant understanding of the church to speak of experiences that can never constitute a church and in which there is no grasp at all of the church's essential nature. Our age is not poor in experiences, but in faith. Only faith can create true experience of the church, so we think it more important for our age to be led into belief in the church of God, than to have experiences squeezed from it which as such are of no help at all, but which, when there is faith in the *sanctorum communio*, are produced of their own accord.

4. *The church and eschatology*

'We walk by faith, not by sight.' This must be so, as long as history lasts; thus for us it is a fundamental perception that history cannot provide the final solution, so that the end of history cannot provide it either. Furthermore, the meaning of history cannot be progressive development, but that 'every age is in direct relationship with God' (Ranke). This provides theological justification for our sociological method of asking about the essential structure of the church, and not giving an outline of its development from the point of view of the philosophy of history. In principle the course of church history does not teach us any more about its eschatological significance than does the understanding of every present moment. In history there are two fundamental tendencies warring against each other, and both are destined to flourish in a constant increase of violence and power. The one is the striving of the *sanctorum communio* to penetrate all human life, whether community or society. It would, however, not be correct to make the final antagonists the empirical church and the world. Rather the rift passes midway through the empirical church; the struggle between good and evil is bound to flare up within the empirical church itself; there will never be a pure church, just as there never has been. The ultimate antagonists in history will forever be the *sanctorum communio* and the *Antichrist*.[165]

Christian eschatology is essentially the eschatology of the church; it is concerned with the consummation of the church and of the individuals in the church. The concept of the kingdom of God does indeed embrace not only the consummation of the church but also the problems of the 'new world', that is, the eschatology of civilisation and of nature. In speaking of the consummation of the church and of communities we are dealing with only a section of the total problem.

The question contains two groups of ideas: that of judgment and that of eternal life, the consummated communion with God.

How does human community present itself at the judgment? Judgment is executed upon persons, which evidently means not only upon individual persons but also upon collective persons. This implies, however, that we have to conceive of the individuals being judged not only alone but equally as a member of the collective persons. A people, a family, a marriage—each undergoes its judgment as a whole. Here what we said earlier about the eschatological character of communities and the temporal character of societies becomes significant. The eternal judgment is passed upon both, but upon communities as collective persons, upon societies only as consisting of individuals. Thus the community, as a collective person, can expect eternal life, but the society is dissolved. How in particular cases it is possible to imagine a collective person as being rejected or accepted while the individual within it is still accepted or rejected on his own account is something that remains obscure. But we cannot conclude from this that the idea of the judgment of the collective person must be rejected. We have seen how the community as a collective person is from God to God, and how it must be thought of as based upon the will of God; and this holds true at the Last Judgment as well. The New Testament, too, is familiar with this idea (Chorazin, Bethsaida, Capernaum in Matt. 11.21ff. and the words to the churches in Rev. 2 and 3, esp. 3.16 and 3.10). The thought that God can condemn a collective person and at the same time accept individuals from it, and *vice versa*, is just as necessary as it is unimaginable.

At the judgment each man stands consciously—perhaps for the first time—before God to receive sentence. Here each man becomes a 'person', perceiving God's holiness and his own guilt; here everyone becomes 'lonely'. But there is a loneliness in face of the grace of God, and a loneliness in face of his wrath. It is eternal death to exist in the loneliness of the wrath, that is, in isolation in guilt, without any ethical connection with the other spirits, but simultaneously knowing one's guilt and being aware of what one is missing. If we assume that the spirit lives on free of the body, then the possibility for communication afforded by the body is entirely lost; in addition to the loneliness before the judgment of wrath there is also the state of isolation.[166] The weight of God's judgment of wrath is nevertheless essentially in the 'loneliness', and not so much in the state of general spiritual isolation. Loneliness is an ethical category and surpasses the wretchedness of spiritual isolation; it is not spiritual, but religious death, and it is conceivable that it will be most felt when it is not linked with the state of general spiritual isolation.

Luther, like Paul before him, assumed a resurrection and a new corporality for the godless as well;[167] the fact that resurrection is possible only through Christ and can thus be taken account of only for the faithful did not prevent either of them from teaching universal bodily resurrection, in order to uphold the idea of the Last Judgment. But the deepest significance in the thought of the new body lies in the Christian concept of person and of community. In the Christian person body and soul are bound together in an indissoluble unity.[168] Real community is possible only through man's being equipped with a body, so we must think of body and soul as being essentially connected. We assume that with the body the sinful soul also dies, and that in the resurrection God, with the soul, also creates a new body, and that this new spiritual body is a warrant and condition for the eternal communion of personal spirits. Whether this idea has its necessary application to the godless is something we cannot go into here. Thus we can summarise: God's judgment extends over both individual and collective persons. In the eternal judgment of wrath God recognises the ultimately recalcitrant will as free; the man who wants only himself gets his own way, but simultaneously finds that in asserting it he has brought about his own religious death; for man lives only in communion with other men and with God.

By the loneliness of the judgment of grace we understand the judgment of faith in the eternal church, the final decision. The significance of this moment is that loneliness is completely vanquished in the church and that individual personality exists only in the reality of the church. At the moment when man must live in loneliness and before God through the unspeakable suffering of the grief of repentance—as we assume the faithful too must do—he enters fully into the church of Christ which sustains him.

Although we are speaking here of a double issue we must not do so without at the same time emphasising the inner necessity of the idea of apocatastasis. We are not in a position to resolve this antinomy.[169] In the concept of the church, as the presence of Christ in the world urging us to a decision, the double issue is just as necessarily required as it appears impossible to us, perceiving that we in no way merit the gift of God's undeserved love we have received, that others should be excluded from this gift and this love. The deepest reason for assuming apocatastasis, however, seems to me to be that every Christian must be aware that he has brought sin into the world, so that he is linked in guilt with the whole of mankind, and has mankind's guilt upon his conscience. No justification and sanctification of man is conceivable if he is not granted the certainty that with him God also draws to himself all those for whose guilt he is responsible. But to speak about this is only to hope. These ideas cannot form any part of the system.

God's judgment and grace cover persons, that is, all the individual persons in the church; the multiplicity of spirit as we have described it earlier, as well as the marriages and friendships that have entered into the *sanctorum communio*, and finally what unites them all, the collective person of the church, spiritual unity. Ultimately, however, these persons are persons solely in the fellowship they have with each other—this is something we must in conclusion emphasise once more—that is to say, in community of spirit. Community of spirit, however, demands whole persons in a corporality which must be thought of as the full expression of the new spirituality. This precludes any mystical ideas of a final absorption in God as the person who is one and all, of fusion of our divine being with his. The Creator and the creature remain distinct as persons. But the creatures too are distinct from one another, and yet taken all together form the mighty unity of the congregation of God. They are now 'entirely justified and sanctified', one in Christ and yet all individuals. Their community of spirit is based upon and is kindled at their mutual love. They surrender themselves to each other and to God, and thereby form community both with man and with God. And this community, which in history is never more than incipiently realised and is constantly breaking up, is real and eternal here. Whereas in the church too the I and the Thou confronted each other as strangers, in an estrangement overcome only in the eschatological signs of sanctification, here the revelation of one heart to the other is consummated in divine love. We behold the community of love in the mutual revelation of hearts which are filled by the Spirit. 'I seeks I. They find one another and flow together . . . reality and truth become the same. . . .'[170] The meaning of love is consummated where one's own person is no longer seen, and so reaches its 'self' in the most intimate communion with the other, a communion which may be called blessed. It remains a community of will of free persons, and its blessedness has nothing to do with a mystic fusion. It is the highest potentialisation of personal life, just as losing this communion means death. The mystic has no understanding of the power and the glory of love. From man's dual destiny of being under God's lordship and in God's kingdom arises his dual function of seeing the eternal truth—as formerly he believed it—and practising the love that is now perfect, the perfect service of the Spirit. The movement upwards cannot be separated from the movement towards our neighbour. Both belong indissolubly together. Ritschl's distinction breaks down. Standing under God's lordship means living in communion with him and with the members of the church. God wills to be the King and Father of his subjects and children, he wills to reign over spirits whose will is free, to have communion with them, but not, as the primal ground of all being, to be the death of all true being. He is the God of living persons.

Now the objective spirit of the church has really become the Holy Spirit; the experience of the 'religious' community is now really the experience of the church and the collective person of the church really 'Christ existing as the church'. How they all become one and yet each man remains himself, how they are all in God and yet each is separate from him, how they are all in each other, and yet each man will be alone, how each has God entirely and alone in the merciful dual loneliness of seeing and serving truth and love, and is yet never lonely but always really lives only in the church—these are things it is not given us to conceive. We walk in faith. But we shall see not God alone but his church too; we shall no longer only believe in its love and faith, but see it. We shall know that God's purpose to rule is constantly over us, and we shall put it into action in the kingdom of the church. Here the kingdom of Christ has become the kingdom of God; here the *ministerium* of Christ, the Holy Spirit and the Word is at an end.[171] Christ himself gives his church into his Father's keeping (I Cor. 15.24), that God may be all in all.

What has become reality here is not the *ecclesia triumphans*, but the kingdom of God in all the world. There is no longer repentance and faith, but service and sight. Here the wheat is parted from the chaff, here the age of the historical church, in all its tribulation, is past. God will wipe away the tears from all men's eyes. The victory is won, the kingdom has become God's.

This is the church's hope, the hope of our present-day church, of the *sanctorum communio*, and it guards this hope as its treasure, its real hope. It will not make any premature attempts to make it present. But in hope it grows strong. It knows 'that the sufferings of this present time are not worth comparing with the glory that is to be revealed to us.'

Notes

Notes to Chapter 1

1. The term comes from Comte, *Cours de Philosophie*, IV, 185, replacing the term 'social physics'.
2. The best historical survey of the history of sociology is to be found in Paul Barth, *Sociologie als Philosophie der Geschichte*, 1896.
3. In addition, the concepts 'sociological' and 'social' cannot be used correctly. They are related to one another similarly to the concepts 'psychological' and 'psychic'. There are social and psychic facts, and there is a sociological and a psychological view of these facts. This clear distinction is hardly ever maintained.
4. Troeltsch, *Gesammelte Schriften*, IV, 705ff., Tübingen, 1925.
5. The expression 'formal sociology' comes from Simmel's main work, *Soziologie, Untersuchungen über die Formen der Vergesellschaftung*, 1908.
6. Vierkandt, *Gesellschaftslehre*, para. 3, 13.
7. Vierkandt, op. cit., 28. Cf. Gustaf Stefen, *Die Grundlagen der Soziologie, ein Programm zur Methode der Gesellschaftswissenschaft und Naturforschung*, 1912, 12: 'Since the subject of sociology is simply the interactions or influences of human consciousness, the only possibility for sociology is that it should form part of the psychological type of science.'
8. Vierkandt, op. cit., para. 7, 47.
9. loc. cit., 14.
10. Tönnies, *Gemeinschaft und Gesellschaft*, cf. *Soziologische Studien und Kritiken*, 1924.
11. Cf., in addition to the work mentioned above, the *Philosophie des Geldes*, 2nd ed., 1907, and the summary in the *Grundfragen der Soziologie*, 16ff.: 'The insight that man's whole being and utterances are determined by his living in interaction with other men must lead to a new view in all the so-called humane studies.' Further, and very significant for the unconscious approach to Hegelian ideas, 18: 'Through the awareness of the social nature of production which is interposed between the purely individual and the transcendental, a genetic method in all humane studies has been reached.'
12. Von Wiese, *Soziologie I, Beziehungslehre*, 1924.
13. Durkheim, *Les formes élémentaires de la vie réligieuse*, Paris; also *Die Methode der Soziologie*, Leipzig, 1908.
14. Gabriel Tarde, *Les lois de limitations*.
15. McDougall, *Social Psychology*, 13th ed., London.

16. A. Comte, *Sociologie*, cf. Tönnies, 'Comte's Begriff der Soziologie', *Studien und Kritiken* II, 116ff.
17. *Sociology;* also, *Introduction to the Study of Sociology*. Cf. Tönnies, op. cit., 75ff., 'Spencer's soziologisches Werk'.
18. *Bau und Leben des sozialen Körpers*, 4 vv. 1875ff.; also *Abriss der Soziologie*, 1906.
19. *Gesellschaftslehre*, 1919.
20. *System der Soziologie*, I.
21. *Die Phasen der Kultur*, 1908.
22. op. cit., 135.
23. We make use of this concept, which is very unclear in Simmel, in the interpretation of Vierkandt and others.
24. It follows, for example, that in order to know a man fully, one must have known him in all possible situations (Vierkandt, op. cit., para. 7, 51), and even then one must be prepared to discover entirely new sides to him in new situations. Clearly this is a profound error: to consider the power of circumstances may be empirically perfectly right, but something decisive has been overlooked. A man who knows others can really do so from a single situation, without knowing from experience how the other behaves in other situations, but simply because he looks at that moment at the personal centre from which every possible mode of action arises. In every action the whole person is concerned, and knowledge of this person does not rest on the wealth of possible modes of action, but on the intuitive views of the personal centre.
25. Cf. for what follows Theodor Litt, *Individuum und Gemeinschaft*, 3rd ed., 1926, 205ff., 221ff.
26. Vierkandt, op. cit., 48.
27. Von Wiese, op. cit., 6ff. Cf. Vierkandt's remarks about the disunity of the person, 50ff.
28. I consider it a misjudgment to distinguish in principle Simmel's formal sociology from the relational teaching of von Wiese and Vierkandt, as has been done by Schumann in *Systematische Theologie*, 1926-7, No. 4. It is true that Simmel's formal concept is extremely imprecise. But he seems to me to be correctly interpreted by the other two, who have good reason for saying they are building on Simmel's foundations. Nor does it seem justifiable to me to put Tönnies and Oppenheimer together. They are allied by a cultural and philosophical interest, but the interesting thing in Tönnies is that he joins this to the formal method, whereas Oppenheimer's method is encyclopædic and universalist. It is true that Tönnies deserves a special place in formal sociology; but still, his place is there.
29. Von Wiese's and Vierkandt's so-called relational teaching is one of

many accounts which have overlooked this strict distinction. This teaching is based on a social-philosophical atomism, which at the same time it tries to refute. Persons are stable and isolated objects, outside the social process, whose social 'capacities' make possible relations with other persons. Cf. Litt, *Individuum und Gemeinschaft*, 3rd ed., 1926, 205ff., 221ff.; Vierkandt, *Gesellschaftslehre*, 51, 48; von Wiese, *Beziehungslehre*, 1924, 6ff.

30. Uncertainty about the object of sociology leads to the prevailing conceptual confusion. While the encyclopædist-universalist group (cf. Troeltsch, *Ges. Schr.* IV, 705ff., Vierkandt, op. cit., 11ff., and P. Barth, *Soziologie als Philosophie der Geschichte*, 2nd ed., 1920) want to use sociology as a generic name for all human studies, that is, for a universal science, but in this way unwittingly render it superfluous as an independent discipline (cf. Oppenheimer, *System der Soziologie*, 135), the formal sociologists on the other hand want to investigate the forms of concrete society. They seem to find an independent subject-matter in this way. But their use of empirical methods prevents it from reaching full individuality, leaving it in the realm of historical research. Schumann, op. cit., has grasped the problem clearly; there are almost as many definitions of the subject-matter as there are sociological works.

31. This method has been applied since the beginnings of formal sociology, at first unconsciously (Simmel, *Soziologie*, 1908, Tönnies, *Gemeinschaft und Gesellschaft*, 3rd ed., 1919, and *Soziologische Studien und Kritiken*, 1924), and later explicitly, in Vierkandt. There the genetic and the phenomenological approach are in conflict, with consequent obscurity. The conflict is in his concept of sociology as a theory of relation, which would in itself require the empirical method. The defect can be seen in Scheler's *Formalismus in der Ethik und die materiale Wertethik*, 3rd ed., 1927, 495ff. Cf. the works of the phenomenologists, Edith Stein, 'Individuum und Gemeinschaft', *Jahrbuch für Philosophie und phenomenologische Forschung*, v, 1922, 116ff., Gerda Walther, 'Zur Ontologie der sozialen Gemeinschaften', ibid., IV, 1923, Samuel Krakauer, *Soziologie als Wissenschaft*, 1924, and Litt, op. cit.

32. It is almost incomprehensible how Max Weber can speak of the sociology of religion when he is describing the relations of politics, economics and religion, i.e., of various distinct spheres of learning, to one another, and is actually doing historical work. Cf. *Aufsätze zur Religionssoziologie*, III; the apparently systematic 'sociology of religion' in *Wirtschaft und Gesellschaft*, 1922, 227-363, is also in the last analysis historical. Cf. the following definition of sociology: 'Sociology should mean a science which interprets social action,

explaining its course and effects causally.' This explains the wide range of Weber's essays. Cf. his 'Über einige Kategorien der verstehenden Soziologie', Logos IV, 1903. Before Weber, sociology of religion had hardly ever been concerned with anything but the history of religion, either from a universalist or an economic standpoint. Cf. Spencer, *Principles of Sociology* v, 1, Schäffle, *Bau und Leben des sozialen Körpers*, 1875, IV, 144ff., and more systematically in 1, 689ff., Spann, *Gesellschaftslehre*, 1919, 323-49. Here too the prevailing interest is the history of religion. A possible exception is Durkheim in his study of totemism as the original form of human society (*Les formes élémentaires de la vie réligieuse*, Paris, 1912). Yet even here it is the history of religion and ethnology rather than a systematic treatment which dominate. So far as I know, it was Simmel who first attempted a systematic sociology of religion in his book *Die Religion*, 2nd ed., 1912. He really discusses questions of structure in religious societies. Troeltsch in his *The Social Teaching of the Christian Churches* (E.t. 1931) unfolded the history of Christian ideas of community in terms of an autonomous systematic sociology, though he did so with an emphasis upon the contingent social structure rather than on the essentially Christian structure. Finally, Max Scheler in the *Formalismus* outlined a systematic sociology, with emphasis on the problem of a Christian sociology, with which we have still to deal. If we recall Schumann's essay, already mentioned, which is concerned with a systematic understanding of sociology, then it may be seen that we are slowly gaining an inkling of the inadequacy of the old concept of the sociology of religion.

Notes to Chapter II

1. Windelband, *History of Philosophy*, para. 13.
2. We must pass over the medieval developments of Aristotle's philosophy, which were of no small significance for social philosophy and can in fact be traced as far as Spinoza's and Leibniz's inquiry into the *principium individuationis*.
3. The Patristic conception of the person is very close to this Stoic view, only the personal element is more pronounced, due to the personal concept of God with its I-Thou relation as the basic one between man and God, as well as the doctrine of personal life after death, which is not found in ancient philosophy. Here it is sufficient to notice the social philosophical teaching of Stoicism which arises from the new concept of the person.
4. Even Kant agrees (cf. *Religion within the Limits of Pure Reason*, III,

1, 2), except that he considers an emergence from the state of nature both possible and required.

5. Exception will perhaps be taken to my ranging Kant among the idealists. I am conscious of his distance from them all, and shall have to speak later of how the idea of transcendence is constantly in conflict with the idea of immanence. But for our present purpose he is the first of a line stretching to Hegel.

6. Cf. Heinrich Barth, 'Kierkegaard der Denker' in *Zwischen den Zeiten*, 1926, 3, 208, who attempts to base Kierkegaard's ethics on Kant. What Barth takes to be formalism is the correlate either to radical subjectivism or to a materialist ethic, which empties the concept of formalism of any significance. In Kant formalism and universality are necessarily connected, and this provides a content for his ethic. When Brunner, in *Die Mystik und das Wort*, 331, identifies the Kantian and the Christian concepts of person, the point of identity lies elsewhere. From many different starting-points in his ethic Kant could have destroyed his own epistemology. Cf. Scheler, *Formalismus*, 512, n. 1.

7. *Idee zu einer allgemeinen Geschichte in weltbürglerlicher Absicht*, 4th proposition.

8. Fichte considered the question of the 'synthesis of the world of spirits' more seriously than anyone else. He was the only one to see that the presence of other living men 'in self-active freedom' was a philosophical problem, which threatened the whole system. How does one man approach the other? Where is their common origin? Fichte's answers are manifold and yet very much alike. (Cf. Hirsch, *Die idealistische Philosophie und das Christentum*, 1926, 'Fichtes Gotteslehre', 140-290, esp. 26off.) The synthesis of the world of spirits lies in God. Only because we all come from God can we reach mutual understanding. Where the essential human encounter takes place, there is God; and in God the complete unity of all men is present in the spirit. Outside God each man is alien to the other, and there is only a plurality of atomistic I's. But this is not all that Fichte says. In his *The Science of Knowledge*, 1801-2, he sees the synthesis of the world of spirits as founded in certitude. Certitude necessarily presupposes universal consciousness as well as individual, and is itself neither of these, but absorbs them within itself. But universal consciousness comprises some kind of synthesis of spirits, not only from the epistemological but also from the ethical standpoint. Basically this is what Kant says, when he links the metaphysical category of the One and the social category of the species (the synthesis) in the concept of rational knowledge; as we have already seen, this was misguided and had unhappy results. Fichte's view must also be rejected as being

epistemologically false. For on an epistemological basis he draws conclusions about a fact which lies beyond epistemological comprehension. It is impossible to move from the idea of universal consciousness to the idea of the other man in the sociological sense. Fichte's basic concept of relation is not a social but a metaphysical category, namely, the unity of an undialectical synthesis, of sameness on the basis of likeness.

9. Cf. Hirsch, op. cit, 66ff., and Eberhard Grisebach, *Die Grenzen des Erziehers und seine Verantwortung*, 1925. The chapter was finished before I read Gogarten's *Ich glaube an den dreieinigen Gott*, 1926, which may also be consulted.

10. Only when God himself gives man the impulse, enters into him, is it possible to speak in the Christian sense of such an identification, and only from the standpoint of 'faith'.

11. This is not the place to discuss in what sense man is and is not a barrier for God (sin).

12. This conclusion cannot help recalling certain ideas of Fichte, the only idealist philosopher who felt the inadequacy of the idealist categories for mastering the problem of the 'other'. In connection with the question of the synthesis of the world of spirits (see above), Fichte concludes that one man cannot exist at all without kindling his own personal being at the other man. The realm of persons is thus closely united by this law of 'collision'; one man cannot be thought of without the other. But there is a decisive difference between Fichte's theory and our own. Fichte says that 'the concept of the Thou arises by union of the "It" and the "I" ' (*Werke*, ed. Medicus, III, 86, 1910, cf. Hirsch, op. cit. 236ff.), thus clearly ignoring any non-synthetic, original concept of Thou. For him the Thou is identical with the other I and at the same time an object. Both these ideas we have already rejected.

The other thinker who strove to achieve a concrete grasp of reality in this problem of the person is Kierkegaard. Our criticism of the idealist view of time and reality is close to his. But we differ where he speaks of the origin of the ethical person. For him to become a person is the act of the I establishing itself in a state of ethical decision. His ethical person exists only in the concrete situation, but it has no necessary connection with a concrete Thou. The I itself establishes the Thou; it is not established by it. Thus in the last resort Kierkegaard did not abandon the idealist position, and thus he founded an extreme individualism, which can only attribute a relative significance to the other (cf. below, on the sociology of the care of souls).

Notes to Chapter III

1. Cf. *Christliche Dogmatik*, Reinhold Seeberg, 1, 484.
2. This distinction, which is of course outdated, is used here for simplicity's sake. It is not important for the general argument.
3. To prevent misunderstanding, we present several pairs of concepts, essential to our argument, which have to be strictly distinguished. Structure and intention: the structure of the whole is visible only in the intention of individual acts, but is in principle independent of them. Thus a person's structural openness is not affected by 'intimate' intentions (to use Scheler's term), just as, conversely, structural unity does not affect social intentions. We must also distinguish between all acts that are real only in sociality, and the will for community. The former are indeed only acts in virtue of willing and thinking, but the will does not extend to the community as content, but the intention of the act, in accordance with its structure, is indirectly related to the community. Similarly, an intimate intention does not lead the agent out of the structural community. But the will for community leads to a concrete forming of basic ontic relationships, and the will to be a person leads to empirical solitude, without any effect upon the essential structure, which becomes visible in the intentions of the acts. Basically, these distinctions end in two different concepts of community, the first purely ontological, the second empirical. It is unfortunate that there are not two different words for these concepts. Later we have to give yet a third meaning to community, as a social type, and not the summary of all empirical groupings. But the context will always indicate the proper meaning. The distinctions must be borne in mind.
4. Cf. Hamann. Humboldt, too, spoke similarly. Cf., for instance, L. G. A. de Bonald, *Essai analythique sur les lois naturelles de l'ordre social ou du pouvoir du ministère et du sujet dans la société*, publ. anon. 1800, 2nd ed. 1817; and P. S. Ballanche, *Essai sur les institutions sociales*, 1818. De Bonald and Ballanche develop some highly imaginative ideas on the original community and its disintegration in present society. Their ideas about universal reason are traditional, recalling Hegel's view of objective spirit and ending in a glorification of the church.
5. Cf. Edmund Husserl, *Logische Untersuchungen*, vol. II, 3rd ed. 1922, 8ff. 'Ueber Bedeutungsintention und Bedeutungserfüllung'; Hans Freyer, *Theorie des objectiven Geistes*, 1923, 51; F. Mauthner, 'Die Sprache' in *Gesellschaft* by Martin Buber.

6. Cf. *Sozialpädagogik*, 2nd ed., 1904, 83ff. In the long introductory chapters Natorp seems to me to go beyond his neo-Kantian scheme. In his account of the three stages of the will, in particular, he penetrates deeply into a phenomenology of the will and of social being as a whole.

7. Scheler is certainly right in describing self-consciousness as a 'singularising act of the individual'. But this is just what expresses a man's intention to detach himself from the Thou as well as to enter into relations with it. This Scheler overlooks, as Litt has rightly pointed out. Litt maintains that in its involvement with the Thou the I learns 'to see itself through others' eyes', or rather, it learns that it can be observed 'from outside'. The danger is that the experience of the Thou is put before consciousness of self. But this is a contradiction: for if I know that I can be observed from outside, then I must clearly already have some knowledge of my 'self'. Natorp, op. cit., 'How could I become a Thou for myself, if there were not first a Thou facing me, in which I recognise another I?' (90) Cf. Scheler, *Formalismus*, 543, and Litt, *Individuum und Gemeinschaft*, 231ff.

8. Natorp, op. cit., 93. A more detailed philosophical discussion of this thesis cannot be given here. Cf. the writings of Natorp and Litt already mentioned.

9. Othmar Spann, *Gesellschaftslehre*, 103ff.

10. A theory of objective spirit will be given later.

11. See note 2 above.

12. The criterion for such acts is certainly not immediacy. Here Litt, rather than Scheler, is right (213). But it seems to me that Litt's fear that to accept the idea of intimate personal acts would run the risk of establishing stratifications in structure and substance within the I, between an intimate and a social part of the person, thus destroying the essential unity of the I, does not enter into consideration for us. So long as the one person is conceived as having his place only in sociality, the direction of the person's intentions cannot affect the issue.

13. There is no difference in principle here between Fichte's earlier synthesis of the world of spirits (in the light of the goal) and his later synthesis (in the light of the origin). Cf. Hirsch, op. cit., 140ff. The question simply proves that it is possible to isolate the I. It is more correct to speak of thesis than of synthesis. Fichte's ultimate basis for the Thou is the union of the It and the I.

14. Cf. Kistiakowski, *Einzelwesen und Gesellschaft*, 1899 cc. 1 and 2.

15. Scheler (*Formalismus*, 540ff.) sees the sense in this assumption. W. Stern (*Die menschliche Persönlichkeit*, 40ff.) agrees with Scheler. E. Stein (*Individuum und Gesellschaft*, 250ff.) modifies the idea in her

discussion of Scheler. Litt (op. cit. 234ff., 26off.) rejects it.

16. Rousseau, for instance, committed the error of confusing these two questions. If with his idea of the social contract (the book written in 1754, printed in condensed form in 1762) he meant to say that all specifically human community has its essential basis in the conscious being possessed of a will, then we should be able to agree with him. His error, however, consists in the fact that (1) the conscious will of the individual is introduced in the wrong place, appearing already in the origin of organic social formations, such as marriage in its most primitive forms, and in particular (2) that this will is conceived of as being purely contractual, which would mean that all empirical social units should be thought of as having arisen from such a contract. This, however, is sociologically untenable. Sociologically a contract cannot be conceived of without the underlying social ethos supporting the idea that a contract is binding (cf. Vierkandt, *Gesellschaftslehre*, para. 29). The interpretation of marriage as a form of economic life (Kant, opposed by Hegel) is one that would never be capable of fully comprehending monogamy (Kant, *Metaphysische Anfangsgründe der Rechtslehre*, para. 24, Hegel, *Naturrecht*, para. 161).

17. From this it follows that the 'social categories', for instance of statistics, such as of drinkers, unmarried people, suicides, etc., cannot be considered as communities either. These distinctions are already treated in the study of logic. Cf. Sigwort, *Logik*, 2nd ed., vol. II, 1893, 662ff.; F. Kistiakowski, *Einzelwesen und Gesellschaft*, 111ff., 117ff.

18. This in opposition to Schumann's recent definition (*Zeitschrift für systematische Theologie*, 1926-7, no. 4) of the social unity which, he says, is present 'if every soul in question knows of every (!) other soul that is at one with it in that unity which is comprised in self-relation to a common aim; or, as we may more briefly say, at one with it in the common act of willing'. Cf. for example Gerd Walther 'Zur Ontologie der sozialen Gemeinschaften', op. cit., 132. The reciprocal act of the will has no place in the list she presents of the thirteen constituents of community.

19. It was Hobbes who was probably the first to express the purely social significance of strife. He saw the origin and sense of socialisation in the *bellum omnium contra omnes*, and Kant, with reservations, agreed with this (*Religion within the Limits of Pure Reason*, III, 1.2). But Hobbes was only seeking to present the theory of the contract, and the status *belli omnium in omnes* (as Kant amended the expression) is something which essentially exists before and outside society. It is to regulate this state, so to speak, that the social contract is entered into (Rousseau, see above). Kant sees

'antagonism' as the spiritual principle that drives society forward (*Ideen zu einer allgemeinen Geschichte in weltbürgerlicher Absicht*, fourth proposition). Attraction and repulsion always go together; in strife life, talent and art develop. 'Man wants harmony, but Nature has a better knowledge of what is good for the human race; Nature wants discord' (Kant *ibid.*).

20. Seeberg, *Christliche Dogmatik* I, 513.
21. Tönnies, *Gemeinschaft und Gesellschaft*, 6th ed., 1926, 103, has distinguished between 'essential will' (*Wesenwille*) and 'arbitrary will' (*Kürwille*). (Eng. tr., *Community and Association*, 1955, 136ff., 'natural and rational will'). The distinction we shall make does not correspond to this, because Tönnies confuses the phenomenological analysis of the acts of the will and the social structures with a genetic method of observation, a proceeding which, following the principles we have so far evolved, must be rejected as unmethodical. Clearly for Tönnies the genesis of social structures assumed a heuristic significance for his phenomenological analysis, so that he was unable to break away from it again. The genetic method does in fact come close to the truth here, but its application to the concept of the church, for instance, would bring results which we shall later show are faulty, as they appear in the works of Troeltsch. Even Scheler often seems to lapse into the genetic method of observation, instead of following the phenomenological one at which he is consciously aiming. In order to overcome this error we shall keep purely to the social acts of the will which we consider essential, and analyse them alone, deducing the typology of the communities from them.
22. Cf. Tönnies's definitions, op. cit., I, para. I and 19; the distinction between the organic and the real formation of the community, and the ideal and mechanical formation of the society. Freyer, in his *Theorie des objectiven Geistes*, 53ff. comes close to the Aristotelian conception.
23. Windelband, *Einleitung in die Philosophie*, 2nd ed., 1919, 'Willensgemeinschaften', 306.
24. See the conclusive proof in Scheler, *Formalismus*, 552ff.; further Vierkandt, *Gesellschaftslehre*, para. 29.
25. von Gierke, *Das deutsche Genossenschaftsrecht*, esp. I, 1868, 12-140.
26. I cannot agree with Schumann's view *Zeitschrift für systematische Theologie*, 1926-7, 691, that associations of authority do not create a unity because A, who is giving the order, seeks to have B's will directed towards the alteration X, whereas B, who is obeying it, only wants the alteration X, which means that the will's object in each case is different. B, however, does not want X, but

wants to conform to A's will, which consists in the guiding of B towards X.

27. Vierkandt, op. cit., 427; Le Bon, *Psychologie des Foules*, 1895 (Eng. tr., *The Crowd, a Study of the Popular Mind*, 1896). Simmel, *Grundfragen*, 41ff.

28. This is why people come to confuse the awareness of unity present in the mass, and the feeling of community; as in my opinion Vierkandt does (cf. 202ff.), in including the theatre, the literary circle, the philosopher's republic and also the idea of the invisible church under the notion of elevating communities. This is clearly to overlook the intermediary concept of the public, which, however, is a subsidiary of the concept of the mass.

29. Schumann (op. cit., 690) answers this question in the negative, but we maintain the opposite. It is a sign of Tönnies's profound view that he writes (op. cit., 5) 'Community is enduring and authentic life together, society is transient and illusory.' This view is confirmed phenomenologically.

30. This in opposition to Freyer, *Theorie des objectiven Geistes*, 53ff. 'It is just as complicated, but just as possible in principle, to formulate the teleological structure of meaning of a moral association or the community of a people, as it is of the aesthetic structure of meaning in a symphony.'

31. Cf. Seeberg, *Dogmenschichte* vol. II, 3rd ed., 263ff.; Troeltsch, *Soziallehren der christlichen Kirchen und Gruppen;* Schilling, *Die Christlichen Soziallehren*, 1926.

32. Troeltsch, op. cit., 93ff.; Schilling, op. cit., 45ff., 79ff.

33. Schilling, op. cit., 59ff.

34. Troeltsch's terminology.

35. Seeberg, op. cit., 503, 3.

36. Schilling, op. cit., 58: 'State law is nothing but an institution of reason, enacted by the wielder of power for the protection of the whole, and for the maintenance of the common weal. This is essentially the view found as early as Tertullian.'

37. Augustine, *de bono conjug.* 1.

38. Schilling, against Troeltsch, op. cit., 77. As proof of this the Fathers often adduced the divine grace of the emperor.

39. Later Aegidius of Rome defended private property in *de regime principium*.

40. Troeltsch, op. cit., 127: 'As presupposing pleasure in possession and gain, trade was suspect to the ascetic view, as taking from one what it gives to the other, and to the attitude of love it was suspect as enriching itself with the goods of others.'

41. The fitting of the monastic orders into the organism is somewhat difficult for a formal concept of equality like that of Troeltsch.

42. Cf. especially Maurenbrecher, *Thomas Stellung zu dem Wirtschaftsleben seiner Zeit*, 1898.
43. Cf. Seeberg, *Dogmengeschichte*, vol. II, 3rd ed., 406ff., 501ff.
44. Thomas, *Summa Theologica*, I, 2 para. 81, 1.
45. Cf. Hegel, *Philosophie des Geistes*, paras. 483ff.; Hans Freyer, *Theorie des objektiven Geistes*.
46. Cf. pp. 87ff.
47. Litt, *Individuum und Gemeinschaft*, 260. 'The structural principle which we called social involvement precludes the forming of any particular supra-personal centre of action, but at the same time renders any return to such centre of action superfluous.' Why then should only the individual person have monadic being? Litt would probably answer: because only the individual has a body. But the community too has a body (see below). Thus in my opinion the introduction of collective persons does not do away with the idea of the monadic image (see also above). Cf. Litt's excellent critique of organology, 279ff., and also Scheler, *Formalismus*, 540ff., on the collective person. Scheler's sociological thesis has as its starting-point the life-community, seen as the entity which engulfs the individual. Opposing this there is the society, which has its basis in individual I's. The highest form of social being is then, in Scheler's view, the Christian idea of community, 'the unity of autonomous, spiritual, individual single persons, in an autonomous, spiritual, individual collective person' (p. 555). Its moral law of life is solidarity (cf. *Phänomenologie und Theorie der Sympathiegefühle*, 1913, 65ff.). At the deepest level there are only two pure collective persons; those of a civilisation, and the church (p. 668). Thus for Scheler the church is ultimately an entity which deploys itself in the moral world, and is morally sacred; with this, however, he has arrived at most of the idea of religious community, but not at that of the church. In so far as the sociological structure is concerned, he has failed to understand it in all its depth, since he lacks an understanding of the concept of Christian love.
48. Freyer, *Theorie des objektiven Geistes*, 61.
49. Hegel's *Philosophy of Right*, tr. T. M. Knox, 1942, para. 156.
50. Freyer, op. cit., 81.
51. Scheler, op. cit., 413ff., 566.

Notes to Chapter IV

1. Two preliminary remarks: in the history of dogmatics the false translation of ἐφ' ᾧ (Rom. 5.12) by *in quo* has had a devastating

effect. It was thought that the core of a physical doctrine of original sin could be seen here, even though I Cor. 15.22 should have proved that this idea was impossible, with its 'in Christ' alongside 'in Adam'. Further, it is to be noted that Paul does not regard the analogy between Adam and Christ as complete. This is clear without his actually saying it. Adam is man by nature, he is also the first man, he stands in history. His sin was the 'first' sin. But in a qualitive sense there are only 'first' sins (see below). Christ was man and God, he stood both in and beyond history. In so far as Adam is *the* man, he can be set over against Christ as the representative of the old mankind, in contrast to the new, in a limited analogy.

2. The concept of the mass presented here is not a sociological concept of a social structure, but gathers together a number of persons from one standpoint.

3. Cf. Seeberg, *Dogmengeschichte* II, 504ff. We cannot go into the matter of Augustine's theological ambiguity.

4. Since scholasticism there have been various efforts to establish an ethical idea of mankind. Anselm, with his background of Realism, sees in mankind a single substantial reality. Through the fall of the one man the one mankind was also bound to fall (*de fide terin* II). Duns Scotus attributes the lost of the divine image to a divine decree, Thomas Aquinas emphasises the physical and moral unity of man in Adam. The physical unity consists of the Adamic nature of man: '*omnes homines qui nascuntur ex Adam possunt considervri ut unus homo, in quantum conveniunt in natura*' (*Summa Theol.* 1, 2, qu. 81.1). Thomas establishes the moral unity as consisting in the fact that the members of a community are regarded as *unum corpus*, while the community is regarded as *unus homo* (*in civilibus omnes homines sunt qui unius communitatis reputantur quasi unum corpus et tota communitas quasi unus homo . . . sic igitur multi homines ex Adam derivati sunt, tanquam multa membra unius corporis* (1, 2, 82.1)). The individual person of one man stands within the collective person of the human race. But from this point Thomas turns for clarity to the biological image of the organism. The member does not have free will, but must act in accordance with the will of the head. If in the first case the Augustinian view of nature is not overcome, in the second case we hear of the moral solidarity of all people, and in the third case the exclusive responsibility is ascribed to the head of the body. Posttridentine Roman theology has taken up the problem at this point, and developed the theory of the decree of God and his covenant with Adam (following Duns Scotus). (Cf. Busch, *Lehre von der Erbsünde bei Bellarmin und Suarez*, 70ff., 171ff., 186; and Ambros. Catharinus, *De casu hominis et peccato originali*, 184: '*ipso existentes*

ratione simul naturae et pacti.' So also Suarez. The biblical basis is
Gen. 2.16ff.) None of these to reach an ethical view of mankind
could succeed so long as they clung to a biological view of man,
connected with the Roman view of infant baptism.

5. Ritschl, *Rechtfertigung und Versöhnung*, 2nd ed., vol. III, 311ff.
6. Cf. Seeberg, *Dogmatik*, II, 49ff., who was the first to express this
idea. Thus, at page 52, 'however paradoxical it may sound, it is
understandable that men have been able to spread their anti-
social egoism in virtue of their social disposition.'

Notes to Chapter V

1. F. Kattenbusch, *Das apostolische Symbol*, II, 928ff., makes it clear that
this word-order was the original one. The earliest source for this is
Jerome, *Epistle* 17, between 374 and 397. The fact that Nicetas of
Remesiana (c.400) uses the opposite word-order is certainly striking,
but this may be explained from the construction of the sentence
(*De symbolo* 10; cf. Burn, *Niceta of Remesiana*, 1905, 48). Moreover,
a few lines earlier the sentence occurs: *ecclesia quid aliud quam
sanctorum omnium congregatio?* (Kirsch, *Lehre von der Gemeinschaft der
Heiligen im christlichen Altertum*, 1900, 217, n. 4, and 215ff.; English
tr., *The Doctrine of the Communion of Saints in the Ancient Church*, 1911,
257, n. 4, and 254ff.). On the question whether it is *sancti* or *sancta*
in the *sanctorum communio*, and who are intended by the *sancti*, see
the relevant literature: Theodor Zahn, *Das apostolische Symbol*,
1893, 91ff.; Kattenbusch, op. cit., 941f.; Harnack, *Das Apostolische Symbol*, 32ff.; Kirsch, op. cit., 220ff.; Seeberg, *Dogmengeschichte* II, 1923, 465ff., n. 4. Without being able to give full
evidence here, it is my view that the original form was certainly
sancti; but it is hard to say whether the saints in heaven or
Christendom was intended. There is much in favour of the first
(Kirsch, op. cit., 220ff.). In our study the concept is referred to the
church of Christ, 'the company of the saints' (Seeberg). Admittedly, this idea of a company in the sense of a co-operative group
cannot be used by us, in view of the definition we have already
given. We shall speak of a communion or a community of saints,
though as we shall see these do not mean precisely the same thing.
2. (1, 82) Calvin, *Institutio*, 1536, III, 14.11.
3. (2, 82) Weimar edition of Luther's collected works, II, 457 (referred
to hereafter as 'W. ed.')
4. (1, 86) *Formalismus*, 91f.
5. (1, 88) Luther, from whom Scheler might have been able to learn

something here, had already made this point. W. ed. IV, 401:
quia spiritualia habent hanc naturam, ut non possint dividi in diversa, sed diversos et divisos colligunt in unum.

6. (2, 88) H. Scholz, *Religionsphilosophie*, 2nd ed., 1922, esp. 115ff.

7. Simmel, in *Die Religion*, 24ff., has some perceptive comments on this point.

8. This definition seems at first to ignore the primitive religions. But this is not really so. Cf. Seeberg, *Dogmatik* I, 70-7. It seems to me right that genuine Buddhism is not included in our definition. Its development into a religion only came after the Buddha was deified.

9. Friedrich Heiler, *Das Gebet*, 4th ed., 53ff.

10. Cf. Durkheim, *Les formes elementaires de la vie religieuse—le totémisme*, 1912. Durkheim attempts to make totemism the sole source of all social life, and especially of the religious social life. The establishment of brotherhood, through a common meal of a cultic animal, with common rights and duties, led later to the animal being regarded as the symbol of a community, and this has certainly had considerable influence on sexual, family and economic life. But the extent of this influence was not as great as Durkheim supposed.

11. Cf. Weber, *Wirtschaft und Gesellschaft*, 228.

12. ibid., 250ff., and Seeberg, *Dogmatik* I, 52ff.

13. Holl, *Kirchenkampf des Paulus in seinem Verhältnis zu dem der Urgemeinde*, Sitzungsbericht der preussischen Akademie, 1921, 920ff.

14. ibid., 932.

15. Cf. especially Cremer, *Bibl. Theol. Wörterbuch*, 'Ekklesia', 480, Scheel, 'Kirche', 13, Sohm, 'Kirchenrecht', 16ff., Köstlin, P.K.E.3, 'Kirche', Traugott Schmidt, *Der Leib Christi*, 113ff., Kattenbusch, *Quellort der Kirchenidee*, Harnack, *Festgabe*, 1921, 143ff.

16. Cf. Harnack, *Mission und Ausbreitung des Christentums*, 4th ed., 1924, I, 410-33.

17. Schmidt, op. cit., 120.

18. Cf. Dorner, *Grundriss der Dogmenschichte*, 1899, 40, B. Weiss, *Biblische Theologie*, §105, Beyschlag, *N. T. liche Theologie* II, 226ff., Gloel, *Der Heilige Geist*, 303ff., Holtzmann, *N. T. liche Theologie* II, 191ff., Feine, *Theologie des NT*, 446ff., Alfred Krauss, *Dogma von der unsichtbaren Kirche*, 124ff.

19. Cf. Seeberg, *Dogmatik* II, 320ff., with which I agree.

20. I agree with Schmidt's exegesis of the passages, op. cit., 135.

21. This does not exclude the Holy Spirit giving Christ to the individual heart, Gal. 2.20, Phil. 1.21, or the Holy Spirit being at work in the church.

22. v. Hofmann, Commentary to I Cor. 12.12, 'Christ is the I of the community of his body.'

23. Cf. Kattenbusch, 'Quellort der Kirchenidee', *Harnackfestgabe*, 1921, 143ff., where a similar conclusion is reached to that of Schmidt in *Der Leib Christi*. Christ and the church are regarded as being identical, without, it is true, any mystical conceptions being linked with this idea (this latter point in opposition to Schmidt). Whereas Schmidt is still chary (p. 154) of making the equation, after the example of Bousset (II Cor. 5.17 and elsewhere), between 'in Christ' and 'in the church', Kattenbusch states that he approves of this (p. 157). ἐνδύσασθαι τὸν χριστόν is incorporation in the church. Thus to Paul it is the same whether a man lives **ἐν** χριστῷ or ἐν ἐκκλησίᾳ; ἐν Ἰησοῦ never occurs as a mystical expression. Cf. Deissmann, *In Christo Jesu: Die neutestamentliche Formel untersucht*, 1892, vi.

24. πλήρωμα here means 'vessel'.

25. Schmidt, op. cit., 154: 'When the community enters Christ, it is not only turned around by his person, but it fuses with him and is absorbed in him.' Feine speaks of the 'mystical depth' of the idea of the church (op. cit. 447). Holtzmann discusses the doctrine of the church under the title 'Mysteriousness' and speaks of 'mystical life of association' (194), and then coins the happy formula, 'the social miracle'. The reference to the mysticism of the idea of the church is very ancient, and owes a lot to the concept of the *corpus mysticum* taken from Eph. 5.32.

26. Cf. Althaus, *Die Letzten Dinge*, 3rd ed., 1926, 155 and 169ff.; also Augustine Ep. 208, 2ff.

27. Cf. Kistiakowski, *Gesellschaft und Einzelwesen*, 1898, cc. 1 and 2.

28. Cf. Hofmann, *Erste Schutzschrift*, 1856, 19. Cf. also *Schriftbeweis* 1, 1852, chap. 6.

29. A. Ritschl, *Rechtfertigung und Versöhnung* 1, 621 (Eng. tr., *A Critical History of the Christian Doct. of Just. & Recon.*, 1872, 546), quoting Hofmann loc. cit.

30. Irenaeus, *Adversus haereses* III, 24.1.

31. Thus Scheler, *Formalismus*, 555ff.

32. Schleiermacher too finds a theological basis for this scattering of the disciples (*The Christian Faith*, para. 122.2): 'We find the disciples in the mood thus to disperse after Christ's death, and up to the time of His Ascension their life together was so much interrupted and decreased as to become quite formless. But even when Christ was alive it could not but be that each felt mainly dependent on Him, and sought to receive from Him; no one of them all considered himself ripe for free spontaneous activity in the Kingdom of God yet to be formed.' Jesus had addressed himself to the disciples' receptivity, they were completely dependent upon him. Only the Holy Spirit brought about their independent activity and

reunion. To this it can be objected: 1. Schleiermacher equates the events of Ascension Day and of Pentecost (paras. 122, 1 and 2). Yet the church was assembled with one accord in prayer and supplication before Pentecost (Acts 1.14-2.1), that is before the imparting of the Spirit. 2. Schl's. distinction between receptivity and spontaneous activity is theologically dubious, as he himself realises (para. 122, 3). In so far as Christ acts, he makes us fully into recipients, but also fully into independent agents. This Schleiermacher also admits later, but the spontaneous action, he says, became truly 'joint' action only after Christ's departure, and it was only then that he could manifest himself as Holy Spirit.

33. If the church's temporal determination is posited in Christ, the action of the Holy Spirit comes under the church's spatial intention.

34. Cf. I Cor. 15.24. See further Luther's exposition, Erlangen ed. 51, 159—and Karl Barth's pertinent observations in *The Resurrection of the Dead*, 1933, 172f.

35. Seeberg, *Dogmatii.*: II, 271ff.

36. There is, however, also an ethical idea of vicarious action, meaning the voluntary acceptance of an evil by one man in another man's stead. It does not involve the other man's self-responsibility, and as an act of humanly heroic love (for one's country, friend, etc.) it remains in the sphere of the highest ethical obligation even of the man acting vicariously. In acknowledging it a man does not set his whole ethical person at stake, but only what he owes to the one who acted vicariously in each case (his body, honour, money, etc.), whereas he acknowledges Christ as acting vicariously for his entire person, and thus owes his entire person to him.

37. Schleiermacher, for example, did not perceive this connection. There are two conflicting lines of thought on the nature of the church. Cf. Seeberg, *Begriff der christlichen Kirche*, 1884, 202ff.—Krauss, *Das protestantische Dogma von der unsichtbaren Kirche*, 1876, 103ff.—A. Ritschl, T. & R. I *Rechtfertigung und Versöhnung*, ET, 445ff., 475f. This can be shown briefly as follows. 'The Christian church takes shape through the coming together of regenerate individuals to form a system of mutual interaction and co-operation' (*The Christian Faith*, para. 115). 'If there is religion at all, it must be social . . . you must confess that when an individual has produced and wrought out something in his own mind, it is morbid and in the highest degree unnatural to wish to reserve it to himself' (*On Religion*, Fourth Speech, 1958, 148). The basis for the formation of religious community lies in the individual's need to communicate. The church is the satisfaction of a need, its

construction is individualistic. The famous words in *The Christian Faith*, that Protestantism makes the relation of the individual to the church dependent upon his relation to Christ (para. 24) points in the same direction; here clearly individual communion with Christ is conceived of independently of the church. Opposing this there is the idea of the church as the entity present before any individual, outside which there is no religious self-consciousness (*ibid.* para. 113), and the entire doctrine of the collective life of sin and grace, of the shared Holy Spirit engulfing the individual. This contradiction was noted by Ritschl, who interpreted it as meaning that Schleiermacher accorded ultimate precedence to the Individual over the communal, in that the latter is given only historical, preparatory significance (paras. 113.2 and 122.3) for the evolution of the Individual. Thus while the community takes temporal precedence over individuals, individuals are nevertheless those who 'would have co-operated in the founding of such a communion if it had not been there already' (para. 6.2), so that the congregation is at every moment created anew by the individuals' need. If this were not so Schleiermacher could not have said that it is the individual's life in communion with Christ which first establishes his attitude to the church, and only thus can he assert that the basic sociological structure of the church is the individual's need to communicate. In his thinking the individualism of social philosophy, which is, however, not 'personalism', although occasionally it seems indeed to become such, as for instance in this very idea of the individual's life in communion with Christ, clashes with a spirit-monism, a pantheism which should, I think, nevertheless in the last analysis be interpreted as a result of this concept of the person. Only thus can one explain such diverse judgments as that of P. Althaus, *Das Erlebnis der Kirche*, 1924, 8: 'Schleiermacher proceeds from the individual and justifies the church as a religious community thus: "Man feels that he must communicate . . . thus the church arises as a free association"—and that of A. Krauss, op. cit., 103: "Schleiermacher thus quite ignores the proposition which previously had had axiomatic force, that in defining the church one must proceed from the individuals who make up the *coetus*. He proceeds instead from the quality of the spirit mightily manifesting itself in them." '

38. E. Lohmeyer, *Zum Begriff der religiösen Gemeinschaft*, 1925, 42ff., 44: 'The possibility one has of drawing back becomes a duty for the believer.'

39. Kierkegaard, who was almost without equal in his ability to speak of the burden of loneliness, makes it the reason for rejecting the idea of the church (cf. *Furcht und Zittern*, ed. H. Gottsched and C.

Schrempf, 1922, 171). 'From the moment the individual has entered the sphere of paradox, it is impossible for him to arrive at the idea of the church' (106; cf. Eng. tr., *Fear and Trembling*, 1939, 107).

40. Scheler, *Formalismus*, 587: 'The idea, on the other hand, that the individual person, resting solely and exclusively upon this his lonely relationship with God, must first master the idea of solidarity by means of this necessary détour, would be a denial of the essential idea of the church itself.' And the note to this: 'This denial has many forms. Historically, for instance, it is just as much implied in the consequential doctrine of election by grace as in that of justification by faith; for according to both doctrines the community of love and salvation, in its solidarity, is not an intercourse with God which is as original and necessary as the immediate intercourse of the intimate person with God. Both are presented as being first derived from this intimate relationship.' In simply equating the teaching of election by grace and that of justification Scheler is overlooking the entire problem of the Word.

41. Thomas Aquinas, it is true, gives another definition of the church's compass, as according to him those who are not predestined are also members of the church. *Summa theologica* III, 8.3: *'ecclesia constituitur ex hominibus qui fuerunt a principio mundi usque ad finem ipsius . . . sic igitur membra corporis mystici accipiuntur non solum secundum quod sunt in actu, sed etiam secundum quod sunt in potentia . . . qui in potentia sunt ei uniti, quae nunquam reducetur ad actum, sicut homines in hoc mundo viventes qui non sunt praedestinati.'* This we cannot accept. Cf. W. ed. VI, 302: 'A head must be incorporated with its body . . . hence Christ cannot be a head in common with any evil member.' The stimulus for the use of the doctrine of predestination for the idea of the church had already been given by the ancient church, by Augustine. But it is wrong to think that Augustine's idea of the *sanctorum communio* is entirely contained in the doctrine of predestination (Holl, *Augustins innere Entwicklung*, Akademische Abhandluangen, Berlin, 1922, 41ff.). On the contrary, his idea of the *sanctorum communio* was merely disturbed by the idea of predestination; he developed a view of the *sanctorum communio* which had a tremendous wealth of content, and compares well with Luther's. R. Seeberg, *Dogmengeschichte* 3rd. ed., Vol. II, 1923, 464ff., and *Begriff der christlichen Kirche*, 38ff. Wycliffe (*Trialogus lib.* IV.22) was the first to present a purely predestinarian idea of the church. He was joined by Huss, and later by Zwingli (Huss, *Tractatus de ecclesia*, esp. chs. 1-7), whose frank division of the idea of the church into three parts (predestined church, individual local church,

universal church), merely succeeded in making the embarrassment quite evident. The definition of the church's compass cannot tell us anything about its nature. Krauss, op. cit., p.16: 'The definition *praedestinatorum universitas* is no answer at all to the question of the nature and concept of the church. We must first have the concept of the whole as such, before we can· reflect upon the individual parts.'

42. Cf. J. Kaftan, *Dogmatik*, 4th ed. para. 63, 597.

43. Seeberg, *Dogmatik* II, 339f.: Ritschl, *Justification and Reconciliation* III, 1900, 320: 'If therefore God eternally loves the community of the Kingdom of God (Eph. 1.4f.), He also loves already the individuals who are to be gathered into it, in so far as He purposes to bring them into the kingdom.'

44. Holl, *Luther*, 293, n. 3.

45. I call attention for all that follows to *Communio Sanctorum*, 1929, by P. Althaus. Unfortunately it appeared so late that I was unable to use it fully, but had to confine myself to references on some points of detail. I was of course delighted to find there the fullest possible illustration, through Luther, of important parts of the present work.

46. Lohmeyer, *Zum Begriff der religiösen Gemeinschaft*, 62.

47. Cf. Karl Barth, *The Epistle to the Romans* (ET of 6th ed., 1933), esp. 451ff., 492ff. I cannot agree with the way in which in that commentary he interprets the command to love, or with the idea of community that he deduces from it. 'Love is the still more excellent (incomprehensible) way (I Cor. 12.31), the eternal meaning of our comprehensible ways, and the realisation of their "highest places". Love is therefore human religious impossibility—when it is apprehended as the possibility of God: in other words, love is the fulfilling of the law' (493ff.). Again, 'In the visible and concrete existence of our contemporaries the problem of God is therefore formulated concretely and in such a manner as to demand a concrete answer' (452). That is certainly a legitimate way of putting it. 'In the concrete fact of the neighbour we encounter, finally and supremely, the ambiguity of our existence, since in the particularity of others we are reminded of our own particularity, of our own createdness, our own lost state, our own sin, and our own death' (494). This too we can accept. But he then goes on to say that the nature of love of one's neighbour is 'in . . . the other . . . to hear the voice of the One' (ibid.). Again, 'we must acknowledge that our most questionable "I" is one with the "Thou" by which we are confronted. . . . In Christ . . . I am not only one with God, but, because "with God", one also with the neighbour' (495). The relationship to the other man 'is to be related to the Primal Origin'

(454), and yet all deeds of love do not aim at a result, but are pure sacrifice, obedience in the sight of him who confronts our sacrifice in his 'freedom . . . as God' (452). While we can agree with this last statement, we maintain that love really loves the other man, and not the One in him—who perhaps does not exist (double pre-destination! Barth, 452)—and that it is precisely this love for the other man as the other man by which 'God . . . must be honoured' (453). What authority has Barth for saying that the other 'in him-self is trivial and temporal' (452), when this is the very man that God commands us to love? God has made our neighbour 'of supreme significance' in himself, and for us there is no other way in which he is important 'in himself'. The other man is not only 'a parable of the Wholly Other . . . the emissary' of the unknown God; but he is of supreme significance in himself, because God considers him significant (ibid.). Am I ultimately to be alone in the world with God? Is not the other man as a real man to receive his rights infinitely through God's command? We are not speak-ing of 'the other man's eternal soul', but of God's will for him, and we believe that we can apprehend the will of God in all earnestness only as it is manifested in the concrete form of the other man. Cf. R. Bultmann, *Jesus and the Word*, 1935, 115: 'Whatever of kindness, pity, mercy, I show my neighbour is not something which I do for God; . . . the neighbour is not a sort of tool by means of which I practise the love of God. . . . As I can love my neighbour only when I surrender my will completely to God's will, so I can love God only while I will what he wills, while I really love my neighbour.' The second difference between Barth and ourselves is in our con-ception of *communio*. 'To be one' with God and with one's neigh-bour is something totally different from having communion with him. Barth, however, makes the two things synonymous. Where there is only love of the One in the other there can be no *communio* for here there is ultimately a creeping danger of Romanticism. Cf. for the whole Kierkegaard, *Leben und Walten der Liebe*, ed. A. Dorner and C. Schrempf, 1924.

48. Schleiermacher motivates love for all men as follows: 'No one can be aware of the divine spirit unless he is at the same time aware that the whole human race belongs to this spirit. The difference between individuals is only one of time, namely that some already have the *pneuma hagion*, whereas others have not yet received it' (*Christliche Sitte*, ed. L. Jonas, vii.ii, 514). This is an impossible method of finding a basis for love, since apocatastasis can at most be an ultimate word of eschatological thinking, not a self-evident point of departure for a dogmatic train of thought. Materially we have rejected the biological formulation of the idea of mankind,

as we have the anthropological formulation of the idea of the *pneuma*.

49. Luther, *Römerbrief*, ed. Ficker, I, 118.

50. *Wesen und Form der Sympathiegefühle*, 1923 (ET, *The nature of Sympathy*, 1954).

51. *The Christian Faith*, para. 165, 1. Cf. in opposition to this Ritschl, *Justification and Reconciliation* III, 277f.; love is a constant attitude of will when it 'strives to . . . appropriate the individual self-end of the other personality, regarding this as a task necessary to the very nature of its own personal end.' This idea of ends was bound to follow as soon as love was conceived of as volitional. Häring, for example, attempts a synthesis: 'Love is the desire for fellowship . . . for the realisation of common ends' (*The Christian Faith*, 1913, I, 340), without making the necessary distinction. Seeberg aptly defines love as the community of ends in which the one who loves makes himself the means for the other's achievement of his end (*Dogmatik* II, 322).

52. Is it mere chance that in I Cor. 13 there is no mention of love's will for communion?

53. Seeberg, *Dogmatik* II, 324.

54. Luther, *Disputations*, ed. P. Drews, 1895-6, 450f.; *christianus est persona, quae iam sepulta est cum Christo in morte eius, mortuus peccato, legi, morti . . . sed hoc ipsum non cernitur, sed est absconditum in mundo, non apparet, non occurit in oculos nostros . . . in praesenti saeculo non vivit, mortuus est, versatur in alia vita longe supra hac posita, coelesti . . . sed e contra christianus in quantum miles et in militia versatur, hic etiam sentit et expetit quotidie militiam carnis suae.* Cf. 452—W. ed. LVI, 58: *haec vita non habet experientiam sui, sed fidem; nemo enim scit se vivere aut experitur se esse iustificatum sed credit et sperat. Römerbrief*, W. ed. II, 457.

55. W. ed. V, 165: *Oportet enim non modo credere, sperare, diligere, sed etiam scire et certum esse se credere, sperare, diligere.* Cf. O. Piper, *Theologie und reine Lehre*, 1926, 5: 'In faith all we can ever do is just believe that God has given our hearts the proper faith. . . .'

56. Cf. Seeberg, *Dogmengeschichte* II, 464ff.—*Begriff der Kirche*, 38ff.—Augustine's doctrine of the *sanctorum communio* is to a certain extent foreshadowed by earlier Christian writers, cf. Augustine, *Bapt.* v, 21 (29) (Migne, PL 43.191): *Sacramentum gratiae dat deus etiam per malos, ipsam vero gratiam non nisi per se ipsum vel per sanctos suos.*

57. Cf. Althaus, *Erlebnis der Kirche*, 16. 'Only the church which worships and loves is an end in itself in the full sense to the eternal God, as his goal for the world.'

58. Recent sociological works have asserted that the idea of the *sanctorum communio* is based upon an indirect, non-immediate

linking together in a communion. Cf. Spann, *Gesellschaftslehre*, 144f. 'The communion of saints: in it, if I understand aright, the saints are conceived of as beholding only God directly, while among themselves they are linked only by their similar bond with the divine Being . . . in accordance with his own wish to be a sacred, distinct state, and not a social one.' Even in the greatest work we have on theological sociology we find the proposition that the saints are solely in God, and are thus linked only indirectly with each other. (Cf. Troeltsch, *The Social Teaching of the Christian Churches*, 1931, 56: 'In the last resort the idea of fellowship springs from the fact that those who are being purified for the sake of God meet in Him.') cf. Scheler, *Formalismus*, 519.

59. W. ed. x, Part 1.1, 100—IV, 280; Holl, *Luther*, 101.

60. W. ed. II, 750. *Sermon von dem Hochwürdigen Sakrament des heiligen wahren Leichnams Christi*, 1519. Here Luther presents some splendid and profound thoughts upon the question.

61. Ibid., 749: '. . . Thus we too are truly drawn and transformed into the spiritual body, that is, into the communion of Christ and all saints. . . .' 750: 'That is to say transformed through love in each other.' Baader expresses this by saying that 'with the blood of Christ's sacrifice' the heart's blood of each individual man was made fluid again and thus made free; in this wise man was delivered and redeemed from the petrifaction of his selfhood. *Schriften zur Gesellschaftsphilosophie, Die Herdflamme*, 781.

62. Lohmeyer, *Zum Begriff der religiösen Gemenschaft*, 83 . . . 'This expression of a state where all things melt into one, which no longer knows the frontiers between the I and the Thou, because in its religious exuberance it overlooks, as indeed it is bound to do, the basic fact of the I's singularity.'

63. W. ed. II, 749: 'Our sins afflict him just as in return his righteousness is our protection.'

64. Ibid., 745.

65. *Tesseradecas consolatoria pro laborantibus et oneratis*, 1520. W. ed. VI, 131: *onus meum portant alii, illorum virtus mea est, castitas aliorum meae libidinis tentationem suffert, aliorum ieiunia mea lucra sunt, alterius oratio pro me sollicita est. Atque ita vere congloriari possum in aliorum bonis, tanquam meis propriis, atque tunc vere et mea sunt, sic gratulor et congaudeo eis . . . eorum merita (!) meis medebuntur peccatis.*

66. Ibid., 132: *quare si dolemus, si patimur, si morimur, huc feratur intutus, et fortiter credamus ac certi simus, quod non nos aut non soli, sed Christus et Ecclesia nobiscum dolet, patitur, moritur . . . comite tota Ecclesia viam passionis et mortis ingredimur.*

67. W. ed. II, 745.

68. W. ed. 10. III, 1; 9th March, 1522.

69. This phrase 'the communion of saints dies with' makes every psychological interpretation impossible.

70. W. ed. II, 746.

71. Ibid., 745f.

72. W. ed. VI, 131: *nam etsi non sentiatur vere tamen ita agitur, immo quis non sentiat?*

73. W. ed. II, 754.

74. Symeon the New Theologian, *Homily* 22 (Migne, PG 120-425): 'I have seen a man who so fervently desired his brothers' salvation that he would often beg God with bitter tears either to save them or let him also be condemned with them.'

75. Lipsius ad loc., in Holtzmann, *Hand-Commentar zum Neuen Testament*, vol. II, Part 2, 2nd ed., 1891, 145.

76. A. Khomiakov, *Collected Works* (Russian) II, 18ff.

77. Cf. I Tim. 2.1; *Mart. Polyc.* 5.1; 8.1; also Matt. 5.44; Luke 23.4; Rom. 12.14. Luther, W. ed. VI, 237, demands that we should pray 'for all the distress of all men, friend and foe'.

78. Ps. 49.7f. I read '*ach*' with the Massoretic Text.

79. W. ed. VI, 238ff.

80. Ibid., 239: 'For verily the Christian church on earth has not any greater strength nor work than such common prayer against all that might strike against it. . . .' Prayer is 'invincible'.

81. Ibid.

82. W. ed. VI, 131: *quis ergo queat desperare in peccatis? quis non gaudeat in penis, qui sua peccata et penas jam neque portat aut si portat non solus portat, adiutus tot sanctis filiis dei, ipso denique Christo? tanta res est communio sanctorum et ecclesia Christi.*

83. W. ed. II, 745.

84. W. ed. VI, 130, where Luther describes the church as the *nova creatura*.

85. Cf. Confession of Augsburg VII: *nec necesse est ubique esse similes traditiones humanas seu ritus aut ceremonias ab hominibus institutas.* I Cor. 1.10 refers to the destructive, evil will, and not to dogmatic opinions. Likewise Phil. 2.2-3.16.

86. Quotation in T. Schmidt, *Der Leib Christi*, 136.

87. Upon this subject Schleiermacher, Fichte, Hegel and Kant all basically say the same thing. Schleiermacher's central concept is the biological notion of the species. Personality is constituted by the 'whole system of psychic and physical organisation, which the spirit appropriates to itself' (*Christliche Sitte*, 150), whereat the person disintegrates. A man is a single example of a species (ibid., 558) and an individual uniquely differentiated from other men. The individual being is an 'organ and symbol' of the species (*Ethik*, para. 157). 'The spirit is one and the same in all men, and

considered in itself does not bear the personality within it at all, irrespective of whether we consider it as πνεῦμα ἅγιον or as κοινὸς λόγος (*Christliche Sitte*, 510; *The Christian Faith*, para. 123, 3). The first statement on the unity of the spirit seems acceptable to us. To the question as to the nature of the Holy Spirit Schleiermacher gives a characteristic answer by identifying the Holy Spirit and the common spirit, and awareness of the Holy Spirit with common awareness. The Christian common spirit tends by its very nature to become the 'spirit of the species'. Hence the Holy Spirit is clearly nothing but awareness of the species. The apersonal nature of this concept of spirit and community is fully revealed in the definition of the Holy Spirit as the 'union of the divine essence with human nature in the form of the common spirit inspiring the life of the faithful in fellowship with one another'. This union cannot, however, be described, as that with Christ can, as formative of persons (*The Christian Faith*, para. 121.3), and the Holy Spirit's activity is exercised 'without regard to personal peculiarities' (ibid.). Under these conditions Schleiermacher's description of the common spirit as a 'moral personality' (para. 121.2) is no longer of any use. As the One in all individuality the Holy Spirit effects a 'true unity' (ibid.), which is increasingly strengthened by men's 'co-operative and reciprocal activity' (para. 121). The individual is taken possession of by the spirit for the community, so that it may best work through him for the whole (para. 123.3). The unity of the common spirit is thus constantly in motion towards itself, or better, is in a continual state of growth (para. 121), to which end the individuals (examples of the species) are made use of by the common spirit.

Schleiermacher's positive achievement was his recognition that the individual has a life which is solely for the community and in the community, and that the effect of Christ and the Holy Spirit is primarily directed towards the church, towards its entire life (para. 121.2; biblical basis in John 16.7ff.; Acts 1.7ff.; 2.4; John 20.22f.). This, as we showed previously, is of course only the one aspect of Schleiermacher's thinking. This insight, however, was won at the cost of grievous errors: 1. The disastrous identification of the Holy Spirit and the spirit of the species. 2. The individual must be an instrument, which for Schleiermacher means that he must be extinguished as a person. 3. In this way Schleiermacher debarred himself from understanding genuine community of spirit and genuine spiritual unity. The idea of spirit, by its application to the species, becomes anthropological and biological in character, the reason for this being the doctrine of apocatastasis which Schleiermacher makes his premise. The idea of spirit becomes a category of the psychology of species and peoples. The species is accorded the final claim upon God, because it is the species; it is the 'value' God wants, which is to be realised and to which the individual is sacrificed. It is clear that this prevents any understanding of the New Testament. The biological notion of the species has no place in a theological inquiry into the church (see above). If we too describe the Holy Spirit as the spirit of the church, then it is in an entirely different sense, as has been shown and will further be shown.

If the common spirit swallows up the spirit of the individual, so that his personality disintegrates, this bars the way from the outset to a social idea of community. In this way community is bound to become 'unity'—that was made clear from the beginning—but this is to mistake the essential structure of all communities, and thus of the church too. Schleiermacher's idea of unity, moreover, is not theological, but psychological, and this confusion goes deep. It rests on his identification of 'religious fellowship' and 'church' (para. 121.3). The unity of the former is psychological, but the unity of the church is hyper-psychological, established by God, objective. If Schleiermacher had seen this fundamental distinction he would never have identified the Holy Spirit and the awareness of the species. The former subsists in principle only in the church. The latter belongs to any community. Seen from without, the church is indeed a 'religious fellowship', but that is in fact an untheological way of looking at it.

Summarising, we may say that Schleiermacher not only fails to penetrate to a conception of social community, and thus to the essential nature of social 'unity', but that in spite of his efforts with regard to group life and the union of mankind, he does not reach the social sphere at all. Thus to call him a collectivist is as incorrect as to call him an individualist. He is a metaphysician of the spirit, and the concept of sociality defeats him. This is characteristic of all the Idealist philosophers. Even Hegel, who talks most of community, does not succeed in overcoming this deficiency. Man's natural wonder at the other man's reality has been lost, or, as Idealist philosophy imagines, 'overcome'.

We can now, very briefly, sketch the further course of the Idealist conception of community (cf. esp. Hirsch, *Die idealistische Philosophie und das Christentum*, 66ff. and 29ff.). It is based upon the idea that persons are analogous and equal in value. These qualities are assured by the person's participation in universal reason (Kant and Fichte), or in the objective and absolute mind (Hegel). There are many I's, but there is no I-Thou relationship. Kant, who introduces the concept of the ethically responsible person in his concept of the kingdom of God (*Religion within the Limits of Pure Reason* III, 1.4), or sees it, rather, as constituted by such persons, does not grasp the idea of concrete community, since his concept of person is apersonal. And yet he came nearest to the Christian idea of community (Hirsch, *Die Reich-Gottes-Begriffe des neueren europäischen Denkens*, 1921, 20ff., 25). Fichte's idea of community is best studied in his theory of the State (*Rechtslehre*, ed. H. Schulz, 1920). The community is a 'great self', a collective person to which the individual persons have to surrender entirely; the persons, however, merge in this 'unity' (see note above on Fichte's idea of synthesis). Hegel was open to concrete individual life, but for him too it is merely a form of the universal spirit; thus it is the fate of all individual life to be drawn up into the spirit of the community. This spirit is by its very nature hyper-individual; it is the objective spirit that has entered into man's historical and communal life (*Rechtsphilosophie* and *Philosophie des Geistes*, paras. 438ff.), 'the reason of man's life as a species' (Windelband, *Geschichte der neueren Philosophie*, 343ff.).—'In and by reason of my particularity my personality springs from what is finite in me. . . . The relationship to the other man arises from the fact that free personality is inwardly related to the unity of the Unconditional' (Brunstädt, *Vorrede zur Geschichtsphilosophie*, Reclam, 27). Everywhere we encounter the concept of unity; the fundamental reason for this is the concept of the immanence of God or the identity of the human and the divine spirit. (So the State is paid divine honours; *Philosophy of Right*, para, 258: 'this real God'—similarly Hobbes). This basic tendency is clearly manifested once again in Hegel's concept of the Christian church. When in Christ the human spirit had recognised that it was one with the divine spirit, and finitude had been destroyed by the death of death, what had now become apparent in Christ had now to be made effective in the church (*Religionsphilosophie*, ed. P. Marheineke, 1832, II, 257ff., 'Das Reich des Geistes'; cf. E. T., of 2nd ed., *The Philosophy of Religion*, 1895, III, 100ff.). 'God existing as the church' (ibid., 261) brings the 'many individuals . . . back into the unity of Spirit, into the church', and lives in it as 'real, universal self-consciousness' (ibid., 257; ET, 101). The awareness of the spirit and of unity is faith, through which 'material history is made the starting-point for Spirit', and in which it returns to itself (ibid.), 266; ET, 121). There is, I think, no doubt, in spite of recent objections, that Hegel simply identifies the Holy Spirit and the common spirit of the church. On his view, the central point of the entire Christian doctrine of the unity of the spirit and of the church must be the Lord's Supper. In it the awareness of reconciliation with God, the return and dwelling of the Spirit in man, is most clearly and really represented (ibid., 274; ET, 132).

88. Hirsch, *Die idealistische Philosophie*, 73.

89. One might well ask whether it is not the Holy Spirit which best characterises the personality of the church, and in the Bible it is in fact the Spirit which is set forth as the uniting principle (see above). But it is the working together of Christ and the Holy Spirit that characterises the peculiarity of the object, and the Holy Spirit is never imagined as the bearer of a 'body'. Seeberg (*Dogmatik* II, 328) raises the question of the Holy Spirit becoming man in the church, and wonders whether the Spirit becomes flesh in the individual members of the church, but rightly points out that this cannot be, owing to the sinfulness of all men.

90. W. ed. XII, 488: 'Since then we are one cake with Christ, then this makes us to become one thing among one another too.' IV, 400.

91. W. ed. VI, 293.

92. Sociologists too have acknowledged the sociological significance of the Lord's Prayer.

93. Cf., as representative of many, René Wallau, *Die Einigung der Kirche vom evangelischen Glauben aus*, 1925.

94. Troeltsch, *The Social Teaching of the Christian Churches*, 171-6.

95. Modern philosophy of value is unwilling to accept any absolute idea of equality. When the 'working out of our deepest personality, that liberating of the soul from everything that is not the soul itself, that living oneself out according to the law of the I' (Simmel, *Religion*, 79ff.) is interpreted as obedience to God's will, when all depends upon 'the disenchantment of the value present in the soul', equality can consist only in the fact that 'each individual soul has allowed its own idea to grow through everything exterior to itself.' The absolute 'communist idea of equality' must be rejected. In principle equality before God and equality before the law mean the same thing; the latter does not imply that 'the breaker of a police regulation and the man who commits murder in the course of robbery are of equal value in the law's eyes,' but that only factors relevant to the law should be taken into consideration; all else is of no significance. Seen theologically, the concept of sin which this implies is quite superficial. Before God one sinner is *de facto* the same as another; each one really shatters the community. God does in fact overlook our differences in value; for him there are no degrees of obedience; there is just obedience or disobedience. The Christian idea of equality cannot be overcome by the concept of value.

96. Usually in Protestant dogmatics the unity of the church as one of its 'notes' merely signifies something like the unifying bond. In

Roman Catholic dogmatics this idea is accorded considerably more importance (cf. the Encyclicals of Pius IX, 1864, Denzinger, 1685-7, and Leo XIII, 1896, ibid., paras. 1954-62;—Bartmann, *Lehrbuch der Dogmatik*, 1923, II, para. 149). A distinction is made between *unitas fidei, unitas cultus, sacramentorum, liturgica* and the *unitas societatis regiminis, caritatis*, which means, however, that the essential interest is in the principle uniting the empirical church (Primacy of the Pope, cf. *Vatic. sess. IV const. dogm. I de ecclesia*, 18.7.1870: Peter and the Pope are the *perpetuum utriusque unitatis principium ac visibile fundamentum;* cf. also, for instance, Adam, *Wesen des Katholizismus,*[2] 1934, 42ff.), and the wish is to show that the church, being united, is also the one and only church (original meaning of *katholiké=una sola*). The Russian Orthodox Church lays an uncommonly strong stress upon the idea of unity. Khomiakov's presentation (E.T., *The Church is One*, 1948), in which he talks essentially of the unity of the church, has a strength and depth making it almost without parallel among works on the church (cf. also Arseniev, *Die Kirche des Morgenlandes*, 1926, 79ff.). But here too the author is really talking of the unifying spirit of love.

97. Cf. Seeberg, *Dogmatik* II, 400.

98. *Religion within the Boundary of Pure Reason*, III, 1.4: 'Sublime as is the idea of an ethical commonwealth, it can never be fully attained or realised by man, but dwindles in his hands down to an institution that does no more than transcribe the Form of the other; for when we come to the material requisite for instituting such a whole, we find that our means are very much abridged, being contracted by the narrow limits of our moral nature. But how should we expect a perfect frame to be hewn from such twisted wood?(!)' Kant's idealistic scheme had a great effect upon theology, and only to-day can it be said to have been overcome. See Rückert, *Ein Büchlein von Kirche*, 1857, 162f.; Hase, *Gnosis*, 3rd ed., 1869 para. 159; Biedermann, *Christliche Dogmatik*, 88[14], II, para. 935: 'The Protestant distinction of *ecclesia visibilis* and *invisibilis* . . . in fact expresses the contrast between the earthly appearance and the idea of the church.' Seeberg's recent discussion (*Dogmatik* II, 345ff.) of the essence and appearance of the church is not based upon Kant's scheme. Rather the essence is what is real in the appearance, which represents only what is possible. Cf. 346: 'The historical church is thus the church in so far as it makes it possible for the true or essential church to exist, and the essential church is the church because it turns this possibility into a reality.' This completely disposes of Kant's idea.

99. Cf. the saying of Tichonius, *De septem regulis* 6 (Migne, PL 18.54):

'If a man believes that the Word has become flesh, why does he persecute the Word in the flesh?'

100. Rosenstock, *Soziologie* I, 1925, 55. 'No genius, no office, no national spirit or party spirit in art or science, strife or politics has any direct connection with the Spirit of God. That spirit is not God. All sociology begins with this bitter insight.' Rosenstock is dealing here with a problem usually foreign to sociology.

101. Luther's second Preface to Revelation, W. ed. Deutsche Bibel 7,421: 'A Christian is hidden from himself, so that in himself he does not see his sanctity and virtue, but his unvirtue and unsanctity.'

102. *Enarr. in Ps.* 128.2, Migne, PL 37.1689f.

103. Dorner, *Kirche und Reich Gottes*, 1883—Seeberg *Dogmatik* II, 334ff.

104. Ritschl's well-known distinction between the kingdom of God and the church (*Justification and Reconciliation* III, 284ff.) is both theologically and sociologically untenable. 'Those who believe in Christ, therefore, constitute a church in so far as they express in prayer their faith in God the Father, or present themselves to God as men who through Christ are well-pleasing to Him. The same believers in Christ constitute the kingdom of God in so far as, forgetting distinctions of sex, rank or nationality, they act reciprocally from love and thus call into existence that fellowship of moral disposition and moral blessings which extends through all possible gradations to the limits of the human race' (285). How can the two be separated? Is not the new morality possible only in conjunction with prayer? Does faith not imply action? Is not the community of love inseparable from the unity of faith, the kingdom of God from the rule of God? The kingdom of God on earth, that is, the church, is the community, placed under the Word, of penitents, of those who pray for one another, and of those who love, and as such in its whole being it is the Body of Christ. Ritschl is thus trying to separate two things that belong together.

105. Hofmann, *Schriftbeweis* II.2, 1855, 67: 'Abram's faith, through which he became the forefather of the church (*Gemeinde*) . . .'; 97: 'The element in the Old Testament which forms the community is the promise to the people who obey the Law . . .' Cf. 130.

106. Hofmann, ibid. 125.

107. Seeberg, *Dogmatik* II, 348.

108. Hofmann, op. cit., 128—The church 'has no other adherents than those living in the flesh', hence those who have died in faith are not in the church. 'There is no other presence of the Kingdom of God on earth between the Ascension and the Second Coming than that present in the shape of the Christian church'; the only

question is whether God sees the Christian church in more places than we do.

109. Cf. Ritschl, op. cit. III, 286ff.; Krauss, *Das protestantische Dogma von der unsichtbaren Kirche*, 107f.

110. Roman Catholic dogmatic theology states that they do (see the quotations from St. Thomas Aquinas, Chap. v. n. 41 above). Dead members, it says, correspond to the necessary bad parts in the human body. Protestant dogmatics came very close to this idea in considering everyone who had been baptised a member of the essential church, but this meant the introduction of an un-Protestant conception of the sacrament. (Lohe, *Drei Bücher von der Kirche*, 1845; Delitzsch, *Vier Bücher von der Kirche*, 1847; Kliefoth, *Acht Bücher von der Kirche*, 1854; Vilmar, *Dogmatik*, 1874; Stahl, *Kirchenverfassung nach Lehre und Recht der Protestanten*, 2nd ed., 1862.)

111. For all these ideas are in the last resort identical as far as subject-matter is concerned. We cannot here go into the much-discussed problem of the visibility and invisibility of the church. There is agreement in recent dogmatic theology that the terms should be avoided to obviate misunderstandings. The special danger of speaking of the church's invisibility is that when the term is used the visible, that is, the empirical, church is not considered as the church, while 'invisible' is used not as the opposite of what is optically visible, but to describe the essence of an object, whether it be an object of thought or of visual perception. The 'essential' church becomes optically visible in the empirical church; its members are seen quite concretely; but they are seen only by faith. It is meaningless to speak, as people often do, of making the invisible church visible. The 'invisible' church is visible from the outset. One can speak only of an embodiment of the empirical church corresponding in a greater or lesser degree to the essence of the church. The invisible and visible church are One Church. Luther says they go together like body and soul (W. ed. VI, 297). This comparison is acceptable so long as it does not lead us to consider the souls of the particular believers who are united in this way as the church's invisible side, which would be an egregious error. We have yet to discuss the extent to which the church is an object of faith. Cf. Ritschl: '*Über die Begriffe sichtbare und unsichtbare Kirche*', *Studien und Kritiken* 32, 1859; 'Die Begründung des Kirchenrechts im evangelischen Begriff von der Kirche', *Zeitschrift für Kirchenrecht* 8, 1869, 220ff.

112. Hirsch, *Die Reich-Gottes-Begriffe des neueren europäischen Denkens*, 1926.

113. Hofmann, *Schriftbeweis* II.2, 95.

114. W. ed. vi, 300.
115. *Ad Carolum imperatorem fidei ratio*, 1530: *sumitur ecclesia universaliter pro omnibus scilicet, qui Christo nomine censentur.*
116. The Eastern church lays a quite peculiar emphasis upon the empirical church as a totality. It is not the individual local church, and even less the individual, but the church as a whole that is infallible. Thus the Pope in Roman Catholic dogmatics is replaced in the Eastern church by the church as an empirical whole: unity and infallibility coincide. In the Protestant idea of the church, where each individual local church is the Body of Christ, it too is infallible.
117. When our church constitution (Art. 4.1) says that the church is built up out of the congregation, this is an expression of the relation between an unorganised and an organised body. 'Church' here does not signify either the single congregation (this follows from 4.2) or the historical universal church. The fact that in 4.4 it can be stated that the congregation has to maintain connection with the church implies that the church is imagined as in principle separable from the congregation; it would be better to exchange the extremely flat 'maintain' for a sentence clearly defining the situation, to the effect that when the congregation is not its living and sustaining basis the church becomes a meaningless organisation (Constitution of the Church of the Old Prussian Union, 1922).
118. Holl, *Luther*, 96f.; W. ed. xx, 336: *Fides, magna vel parva habet totum Christum.* iv, 401: *nunquam habet aliquis sanctorum totum Christum.*
119. *Religionssoziologie* iii, 306f.
120. Luther could say that if others were of a mind to quote Scripture against Christ, he was for quoting the *dominus scripturae*, Christ, against Scripture. *Disputationes*, ed. Drews, 12, thesis 49.
121. *Second Swiss Confession*, I. Cf. Karl Barth, 'Menschenwort und Gotteswort in der Predigt', in *Zwischen den Zeiten* iii, 2, 1925; 'Das Schriftprinzip der reformierten Kirche', ibid., iii, 3, 1925; Thurneysen, 'Schrift und Offenbarung' ibid., ii, 6, 1924.
122. Cf. P. Althaus, *Wesen des evangelischen Gottesdienstes*, 1926, 17ff.
123. I read καιρῷ, not κυρίῳ.
124. Luther, *Disputationes*, ed. Drews, 689, Theses 41 and 42: *non est negandum miracula fieri posse per impios in fide mortua, praesertim si sunt in officio vel in coetu ecclesiastico, sicut sacramentum et verbum i.e. vita aeterna, quae superant omnia miracula etiam per Judam Scharioth conferuntur.* 730. Theses 9-12.
125. Mulert, '*Congregatio sanctorum, in quae evangelium docetur*', (*Festschrift* for Harnack, 292ff.), has been at pains to reveal contradictions in

the '*in qua*' which were contained, he said, in the very heart of the Reformed idea of the church. He thinks that in fact preaching does not take place in the *sanctorum communio*, but in the empirical church and that thus while it sounds as if the *sanctorum communio* is the wider circle by comparison with the circle of the Word, in fact the circle of the *sanctorum communio* is smaller than that of the empirical church. He is dominated by the idea of the *coetus*, which is quite irrelevant here. His later formulation, *congregatio, in qua*, does not represent any dogmatic advance.

126. *Wider den hochberühmten Romanisten*, W. ed. VI, 298.
127. See the essays of Barth, mentioned above; also Lohmeyer, op. cit., 4ff.
128. *Masse und Geiste*, 1922.
129. This is what makes instruction for confirmation particularly significant. It—and not confirmation itself—is the means whereby the church meets the responsibility it assumed for the child in baptism. The fact, however, that this instruction is given essentially with a view to confirmation shows, in my opinion, that the nature of both is generally misunderstood. Confirmation was and is largely regarded as the moment when the young person makes his profession of faith, that is, the faith held by the church. Such a conception does not seem to me to be adequate to what the congregation as such can do. At the children's baptism the congregation vows to educate and instruct them in the Christian doctrine, but it cannot vow that it will bring them to a free profession of their state as Christians. Confirmation is rather an endorsement by the children of the fact that they have been instructed by the congregation, and so a demonstration of their gratitude towards it; the congregation makes a further vow to take them up, this time as members who are already instructed and are beginning to have a will of their own. It intercedes for them and is aware of its full responsibility for their life. It is *confirmandi*, and not *confirmantes*, who are in question. If the wish is nevertheless to insist upon a profession of faith by the children who are being confirmed, this could only be seen in their expression of a desire to remain associated with the congregation. Hence confirmation is essentially a vow and a prayer by the congregation for the children instructed by it, and perhaps further a profession on the children's part of being members of the church; for the time, for truth's sake, more should not be required. This, however, is not to say that the church's confessional character should be abandoned. Rather the first partaking of the Lord's Supper should be regarded as the first act of free confession, which means that the combining of confirmation with Holy Communion is wrong. (Here I find myself

in agreement with L. Thimme: *Kirche, Sekte und Gemeinschafts-bewegung*, 1925, 300.)

130. Cf. further Münchmeyer, *Das Dogma von der sichtbaren und unsicht-baren Kirche*, 1854, 114. We have an excellent critique of the book in Ritschl's *Über die Begriffe sichtbare und unsichtbare Kirche*.

131. Cf. Althaus: *Communio Sanctorum*, 75ff.

132. Indicative! καταγγέλλετε, Schmiedel ad loc. in H. J. Holtz-mann, *Hand-Commentar zum Neuen Testament*, vol. II, part 1, 2nd ed., 1891, 131.

133. Hollaz's idea that the *influxus* of Christ upon the faithful is the foundation of the most intimate communion evidently has its origin in the idea of the Holy Sacrament. *Examen theologici acroamatici* IV, 1293.

134. G. Hilbert, *Ecclesiola in ecclesia*, 2nd ed. 1924—Thimme, op. cit., 254ff.

135. W.ed. XIX, 72ff.

136. W.ed. II, 39.

137. Let me add that in my opinion the greatest task at the moment is to make private confession once again into a living source of strength for the church. In it the one man assumes the status of a priest for the other, by virtue of Christ's priesthood, as the church that makes intercession and forgives sins. The fact that such an act does not take place only generally in worship, but particularly in the affliction and anxiety of a concrete encounter between two persons, is of great significance for the realisation and experience of the Christian idea of community. We have good reason to listen here to Lohe's impressive words in his *Drei Bücher von der Kirche*, 1845, Book 3.

138. W.ed. II, 470.

139. H. Barth, 'Kierkegaard, der Denker', *Zwischen den Zeiten* IV, 1926, 3, 204.

140. Cf. K. Barth, *Church Dogmatics* I.2 (1956), paras. 21 and 22.

141. Empirically, both types usually have an element of community, sometimes to such an extent that the description 'association' is sociologically inaccurate. Cf. Spann, *Gesellschaftslehre*, 419, who, with the Roman Catholic Church in view, defines the church as the institution for religious community-life (420). He does not make any clear distinction between the association and the institution, as is plain from his definition of the association as a 'voluntary institution' (417). Cf. Gierke, *Das deutsche Genossen-schaftsrecht* I, 143-6, 844-65; II, 526-72.

142. Cf. Chap. III n. 28 above.

143. It is true that the new church constitution does speak of exclusion and suspension of the right to vote (para. 15, 2, 3), but never of

exclusion from the congregation. On excommunication see n. 150 below.

144. We are not speaking here of whether this is right or wrong. Personally I cannot see in this feature of the church any of the weaknesses that are so often condemned. I see it rather as a strength rooted in the church's historicity, the strength it has of bearing its forefathers with it, at the risk of being outwardly old-fashioned.

145. 'Kirche und Sekte in Nordamerika', *Die Christliche Welt*, 1906, 558ff., 578ff.; *Religionssoziologie* I, 211. 'A church is in fact an institution of grace administering the religious goods of salvation like a trusteeship. Membership is (according to the idea of the church) obligatory, and is thus no guarantee of the qualities of the members themselves. One is born into it.'

146. *Soziallehren*, 362ff.

147. In applying the idea that the church is an institution one must distinguish between the individuals' relation to the institution and that of the individuals among themselves. The form of the contract here is other than with the association, in so far as it is entered into between the individual member and the management of the institution, but not between him and the other members. Thus it is only the contract between the institution and the member that is 'social'. The relation of the individuals among themselves remains unregulated, and seen from the point of view of the institution itself is purely accidental. Each man lays claim only to reception of the gift; individual wills run parallel. Thus it seems possible to conceive of the participants, seen as a unit, as constituting a mass—which would be sociologically impossible in an association.

148. An institution which educates its members for community is atomistic in construction.

149. Cf. Althaus, *Communio sanctorum*, who uses other terms but reduces the difference between the Roman Catholic and Protestant idea of community to our distinction between society and community (36); whether he is right is something upon which I still have some doubts. It probably depends whether one considers the Roman Catholic Church at the point where it is degenerate, or at the point where it has retained some original good.

150. The answer to the question of Protestant excommunication varies according to the church's inner and external circumstances. Paul excommunicates (and even perhaps passes sentence of death) so that the soul of the man excommunicated may be saved at the last day (I Cor. 5). That is the only principle we have for our guidance upon this point. In a pure confessing church, excommunication is possible and meaningful, but only of course in accordance with the *iudicium caritatis* on who belongs to the church (cf. Luther's hopes

NOTES

for a confessing church in which excommunication might be possible. W.ed. xix, 72ff.—W.ed. x, 2, 39). The man, however, who proves himself by going to church, taking Communion and living a pure moral life can be regarded as a member of the church (thus Calvin). For our national church such a definition would be quite meaningless. To-day it is surely no longer considered an ostentatious act not to go to church or to take Communion, as it was in Calvin's time. In a national church, excommunication, being impracticable, would be devoid of meaning from the outset. To-day the *iudicium caritatis* would have to cover a much wider field than it did previously, and embrace all those who have never formally renounced the church. If excommunication is practised in 'the church within the church' there can be no objection provided it is practised in the Pauline sense. *Non personam ipsam quae in manu atque arbitrio dei est in mortem abdicamus, sed tantum qualia sint cuiusque opera aestimemus ex lege dei, quae boni et mali regula est.* Calvin, *Institutio*, 1536, iv, 12.9. It is not permissible simply to apply in reverse the New Testament idea 'the tree is known by its fruit'. Abraham and Hosea, for instance, would certainly have been excommunicated from a Calvinist church. Cf. Kierkegaard, *Fear and Trembling*.

151. *Social Teaching of the Christian Churches*, 78ff., 99f., 285ff.; 'Repeatedly we are reminded that Christendom is a great family' (287). —T. Meyer, *Die christlich-ethischen Sozialprinzipien und die Arbeiterfrage*, 1904, esp. 70ff.

152. It is a mistake to identify the society-group and the authority-group because the latter bears reference to the relation of strength between the wills, the former to the way in which their direction is determined. It is of course only the authority-group (by virtue of the spirit-structure peculiar to it, where the one who commands himself sets in motion the will of those who obey, and thus serves them) that makes possible the unity between the will for community and the will for society. All three forms are nevertheless to be upheld in complete purity.

153. *Elementa theol. dogmaticae*, 2nd ed., 1764, para. 2.

154. Weber, *Religionssoziologie* I, 211.

155. Troeltsch, op. cit., 993, 331.

156. *Luther*, 244.

157. Cf. Thimme, *Kirche, Sekte und Gemeinschaftsbewegung*, 250. He rightly rejects Troeltsch's concept of the sect, but without, as it seems to me, a sufficiently clear grasp of the sociological questions involved.

158. *Soziallehren*, 967.

159. op. cit., 983

160. *Masse und Geist*, 1922.
161. *Die kommende Kirche*, 3rd ed., 1925. Cf. 68f.—another very characteristic expression is to be found on 29, where Stange says that the state is lacking in the 'earnest wish to represent the kingdom of God'.
162. *Die Meisterfrage beim Aufbau der evangelischen Kirche*, 1924. Every emphasis is laid upon the community movement. The author's understanding for the church is expressed in the statement that it is 'an essentially Roman Catholic' phenomenon and is surpassed by the congregation. Cf. the table on page 61 which is meant to make the relation between the church and the congregation quite clear. Cf. Richard Karwehl's essay: 'Zur Diskussion über die Kirchenfrage', *Zwischen den Zeiten V*, 2, 178ff.
163. Cf. E. Vurpillot's excellent work, *De la nécessité d'une 'doctrine' protestante de l'église*, Montbéliard, 1926, 11.
164. Here once again the inadequacy of the concepts of invisible and visible church becomes clear. Nonetheless I find no justification for concluding from this, like many recent writers, that the empirical church has absolute doctrinal power, that its dogma is absolutely binding and that it alone can provide by its doctrinal power a basis for the certainty of faith of individuals. One of my reasons for not so concurring would be the monadic image. Cf. the unusual work of Erik Peterson, *Was ist Theologie?*, 1925, 22ff.; O. Piper: *Theologie und reine Lehre*, 1926, 2ff.
165. Establishing the dual course of history. Cf. the two most recent important eschatological studies: R. Seeberg, *Dogmatik* II, 606ff., and P. Althaus, *Die letzten Dinge* 3rd ed., 1926, 119ff., which show a great measure of agreement upon this issue.
166. Seeberg, op.cit., 584ff.
167. Althaus, against Stange, op.cit., 285ff.
168. C. Stange, *Unsterblichkeit der Seele*, 1925, 121ff.
169. Cf. Seeberg, op.cit., 625ff.—Althaus, op.cit., 203ff.
170. Seeberg, *Ewiges Leben*, 1915, 93.
171. Luther, *Disputations*, 116, Thesis 24.

Index

Index of Scripture References

INDEX OF SCRIPTURE REFERENCES

INDEX OF SCRIPTURE REFERENCES

Index of Names

INDEX OF NAMES

Index of Subjects

action, centre of, 51, 68-9, 82, 83-4
actualisation, 111, 115, 116
Adam, mankind of, 82, 85, 107
adiaphora, 186
agape, 119
antagonism, the basic law, 27, 54-5, 215
Antichrist, 199
apocatastasis, 201, 227, 231
Apostles' Creed, 139
Ascension, 111, 222-3
association, church as, 175-6, 178-9
atomic view of society, 17, 18, 21, 241
authority, 173-5, 177; association of authority, 41, 58, 59, 62, 126, 166, 181-4, 216

baptism, 166-7; infant, 75, 166-7, 179
barriers, 29, 31, 33, 44, 121
'being at one', 123
' being for one another ', 129
being in Adam, 74-7
being in Christ, 100, 222
being in the church, 100, 135, 222
' being with one another ', 127, 129
Bible (and preaching), 161
blessedness, 203
body (of collective person), 51, 68-9, 218
body: ' new ', 46, 200-1; spiritual, 201
Body of Christ, 99-102, 108, 135, 139, 145, 146, 147, 151, 153-5, 168, 170, 197
bourgeoisie, 191-3
Buddhism, 221

capitalism, 190
Catholicism, 88, 124, 174, 177-8, 186-7, 189, 219
certainty, 158, 211
charisma, 162

'Christ existing as the church', 85, 100, 101, 102, 135-6, 139, 143, 145, 147, 149, 160, 180, 197, 203
Christ in the church, 135, 222; in Israel, 108, 222; in others (Thou), 119, 147; and time, 112
Christology, 35, 103-4, 122
church, 38, 41, 49, 52, 57, 60, 67, 87-90, 111-12, 138-9, 148; as association, 175-6, 178-9; confessing, 189, 241; 'gathered', 151-2, 169, 171, 187-9; as institution, 175-9, 186-7, 241; missionary, 157, 184; national, 151-2, 167, 171, 186, 187-90, 242; in New Testament, 97-102; of Old Testament, 151; and state, separation of, 184; as trusteeship, 176; universal, 154-5; visible and invisible, 60, 133, 152, 197-8, 237, 243; word of, 166, 173-5; and world, 63, 199
church, concept of, 37, 38, 44, 52; Catholic, 186-7; Kant's, 146; Luther's, 146, 152, 153; misunderstanding of, 87; predestinarian, 117-18, 136, 148
church authorities, 189
church council, 149, 174, 238
church discipline, 179, 184
church history, 148; 'counsel of our neighbour', 172
church taxes, 176, 179
'church within the church', 169, 242
churches: individual local, 153-5, 159-60; unification of, 141
co-operative association, 59
cognition, 37
collective person, 84, 102, 138, 200, 218
common awareness, 231
common spirit, 231-2
communication, need for, 96, 223

252

INDEX OF SUBJECTS